LETTERS OF THE REVD THOMAS HAYTON
VICAR OF LONG CRENDON,
BUCKINGHAMSHIRE
1821–1887

THE LETTERS OF THOMAS HAYTON

VICAR OF LONG CRENDON
BUCKINGHAMSHIRE
1821–1887

JOYCE DONALD

BUCKINGHAMSHIRE RECORD SOCIETY
No. 20
MCMLXXIX

ISBN 0 901198 16 1

PRINTED BY
BLUNDELLS PRINTERS LIMITED, CHESHAM, BUCKS
FOR THE BUCKINGHAMSHIRE RECORD SOCIETY

CONTENTS

ACKNOWLEDGEMENTS

In the first place I wish to thank Mr Christopher Hohler for his encouragement when I first began to collect the letters of Thomas Hayton, and for his help in deciphering Hayton's almost illegible handwriting.

I must thank Mr G.R. Elvey the present General Editor, for his very great assistance in the lay-out of the letters, suggestions for the Introduction, and his help in preparing the letters for the press.

I wish to thank the archivists of the Bodleian Library, St George's Chapel, Windsor, The Charity Commissioners, the Church Commissioners, the National Society, the Lincolnshire Archives Committee and the Oxfordshire Record Office for their kindness in allowing me to look through their manuscripts. Also, to an unknown archivist of the P.R.O. for introducing me to the early Ministry of Health papers which provided a goldmine of letters.

Finally, I wish to thank Mr Hugh Hanley and his staff at the Buckinghamshire Record Office for their help and encouragement.

INTRODUCTION

This is mainly a collection of letters written by the Revd Thomas Hayton, perpetual curate of Long Crendon from 1821 until his death in 1887. They are supplemented by items of news, and articles believed to be his work which appeared in local newspapers.

Almost all the letters were addressed either to his diocesan (up to 1845 the bishop of Lincoln; after that the bishop of Oxford), the Board of Queen Anne's Bounty, the Charity Commissioners, the Poor Law Commissioners, or the Dean and Chapter of St George's Chapel, Windsor. All the letters that have been found in the archives of these addressees have been transcribed, and are here printed, with a few exceptions, brief calendars of which are given in the appendix. They are arranged in chronological order. Small errors of orthography or spelling have been assumed to be inadvertent, and corrected accordingly.

Very little is known of the early life of Thomas Hayton. He was born in 1793 at Wigton in Cumberland, a pleasant town, renowned for its market, about twenty miles east of Maryport. His father was a butcher and grazier, but unfortunately died along with his mother in 1802, leaving Thomas and his younger sister Jane to the care of their maternal grandfather, Henry Twentyman of Blencogo. John Hayton appears to have been prosperous, as in his will Jane was left £600 when she reached the age of twenty-one, and Thomas was to get his houses, shops and fields. Nothing is known of Thomas's early life, but Crendon legend says he studied law in Carlisle, and it is known that he took part in the quelling of the food riots in 1812. In 1813, when he was nearly twenty, he went to St Bees School, probably as an usher or pupil teacher. In 1815, he matriculated at Oxford and went to Queen's College which had had links with St Bees since the seventeenth century. By this time he would have got his inheritance, and one suspects that it did not last long. He left in 1818 after an undistinguished career, and was ordained deacon in the same year.

To appreciate the letters of Thomas Hayton it is necessary to understand the unusual social conditions in Crendon during the early nineteenth century. The church, with the tithes, had belonged to the Augustinian abbey of Notley since the twelfth century. After the Reformation it was obtained, along with the abbey lands, by

Lord Williams of Thame. During the seventeenth century it passed through the female line to the Earls of Abingdon. All this time the incumbent of this large parish of 3350 acres was forced to rely on the generosity of its lay patrons. After the formation of Queen Anne's Bounty in 1703 it was possible to obtain grants for the raising of clerical stipends. In 1740 the living received £400 from its patron and a friend, and the same sum was contributed by the Bounty Office; this was to be laid out in land. In 1742 a new vicarage was provided, but in reality it was only the dilapidated farm house which was the dwelling house of the glebe farm. Hayton was right when he said that no minister had ever resided. Successive perpetual curates were vicars of Thame or neighbouring parishes and the church was served by young men from Oxford, waiting for something better to turn up. In 1783 a John Holland, vicar of Aston Rowant, had been the curate, but had never resided. The parish register shows the names of at least twelve men who took the services for him. Holland soon got disillusioned with the living and in 1799 he wrote, 'the curate has great cause to lament that so small a Living is so encumbered with Buildings equal to an Estate of six times the value of this which he is necessitated to keep in repair'. Meanwhile the estate of the Earl of Abingdon (with the exception of the Notley farm) had been bought towards the end of the eighteenth century by the Duke of Marlborough. In 1810 he gave a yardland to the curacy, aided by Queen Anne's Bounty, and in 1816 a parliamentary grant of £200 was given, but in the same year Holland wrote to the Bounty Board complaining that although the living was now £100 a year, he had expended £20 to little purpose. Such was the Crendon living when Hayton took over in 1821. Had he come thirty years earlier, no doubt he would have settled down happily with three or four curacies and resided well away from the parishes. It was his misfortune that he should have come under Bishop Kaye of Lincoln, a reformer and an active opponent of pluralities.

With no lay patron residing in the village, the church itself was in a deplorable condition during the early years of the nineteenth century. In 1827 after the archdeacon's visitation it was ordered to be thoroughly repaired. The windows in the chancel, which had been partially blocked, were to be restored to their original state, the dripstones and battlements of the tower repaired, and new south and north doors made. The expenses were to be met by a church rate, which at that time aroused no opposition from the dissenters. However with the exception of the Dormer monument, few repairs were done before Hayton's death.

The Revd F.G. Lee, the antiquary, wrote just before the

restoration of 1888–89, 'Internally, the church is in sad desolation, the Tudor changes cleared it out of all its more interesting and precious contents. The church is now as bare as an empty barn for the square and vulgar pews of deal — as uniform as the divisions of a chess board — are a permanent eye-sore in every part; while the galleries, one at the west and the other perched high in the south aisle — the latter like a square lidless box, approached by stairs — certainly do not add to the effect or impressiveness of the interior'.

It is not be be wondered at that there was an increase in dissent. There had been conventicles in the village since 1669, and in the eighteenth century Crendon was connected with the Baptist Chapel at Ford. At the end of the century there was a split in this Chapel; some members moved to Dinton and formed the Particular Baptists. The first Chapel in Crendon was started by Thomas Howlett, a wealthy farmer from Scotsgrove, and the first minister was William Hopcroft, a tailor living in the High Street who had been converted by listening to a sermon in Thame. The Chapel was built down Frog Lane, and on that proving too small, another one was built on the Chearsley Road. In a Census taken in 1830 of 'Chapels not of the Church of England' the Baptists were given as 156, including children, and the Wesleyans (who had a Chapel on the Chearsley Road) as fifty-six in all.

What was unusual about the Crendon Baptists was that most of their congregation consisted of the more affluent tradespeople and farmers. In many villages their congregations were small and consisted of poorer cottagers, but in Crendon the Chapel was in the unique position of having more money than the Church.

In 1854 a new Chapel was built in the High Street on land given by Joseph Dodwell. It is a dignified building holding 300 people and in a prominent position; and the Baptists could employ a whole time minister. In 1860 the great Mr Spurgeon came to the village to preach two sermons, and a marquee was hired for the occasion. As a result of all this activity, relations between Church and Chapel deteriorated still further. The conduct of the vicar set a deplorable example: 'when the Chapel was opened he organised a procession of his supporters who carried about the effigy of a calf stuffed with straw [1], which in some way was supposed to reflect on the Baptists, and was burnt on the open space before the site on which the Church Room now stands.

Hayton was in the unenviable position of taking second place in the religious life of the village. His very aggressive nature sensed insult when probably none was intended. The whole village

1. They made a calf in Horeb; and worshipped the molten image. Thus they turned their glory into the similitude of a calf that eateth hay. Ps. 106, vv. 19, 20.

became engaged in a deadly feud and his attitude was not helped by Bishop Wilberforce who alluded to certain villages as 'full of dissent and ungodliness'. In these ecumenical days it is difficult to realise the appalling quarrels between the sects. In 1869 the Thame Gazette wrote: 'T'is strange but t'is true that you no sooner reach Crendon than you become the object of abuse; some attribute it to Crendon water, others to a peculiarity in the atmosphere'. As one elderly Baptist told me, 'You can have acquaintances among the Church people, but friends, never'. There were Church shops and Chapel shops, and people buying groceries would go out of their way to patronise one from their own religion. For the Sunday School outings there were Church waggonettes and Chapel waggonettes drawn by Church horses and Chapel horses. Crendonians kept to themselves and did not mix with outsiders. One reason for the atmosphere was the distance between the different 'ends' of the village. There were many living at Church End who had never been to the bottom of Frog Lane, and Lower End was despised by the rest of the village.

The manor of Crendon had been divided into three parts since the thirteenth century. At the beginning of the sixteenth century the land then belonged to All Souls College, Oxford, the Dean and Canons of Windsor and the Dormer family, who in 1760 sold to George Grenville of Wotton Underwood, whose son became the first Duke of Buckingham. There was no resident land-owner and all the land was sub-let. In 1821 the manor belonging to Windsor was let to the Stone family. It is the attractive manor-house lying next to the churchyard; William Stone was an active farmer. The All Souls portion which consisted of an Elizabethan farm house, next to the present Court House, was rented by a Thomas Huxley and sub-let to the Dodwells. The third portion, belonging to the Duke of Buckingham, was also sub-let.

Outside these manors was the land which had belonged to Notley, owned since 1817 by Lord Churchill. Notley itself had been sold in 1790 to the Reynolds family who were active farmers and took little interest in the village. The remainder of the Notley land, the farm house, known at this time as the 'Duke's farm', was let to John Dodwell.

In 1824 there was an enclosure of the common fields. The rights of common grazing were extinguished and the large open fields were divided by neat hedges. The whole cost of this Private Act, together with the costs of the Commissioners, had to be met by selling land. Altogether over 400 acres were sold. The main result was that Lord Churchill got 554 acres in lieu of tithes, and the Church got seventy-eight acres in lieu of tithes on 'half of the wool', consolidated into one block on the north side of the Chearsley Road. The enclosure brought great social changes. As the land was now in blocks is was possible to build farm houses out in the country, and farmers could leave their old houses in the village. More land was sold for investment and then sub-let, and a new breed of farmer arrived in the village who had little concern for village people. These were the 'rack-renting farmers' who were so chastised by Hayton and in revenge did their best to put him in his place.

It must be realised that there were no resident landowners in the village and in these circumstances, which were not of his creation, Hayton's position in the community was difficult and insecure. In what concerned his priestly office none of his parishioners might interfere; but this was a narrow territory, outside of which lay a wide sphere of activity, where he needed and was entitled to expect, the support of his churchwardens. One of these he had a right to nominate, but the other, then as now, was elected by the vestry, in which all had a right to vote, whether or not they were members of the Church of England. The second, or 'people's' warden was therefore oftener than not a dissenter. With division even in the administration of Church affairs, Hayton had no reliable basis of operations, and such authority as he contrived to wield had to depend largely on his own personal qualities. Unfortunately these contained 'a chip on the shoulder' and a good deal of northern aggressiveness. On his arrival in the village in 1821, he wrote in the parish register, 'A most illiterate and irregular book, a disgrace to the church as well as the inefficient Minister who ever he was'.

Until 1877 there was no official school in the village. It is to Hayton's credit that he was a passionate advocate of education; he even sent a subscription of £1.10s.0d. in 1836 for the building fund of the British School in Thame. In 1868 he became a member of the newly formed Birmingham Education League which favoured undenominational education. Crendon possessed many small lace-making schools (the location of six is known) which were held in small cottages; the children were taught the alphabet, but the main object was to teach lace-making. However, the chief means of education were the Sunday Schools, where the children were at least taught to read the Bible. Writing was not considered important, and in some cases was actually frowned upon as being subversive and unnecessary. The Church Sunday School was taught in the aisle of the parish church, later on in the Court House. The Chapel School was first started in 1817 and was held in the chapel itself and later on in the gallery of the present Chapel. Up to the first

World War there were many people living whose education was solely from this source. The Board School started in 1877 and there was keen competition for seats on the School Board; both Church and Chapel put up their own supporters. In the election of 1882, there were ten candidates for five seats. There was a great aftermath with a court case for assault, the candidate at the bottom of the poll being struck by a relative of the successful candidate.

Much has been written about the idyllic nineteenth century village, but Crendon and most other Buckinghamshire villages were plagued by appalling poverty. Population steadily grew during the first half of the century, but that of Crendon increased by 71%, much more than in neighbouring villages, as this table shows.

Place	Population in 1801	Population in 1851	Percentage increase
Chearsley	214	292	36
Chilton	316	398	26
Brill	859	1311	54
Oakley	305	442	45
Crendon	991	1700	71

Up to the eighteenth century the manorial court had restrained the inflow of strangers and the building of new cottages, but by now its grip had relaxed, and the parish vestry was content for Crendon to be an open parish. In 1847 the *Bucks Advertiser* wrote: 'There are no fewer than 400 people residing in the parish who are non-parishioners. They are chiefly agricultural workers who with their wives and children from want of habitation in their own parish have been drawn to Crendon to obtain a home'. Hayton sometimes speaks of the 'waif and strays' who had drifted in from nearby parishes, though some continued to work in the village they had come from. The village was also burdened with 'tinkers' who settled in Lower End.

Cottages were easy to build in corners of gardens or orchards and provided a modest rent of 1s.0d. a week for the landlord. All they needed was on the site; a few stones for foundations, an earth floor, wichert walls, dug up there and mixed with chopped straw, and a roof of willow poles thatched with local straw. There were also many alleyways and yards, for 'backland development' was much practised, resulting in dense infilling with cottages having 'one up and one down'. Bradens Yard, off the High Street, once six cottages, is a typical example; the two cottages left are now scheduled buildings.

People married early and produced enormous families, many of whom died. Hayton did his best to help the poor and took their side against the new bureaucratic authority that had come into being after the Poor Law Amendment Act of 1834. He fought the terrible epidemics of cholera, smallpox and typhus that swept through the village. In 1842 the Poor Law Commissioners ordered a Sanitary Enquiry and Mr Parker, an Assistant Commissioner, wrote: 'Fever is usually endemic in this parish, and during the past year the mortality is alarming; an aged man stated that he had lost by the prevailing fever fourteen children and grandchildren'.

There was no doctor in the village and, until the 1840s, no hospital within reach. Those on 'outside relief' had the doctor for the 'north district'; no nursing was provided, but often widows on relief were forced to help with nursing, the penalty for not complying being the loss of their weekly allowance. There was no sanitation and the privies simply overflowed out into the roads. The present Mill Terrace used to be known as Casualty Row, due to its appalling death record. Older people still remember it by that name.

In 1865 there was another bad outbreak of smallpox. Conditions were chaotic; the vicar wrote:

'What has been done about smallpox? No officer, except the medical one has ever put his foot where smallpox exists . . . other cases have arisen . . . the Guardian sends 1/— every morning and ten loaves weekly, being 1/— a head. The family is destitute of clothing.'

The main work in the village was on the farms, but it was precarious as labourers were often laid off during the winter months. The women worked at their lace pillows, but it was badly paid work as the machine-made lace from Nottingham was rapidly taking the place of the fine Bucks lace. They did dairy work, but there are no examples of women working on the land. There was also needlemaking, a most unusual trade for a Buckinghamshire village. It had been started about 1600, and concentrated on the larger types, like sacking, glovers' and sail needles. During the Peninsular War the trade was at its peak and gave a great deal of employment. It was worked on the domestic system; the living rooms of the needlemakers were the workshops, with small hovels at the rear for the heavier work. There were many small manufacturers in the village who would supply the wire and sell the needles up in London. But by 1820 the trade was declining and being taken over by the Redditch and Alcester firms who had the advantage of water-power. Many Crendon families had started migrating to that area, and by the 1841 Census only about forty-five men were in the Crendon trade. However, in 1848, a Redditch firm, Kirby Beard & Co came to the village and set up a factory on the Chilton Road. By the 1851 Census over one hundred people were employed in the factory, but it did not last: people had been brought from the Midlands to teach modern factory methods and this was resented by the inhabitants. In 1862 the factory departed, taking with it about forty workers.

The two main Crendon families were the Shrimptons and the Dodwells. The former produced 204 babies between 1754 and 1835; the majority became needlemakers, and by the first quarter of the nineteenth century many had migrated to the Redditch area. They were an extremely musical family and founded the Crendon brass band. William Shrimpton who had lived in the village wrote in *Notes from a Decayed Needleland* that 'Hayton as a young man frequently engaged in wrestling contests with the Shrimptons, and was an ardent advocate of bell-ringing and cricket and it was through his instrumentality that a number of bell-ringing contests were arranged and carried out at Crendon, this peal of bells being admirably adapted for these friendly contests'. On the whole Hayton got on well with this family; they were 'Church' (when they went anywhere) and they knew their position in life, which pleased Hayton's vanity.

The Dodwells were the descendants of a Thomas Dodwell who came to the village about 1660. His son and grandson kept the Star Inn; in 1772 his great-grandson married and produced seven sons and three daughters. They all became Baptists, though not all baptised into the Chapel. The whole family were hard-working and respectable; most were very successful in work. John, the eldest, obtained the lease of the 'Duke's farm' from his maternal uncle Thomas Cannon, and became very successful in his farming life despite the depression. His son Joseph became the richest man in the village and re-named his farm 'The Manor House'. He became a noted breeder of shorthorns. He was interested in coursing, and had days out in the fields leading to the Thame water meadows; a marquee was provided for lunch; Thomas Hayton was not invited. His younger brother John Dodwell took over after his death in 1867 and bought the property from Lord Churchill in 1874, including Westfield Farm (the land which had been given in lieu of tithes). The other brothers were almost as successful and many sons followed in their father's footsteps. Those who were not farming became grocers or bakers whose shops were patronised by the Baptist Community. They were all admirable members of the Chapel, untouched by scandal (possibly Joseph may have informed on Hayton for his escapade in 1843).

xiv

Skeleton pedigree of the Dodwells

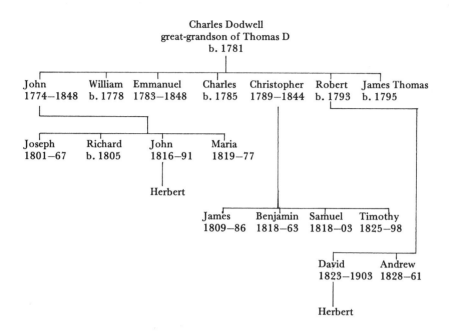

There was little social activity in the neighbourhood. Hayton did not mix well with his fellow clerics. His nearest neighbour was the Revd George Chetwode of Chilton, second son of Sir George Chetwode. He was rector of Ashton in Lancashire, but preferred Buckinghamshire. He rented Chilton House, the vicarage being too small. He was a J.P. as was his near neighbour, John Kipling, vicar of Oakley, who had a quarrel with Hayton over curacies. Another J.P. was John Baron of Brill, who sat on the tribunal that went into the details of Hayton's misdemeanours. These were all well-off and represented the Establishment; they had no time for the son of a north country grazier. Hayton's great friend was Timothy Tripp Lee, vicar of Thame and the father of eleven children. His son Frederick had fallen under Bishop Bagot's displeasure owing to his bankruptcy; he was refused a licence and ended up as an unpaid and unlicenced curate to his father. His son was Hayton's godson and became the well-known F.G. Lee, antiquary and author of the well-known book on Thame Church. He was vicar of St Mary's Lambeth, but afterwards turned Catholic. Hayton was also friends with John Willis of Haddenham, having lived in that village for at least ten years. Willis had also fallen under Bishop Kaye's displeasure and been banished from the parish for one year.

Hayton's name often appears in the parish register as taking various services.

In politics during the first half of the century Crendon supported the Tories. The Duke of Buckingham held land in the village during this period and consequently had considerable influence. His son Lord Chandos was member for the County from 1818 to 1839. He voted against the Catholic Emancipation Bill of 1828 and pleased many of the dissenters. The Poll Book of 1831 shows that he was supported by Thomas Hayton, who must have known that he would vote against the Reform Bill of 1832. However, he brought in the famous Chandos Clause which gave the vote to £50 occupiers of land. Lord Chandos must have displeased Hayton, who became extremely radical during the election of 1835. He wrote a pamphlet called *The Political Trinity* against the three Tory members, Chandos, Young and Praed. On 1 February 1847, the first day of Free Trade after the repeal of the Corn Laws, loaves of bread were hung on poles on the church tower, and the bells were rung all morning at the prospect of cheaper food. For most of his life Hayton continued to be a radical, but in extreme old age he turned Tory, and on Primrose Day he would open the vicarage garden to show great banks of that flower.

I do not think that throughout his long stay of nearly seventy years Hayton had any friends of his own standing in the village — I doubt if he did his duty particularly well: during his temporary banishment his successor baptised many young adults who long ago should have been brought to the font. He was a typical sporting parson and had held a game licence since 1823. He had the game rights of the glebe farm on the Chearsley Road. There is a delightful photograph of him as an old man sitting in his pony cart and surrounded by his bag for the day. Wilberforce disliked his type and would not ordain anyone who shot or hunted.

There is a tradition in the village that Hayton rented a room opposite the vicarage 'to write his sermons'. But Hayton did more than write religious essays. In the first edition of Crockford it was mentioned that he wrote pamphlets on the Poor Law. He was a friend of John Gibbs, the editor of the *Aylesbury News and Bucks Advertiser*, and he wrote many articles for the paper under the pseudonym of Z. Two of these attacking Lord Chandos are stuck in the Parish Register. After 1850 he wrote for the *Bucks Chronicle*, chiefly attacking Joseph Dodwell and the Thame Union. He also wrote an article criticising the Ashendon Petty Sessions for a sentence passed on one of his choir boys. He was very pleased with his writings, and many volumes of the Parish Register are adorned with stuck-in newspaper articles attacking one of his present hates.

Hayton was very proud of his sermons. Only one remains, but this shows that he gave good measure. It must have taken at least forty-five minutes to deliver, and dealt with the Old Testament story of David. A neat little notice was written on the back with a list of the dates on which this particular sermon had been preached. He was a popular preacher and his name often appeared in the *Thame Gazette* as 'our eloquent minister'. Like others of the period, he would discard his surplice and preach in a black gown. I doubt he had a large congregation. In his answers to Visitation Enquiries he blames the dissenters and talks of the 'waifs and strays' who knew no religion. His communicants vary from thirty-five to forty-five. He had a small choir who sat in the gallery on the west side and also a small orchestra. In the 1860s they acquired a harmonium. The Holy Communion was held eight times a year, with offertories only on special occasions, never for diocesan purposes (as Hayton disliked bishops). In 1870, £4.10s.0d was raised for the Radcliffe Infirmary at Oxford. Hayton was a martinet for discipline, and disliked the habit of the bell-ringers of sneaking away after their peal and before the service. He therefore purposely blocked up the door in the north transept so that they had to listen to the entire service.

The Church still played a large part in the life of the village. The Government was in the habit of ordering 'National Days of Prayer' either of thanksgiving or humiliation. One was ordered for the Irish famine of 1847, others for the cholera epidemic of 1849, the Crimean War of 1854 (when Hayton instructed his parishioners on the events of the war) and for the cattle plague (foot and mouth) of 1866, when the village was badly hit.

During the nineteenth century, the Church began to enter into the social life of the village. The bell-ringers had an annual dinner, and with the advent of a Sunday School the scholars had their annual treat which was held in the vicarage garden. For propaganda purposes they were compelled to walk round the village and back by the High Street. The Baptists did the same, ending up at the Manor House where they were entertained by Mr Dodwell. A dinner was provided for the teachers and the choir. A Mutual Improvement Society was started in the fifties; it was supposed to be undenominational, and lectures were given on such subjects as 'The Education of the Female' and 'Self Culture as a means of Elevating the Working Class'. It was held in the old Baptist Chapel Room in Burts Lane, and was supported by Hayton. Penny Readings were held in Crendon and many surrounding villages, and Hayton was in great demand for recitations, his material consisting of 'The Fate of McGregor', 'Orphan Boy', 'Eve of Waterloo', Tennyson's 'May Queen' etc. These meetings were 'calculated to improve the morality of the young and to draw them from places of ill resort'.

The great day for Crendon was the Club feast which was held on the Friday and Saturday after Whitsun. It had started towards the end of the eighteenth century with the advent of Benefit Societies, but it was probably the remnant of an earlier festival. Each of the Societies had its own clubhouse in one of the village inns, and each one had its own band which played the members to Church, where they were regaled by a lengthy sermon from the vicar. The older village people can remember it as the day when open house was kept, and absent relations poured back into the village.

Hayton had what we would consider a large staff — two maids, a gardener, and a boy who looked after his pony-cart. He had a garden with a very large bed of pampas grass. Also a vegetable garden which grew delicious strawberries, and every year some were given to his churchwarden, Stephen Cook dairyman, in return for which Hayton received bowls of cream.

Little is known of Adelaide Hayton; tradition says she was kind and gentle, different from her boisterous husband. She once dared to leave him and in the 1851 Census, Hayton described himself as unmarried — but she came back and became the perfect vicar's wife, presenting prizes on all suitable occasions etc. Hayton was the wrong man for Crendon — opposition brought out all that was bad in his aggressive character, and he especially resented the worldly wealth and success of the dissenters. His letters contain so much detail that they cast a bright light on the realities of village life and the things that matter in a rural community.

Hayton's letters to the Charity Commissioners form a substantial part of his correspondence. In 1818 Lord Brougham set up a Commission to look into the charities of England and report on their administration. In 1835 twenty-six reports were made, and the report on the Crendon charities showed many abuses. One charity, left by William Batten for the repair of Thame Bridge, had been lost, and the five other charities were shown to be badly mismanaged. The parish authorities were required to give an undertaking that the practice of carrying the income from the charities to the relief of the poor-rate should be discontinued. The revenues were to be applied to the purposes for which the charities were given. The main village charity, left by Sir Robert Dormer in 1620, was for the upkeep of the family tomb, one shilling a week for eight poor and elderly persons, and for a Court dinner every third year. But the Commissioners found that the first priority was always for the dinner. It was not until 1848 that proper accounts were kept for this charity; the account book has now been found in the village. Although carefully kept, it shows that the 1s.0d. a week given to the poor and aged had in many cases been given to young men with large families.

In 1853, the Charitable Trust Act was passed. Three Commissioners were appointed, two of them barristers and the third a member of Parliament. Their aim was to prevent abuses and see that the trusts were properly administered, and used for the purpose stated by the founder. In 1857 an expensive lawsuit, as will be seen, was fought to stop the continuous misuse of the funds of the Dormer Charity; until 1860 the Commissioners had no power to establish Schemes of Administration, or to reform obsolete charities. Unfortunately the poor were the losers: from August 1854 to December 1857 they received no money, although £84 was collected for the Dormer Monument. Another part of Hayton's correspondence was with the Poor Law Commission, afterwards the Board of Health. The letters are in the Public Record Office, among the early Ministry of Health papers, and are catalogued under the heading of the local Union Workhouse. The enormous mass of correspondence that poured in daily was sorted into regions, each one assigned to an Assistant Commissioner, or else waited till the afternoon for submission to the Board. This consisted of the three Commissioners, George Nichols, J.G. Shaw-Lefevre and T. Frankland Lewis (two formed a quorum). The answers for the attention of the clerks were written on the backs of letters and envelopes, often crossed and re-written, and show the difficulties experienced in the first two years. One can see the changes in the parish, which since 1601 had been responsible for the maintenance of its poor, and now found itself taken over by bureaucrats.

In November 1887 Hayton died at the age of ninety-four. The new Incumbent, the Revd F. Ogden, arrived in the village; his sister Mrs Chapman had previously bought him the advowson for £500. He was practical, prim and pompous. His two sisters cleaned out the parish chest and a bonfire was made of its contents. Nothing now remains of Crendon's past except the parish registers and the Enclosure Award. In 1888 Arthur Blomfield, the architect, produced plans for the restoration of the church, which was completed by 1889. This meant wholesale destruction of much that was interesting: traces of wall paintings disappeared, all the pews were removed and the interesting series of slab tombs was expelled from the body of the church. The church is lucky in having the original drawings by Blomfield which show how much was destroyed, including a delightful gallery over the west door supported by Ionic pillars.

LIST OF ABBREVIATED SOURCES AND AUTHORITIES

Best	C.F.A. Best, *Temporal Pillars* (1964).
Bodl	Bodleian Library, Oxford.
B.R.O.	Buckinghamshire County Record Office.
Charity Com	Charity Commissioners 252518 A/1.
Ch Com.	Church Commissioners.
D.N.B.	*Dictionary of National Biography.*
E.D.	P.R.O. Records of the Board of Education.
H.O.	P.R.O. Records of the Home Office.
L.A.O.	Lincolnshire Archives Office.
M.E.B.	*Modern English Biography* (reprinted 1965).
M.H.	P.R.O. Records of the Ministry of Health.
N. Soc	National Society for Promoting Religious Eductation.
O.R.O.	Oxfordshire Record Office.
P.R.	Parish Register.
P.R.O.	Public Record Office.
V.C.H.	*Victoria County History of Buckinghamshire.*
Wilberforce	*The Letter Books of Samuel Wilberforce,* ed. R.K. Pugh, Oxfordshire and Buckinghamshire Record Societies (1970).
Windsor	*The Manuscripts of St. George's Chapel Windsor,* ed. J.N. Dalton (1957), XVII, 22. 1 & 2.

THE LETTERS OF THE REVD THOMAS HAYTON

[1] To the Bounty Board

14 March 1822

My Lord [1],

When I had the pleasure of being licensed to the Parish Church of Long Crendon your Lordship led me to conceive, that there would be an increase in salary for me from the Bounty Office [2], in consequence of the number of the inhabitants of Crendon & of my continual residence — As I have been, at Lady Day next, in possession of the Living a year & as I have not yet received anything from the Office (not so much as the interest of £200 which was granted the said Curacy some time ago [3]) I shall feel most dutifully obliged for your Lordship's interference on my behalf.

I am, my Lord, your Lordship's faithful & obedient servant,

Thomas Hayton

Ch Com. F.1278

1. George Pelham (1766–1827), Bishop of Lincoln 1820–1827.
2. Bounty Board, founded 1704.
3. Parliamentary Grant of 1813 to help the poorer clergy.

[2] To Mr Hodgson [1]

Crendon, 14 March 1822

Sir,

Having been the resident Incumbent of the living of *Long Crendon* in the county of Bucks for the space of a year & it is my intention to reside regularly & as the interest of £200 granted to the said Living from Queen Anne's Bounty will be due I shall thank you very kindly to think of me; for the salary which I receive is nominally small & in reality, during these times is still less.

Believe me Sir, very respectfully yours,

Thomas Hayton

Ch Com. F.1278

1. Christopher Hodgson (1784–1871), Secretary to the Governors of Queen Anne's Bounty from 1822 to 1871.

[3] To the Bounty Board

27 March 1822

Dear Sir,

Agreeable to your request I have sent a certification of the number of the inhabitants of my parish — and humbly hope you will obtain [. . . *torn* . . .] augmentation from the Office.

I am Sir, very respectfully yours,

Thos Hayton

N.B.

Let it not be forgotten that I am regularly resident — where no Minister ever resided before viz in the village of Long Crendon.

This is to certify that the number of inhabitants in the parish of Long Crendon was twelve hundred & fourteen in the census of 1821 — and that the number at present is upwards of twelve hundred & twenty [1].

Witnessed in hand Richard Gunn, churchwarden

27 March 1822

Ch Com. F.1278

1. The Bounty Board in 1811 received discretionary power to give a preference to Livings under £150 a year where the population exceeded 1000. (Best, p. 213).

[4] To the Bounty Board

Crendon, 15 February 1823

Sir,

I find there is a charge of eleven shillings as land tax [1] upon my Living of Long Crendon which was augmented by Queen Anne's Bounty — pray, is there not fund whereby such tax may be discharged? — and, as the Curacy does not *now* produce fifty pounds a year & as the number of inhabitants exceeds twelve hundred, cannot you interest yourself on my behalf? I cannot learn why my petition for augmentation [2] was rejected last year, Mr Smith, the Bishop's secretary, referred me to you, but my income will not allow such journeys. Respectfully requesting your help, believe me Sir,

your obedient servant,

Thomas Hayton

Ch Com. F.1278

1. A rate levied on land at 4s.0d. in the £.
2. The Bounty Board did not approve of augmenting livings otherwise than jointly with lay patrons.

24 February 1823

Long Crendon

Revd. Sir,

I advise you to refer to Mr De Costa Land Tax Office Parliament Street as to Exoneration from that Tax. Your Living is not augmentable according to the Rules of the Governors — it has been brought forward twice and disapproved on that account.

C.H. Sec.

Ch Com. F.1278

[6] To Mr Hodgson

Crendon, 15 May 1824

Sir,

About two years ago my Living of Long Crendon in the County of Bucks was intended to have been augmented by the Governors of Queen Anne's Bounty; but such intention was soon after notified to me as being laid aside. Mr. Smith, Secretary to the Bishop of Lincoln, could not tell me the reason why it has not been mentioned but requested me to confer with you on this point as the small Income & the number of inhabitants give it a priority of claim. I now let the glebe land only at £50 per annum & the number of Inhabitants amounts to thirteen hundred!! The Bishop promised his interest to the furtherance of this matter, but at present all is as silent as the grave about it. If you can possibly give me any information or would use your interest to the promoting of so desirable an object I would take it as a very great favour, & will take an early opportunity of personally thanking you.

Yours very respectfully,

Thomas Hayton

Ch Com. F.1278

[7] To Mr Hodgson

Crendon, 20 April 1825

Sir,

In your last letter to me you mentioned that the only way the Governors of Queen Anne's Bounty could listen to an Augmentation of my Living was by a donation on the part of the Patron or some other person. — I have now to inform you that Lord Churchill, the Lay Rector & Patron [1] is willing to grant to the Perpetual Curacy six or eight acres of land to the value of two hundred or so, if the Governors will allow a sum of money for the Augmen-

3

tation of the Curacy. The number of inhabitants is upwards of thirteen hundred: I have double duty half of the year and the Glebe land & farm house is let for £50 per annum. The open field of Long Crendon is now under an Act of Inclosure [2] & the respective allotments are expected to be known at Michaelmas next: therefore this is a good time for the purchase of land: & I humbly request you will lay my case before the Governors as early as you conveniently can.

    Believe me, Sir, yours respectfully,

    Thos Hayton

Ch Com. F.1278

1. Francis Almeric Churchill (1779–1845); third son of George Spencer, 4th Duke of Marlborough. Created Baron 1815.
2. B.R.O. Long Crendon Enclosure Award.

[8] Bounty Office to Hayton

                   2 May 1825

Revd Sir,

  In consequence of your letter I have forwarded to your Diocesan the usual Printed Queries to be transmitted to you — when answered and returned the Papers will be laid before the Governors at the 1st opportunity & you will soon after be informed of the result.

  It may expedite the Business if in the meantime you will send me the names of 3 Clergymen & 3 Laymen of Character in the neighbourhood whom you can recommend to your Diocesan as proper persons for Commissioners to view and value the Estate proposed to be given and make their report thereof to the Governors. I will send the usual Commission Queries to the Bishop who will sign & transmit the same to you, if his Lordship approves the Persons names for Commissioners.

    I am etc.

    C.H.

Ch Com. F.1278

[9] To Mr Hodgson

             Crendon, 7 October 1825

Dear Sir,

  In answer to your enquiry of the 24th September, I have to observe that in addition to the value of Lord Churchill's proposed donation, I will advance £50 in order to make the sum of £800.

  The Commissioner [1] has left a portion of land to be sold adjoining my allotment [2], by the purchase of which the Living would be greatly benefited. May I then be allowed to request you to inform me when I may expect to hear of the Governors' decision in order that arrangements may be made accordingly.

I am Sir, yours very respectfully,

Thomas Hayton

Ch Com. F.1278

1. Thomas James Tatham, Commissioner for the Crendon Enclosure.
2. The curacy had been allotted seventy-eight acres in lieu of small tithes.

[10] To the Duke of Buckingham [1]

Crendon, 5 July 1826

The Revd. T. Hayton respectfully acknowledges the Circular of the Duke of Buckingham [2] and begs leave to observe that there is a manuscript in the Bodleian Library which contains ample details respecting the Abbey of Notley (the only notable relic of antiquity in this parish) and Mr Hayton would esteem it an honour, as it would be a pleasure, in endeavouring to make extracts suitable to the purpose of the Duke of Buckingham, should his Grace express his wishes to that Effect.

Huntington Library, California, Stack L 13 Section E Shelf 1

1. Richard Grenville Temple Nugent Brydges Chandos, 1st Duke of Buckingham.
2. A questionnaire was sent out to clergy with a view to the Duke writing a history of the county.

[11] To Bishop Kaye [1]

Long Crendon, Lower Winchendon, Chearsley
23 April 1827

My Lord,

The subject of your Lordship's communication of the 20th inst I will endeavour to explain with candour and sincerity.

The Glebe House for the Benefice of Long Crendon is perhaps one of the meanest edifices of the same nature in the whole range of your diocese. There is a kitchen & a parlour (about 8 feet by 10 each) with a small pantry below stairs; above there is the same number of rooms, such as I am sure your Lordship would scarcely deem suitable even to your lowest menial. Indeed no clergyman within the memory of man, previous to myself ever resided in the village of Crendon, much less in the Glebe House [2]. When I first succeeded to the living there was no money for dilapidations; the annual amount was £50! for 3 years did I serve Long Crendon without a shilling reward. Nay I was creditor if my services were worth anything. I repaired – I built stalls and Cow-houses, only last year to the amount of £70 & upwards!! I represented my case to the Patron; I effected an Inclosure and have obtained 20 acres as a Benefaction from the Patron. The anxieties I have undergone I need not

5

specify to your Lordship — suffice it to say they were many & trying and not yet entirely dissipated. I mentioned to an Archdeacon my want of a House; he observed that it was a matter of regret, but to mortgage so small a Living would never do, or something to that effect; 'He would however, speak to the Bishop & see whether a sum of money could be procured from the Fund for building churches [3], as he believed there was a clause in reference to poor parsonages'. And Long Crendon, my Lord, has been for a long time one of the poorest in the Diocese, though *now* it averages £150 per annum but would not be £100 if there was no House for a Tenant — nay, I hesitate not to assert that no Tenant could be procured on such terms — it was a matter of difficulty to get one at all — & five years have I lodged in the village in one small apartment less than the least of a Cambridge or Oxford attic; nor have I omitted to perform punctually my duties during that time saving 3 or 4 Sundays when I was afflicted most severely with a Typhus fever, nor have I but once since my ordination to the village been able to see my friends in the North of England. I trust, therefore, your Lordship will extend to me as one of the working clergy the privilege of choosing my residence, till some arrangement or plan may be adopted by which both myself and the Occupier of the Land may be suited.

The curacies of Winchendon and Chearsley, formerly Chapels of Ease to Crendon have always been or nearly always, in consequence of their poverty served with Crendon; and when not so, the incumbent was compelled to give a Title annually! and as there is no parsonage house in either village, the Curacies have been served from Oxford (a distance of 15 miles). There is no clergyman in the neighbourhood who can serve either one or both but myself, and I leave it to your Lordship's consideration whether of the two evils my continuance of the curacies is not preferable.

This subject was discussed between me & the late Bishop of Lincoln, when I explained to him the smallness of my Income — the regularity which had been paid to the Curacies — the satisfaction which had been given & the whole hearing of the case; his Lordship immediately granted my request to hold them, thinking that a case was sufficiently made out to create an exception to his rule. I am regularly licensed, my lord, at £60 a year, nor can the Living afford more; I have no private fortune nor expectations whatever either from College or from friends: I have been engaged to be married, experiencing the malady of hope deferred & have taken a House within 10 minutes walk of both the villages, & had appointed August for its consummation, depending on my living and stipendiary Income for its support [4]. I entreat, therefore, your Lordship not to wrench from me that on which my hopes are rested, not be inflexibly determined that I must forego my curacies (for I cannot give up one without the other) nor inflict a twofold blow on those little prepared to meet it; nor have I the vanity to think that such a measure will be a source of regret to the Incumbent of the Livings, who I am conscious, appreciates the faithfulness of my services, & the preference of whose regard I frequently experience. There are many other topics which I would press upon your Lordship; as countrymen a partiality on my behalf would be forgiven, even by the strictest disciplinarian: but I hope what I have said will induce your Lordship to comply with my request, to yield to my entreaty, & thus confer a favor of no small importance on my Lord

your Lordship's faithful & obedient servant,

Thomas Hayton

N.B. As soon as my Living acquires the highest amount (& I expect another augmentation should the Title to the Patron's benefaction be admissible) I will willingly & with alacrity use every means to have a Parsonage suited to the Living. T.H.

L.A.O., Cor. B 5/3/21/1

1. John Kaye (1783–1852), son of Abraham Kaye, linen draper of Hammersmith; Master of Christ's College, Cambridge, 1814–30; Bishop of Bristol 1820–27; Lincoln 1827–53; theological writer; active in politics, evangelical in sympathies, resolute opponent of pluralities and non-residence. See *D.N.B.*
2. The old vicarage in Carters Lane was exchanged in 1741 for the present vicarage in the High Street (L.A.O., Episcopal Act Book 1723–1761).
3. In 1818, Parliament voted one million pounds to build new churches.
4. In July, 1827, Hayton married Adelaide, daughter of John Stevens of Rickmansworth.

[12] *To Bishop Kaye*

Haddenham, 25 June 1829

My Lord,

In the Archdeacon's [1] late parochial visitation, he intimated the propriety of my serving but two Churches. Your Lordship is already in possession of the circumstances of the case: but I think it fitting briefly to advert to them, previous to the Confirmation at Risborough, that I may know your Lordship's decision thereon, to which I will of course, bend with the most dutiful and respectful submission.

I have certainly been a slave in the vineyard for eleven years. My living of Crendon has fluctuated from £50 to £180 per annum: the two curacies from £60 (at which I am licenced) to £70, as Mr Kipling [2] pleased. The Archdeacon told me that your Lordship would doubtless allow me the whole amount of one curacy if the other was given up, as there were no outgoings attached to either, no Incumbent resident on either, & each being under the annual value of £75. But this matter I leave entirely in your Lordship's hands, being convinced that you are a friend to the lower orders of the Clergy & an advocate for the principle of 'all things being done decently & in order'.

With profound respect, allow me to subscribe myself

your Lordship's faithful & obedient servant,

T. Hayton

P.S. If your Lordship will allow me an audience at Risborough I will explain my intentions so that my residence at Crendon may be effected.

L.A.O., Cor. B 5/3/21/1

1. Revd Justley Hill (1781–1853), archdeacon of Buckingham 1825–1853.
2. Revd John Kipling (1767–1839), vicar of Oakley and perpetual curate of Chilton, Chearsley, and Lower Winchendon.

[13] To Bishop Kaye

Haddenham, 13 July 1829

My Lord,

Previous to your Lordship's final decision respecting the Curacy of Lower Winchendon, I think myself perfectly justified in urging every consideration on my own behalf, inasmuch as the privation of thirty pounds a year is of very great importance indeed to a person of very limited Income.

Since I saw your Lordship, I made further inquiry respecting Mr Kipling's Income, & I find that my statement was more than borne out by the reality; and when I say that the Living of Crendon was about £180 per annum, I forgot to observe that this was the gross amount; & that the deductions for repairs of barns & for new hedges upon the lately inclosed land would amount to nearly £60. I think also that I ought not to omit mentioning Mr Kipling's repeated promise to me for upwards of six years, that he would cede the Livings of Chearsley & Winchendon in my behalf; & that had not such a promise been existing, I could have procured two years ago a Curacy of £100 a year, with a good house upon it within such a distance of my Living that your Lordship would have allowed my residence there. I leave, however, the matter entirely in your Lordship's hands for an equitable arrangement.

I am most faithfully your Lordship's obedient servant,

T. Hayton

[Minute by the Bishop]
July 23rd 1829

Told him he must give up Chearsley and retain Winchendon with a stipend of £50. Told Mr Kipling the same.

L.A.O. Cor. B 5/3/21/1

[14] To Bishop Kaye

Haddenham, 22 October 1829

My Lord,

The Head-mastership of the Latin School at Aylesbury is now vacated. I wish to ascertain from your Lordship, whether I should be permitted to hold my curacies in conjunction with it, in the event of my being the successful candidate. The distance from Aylesbury to Winchendon is five miles, to Crendon about 7 and a half [1]. If your Lordship would allow residence at such a distance, might I be excused in requesting of you a testimonial of *character* & *abilities*. The former, from obvious causes, must be of a negative kind; the latter perhaps you might feel justified in avouching for, when I inform you that, without intending it, I received a second class degree at

Oxford; & will now have testimonials from three heads of houses & others not a whit inferior in respectability & literary attainments.

An early reply will greatly oblige my Lord,

your Lordship's faithful & obedient servant,

T. Hayton

[Bishop's minute]

Answered in the negative

L.A.O Cor. B 5/3/21/1

1. An Act of 1813 (53 Geo III c. 149) insisted that curates must reside in their parish.

[15] To Bishop Kaye

Crendon, 22 March 1831

My Lord,

I hope your Lordship will excuse this liberty I take in addressing your Lordship, but as it is a case I have every reason to suppose your Lordship must be unacquainted, I feel myself justified as a Parishioner in stating the circumstance — Long Crendon the Parish in which I reside contains fifteen hundred Inhabitants, and I regret being under the necessity of informing your Lordship that we have not had a resident Clergyman for these four years — The excuse hitherto has been that the Vicarage House was not in repair; but such is not the case now the same having undergone a thorough repair — The shortest the Clergyman resides from the village is four miles. Consequently the sick are not properly attended to, the distance being a great obstacle in the way of his attendance. I have also to add, that there is but one sermon; and prayers occasionally: I trust, therefore, your Lordship will see the necessity for his immediate residence — I would not have troubled your Lordship, did I not as a strict Churchman see the necessity of doing so, feeling grieved at the decrease of the members of the established Church, and the increase of other sects. I am sure I may express in the name of all the parish, their anxiety to have a resident Clergyman, as some of them are compelled to go to a neighbouring Church.

I have the honour to remain your Lordship's most obedient & faithful servant,

A Parishioner of Long Crendon Bucks

L.A.O. Cor. B 5/3/21/1

[16] To Bishop Kaye

Haddenham, 28 March 1831

My Lord,

Your Lordship's letter of this morning has just anticipated a communication which I have been on the point of transmitting during these last ten days; to the effect of informing your Lordship what I had done to the Parsonage House at Crendon, of the motives which induced me so to act, and requesting your Lordship's advice & assistance under such circumstances.

Your Lordship is already aware of the difficulties I had experienced in procuring a Tenant to the Glebe, and the loss I experienced in consequence of it. A respectable person (who would put the land into condition) offered himself as Tenant provided I would make the House decently habitable. With the Patron's leave (Lord Churchill's) & I ought to have had your Lordship's also, if I had not thought the matter beneath such a formal application — I pulled down an old parlour with the intention of making it to the Tenant's wishes. Finding nearly the whole of the building in sorrowful decay [1], I was determined to make a sacrifice of one year's income, I have accordingly done so; — and, to my own present embarassment & my deep-seated grief — much more has been expended. The house I have actually remodelled! — in the first place to fulfil my agreement with the Tenant, and secondly, with a hope of eventually living there myself. My desire of writing to your Lordship was to ascertain whether a representation of my case might not influence the Governors of Queen Anne's Bounty to give me a donation to fulfil my plans — to make another Kitchen & an out-house or two (*absolutely necessary*) to the value of £50 more or less [1]. I have it is true borrowed money to effect what I have done at £8 per cent: which I should have told your Lordship at the coming Visitation. I wish everything to be canvassed fairly & freely; & I appeal to Lord Churchill & to many neighbouring Clergymen whether or not I have not made sacrifices uncalled for & unwarrantable, & which worldly men attribute only to my folly. At this I grieve not whilst hope and health are granted me. I court enquiry not only into the facts of the case, but to every particular of those facts. — No one can be more sensible of the propriety of residence than myself; & all my wishes & desires have been to this effect. — If the Church would purge herself from her impurities on this head, I should rejoice; her enemies would not then have such room for complaint, & her friends would not blush when pressed with such topics. But to return I throw myself upon your Lordship's good sense: The Tenant is new, just entering upon the House, *as it is — unfinished;* he has left an abode 9 miles distant from this residence. I myself cannot leave this house I at present occupy before this time 12 months. — Had your informer the interests of Christianity at heart, I would have excused his mischievous interference — Lord Brougham's Judas' quotation very aptly applies.

For these last 3 years I have been at Crendon, upon an average 5 days in the week, & I challenge any slanderous complaint to the utmost development of his dastardly insinuations 'An enemy hath done this' & your Lordship I trust will deem it proper to exhibit before me his communication.

> I have the honour to be, my Lord, your Lordship's faithful & obedient servant,
>
> Thos Hayton

P.S. The author of the letter must have told a deliberate untruth; for at the time of it being written there were no windows in the house, the scaffolding still before it, & not a fixture in it. As your Lordship must frequently meet Lord Churchill in the House of Peers an enquiry whether I had not written to his Lordship stating my wish to reside & requesting some little assistance might be a little satisfaction.

To the Lord Bishop of Lincoln
Warren's Hotel, Regent Street, London

L.A.O. Cor. B 5/3/21/1

1. Once a residence had become too mean for contemporary ideas there was absolutely no means of putting up a new one except for a benefactor (the patron perhaps) to give one (Best p. 205).

[17] *Bishop Kaye to Hayton* [on back of letter]

Reverend Sir,

You form a very erroneous judgment when you thought it a matter of little importance whether you acquainted me with your intentions respecting the Vicarage house at Crendon, before you proceeded to carry them into execution. If a Clergyman lets his Vicarage house without the Diocesan permission, he lets it at his own risk. The steps which you have taken may be the best possible under the circumstances of the case but they ought not to have been taken without previous communication to me. I shall, however defer my final determination in the matter till my Visitation, which I hope to hold in June. I know not whether the Governors of Queen Anne's Bounty have in their hands any money which has been allotted to the augmentation of Crendon but if they have they will not allow it to be expended on the House, unless you mean yourself to reside.

L.A.O. Cor. B 5/3/21/1

[18] *To Bishop Kaye*
Haddenham, 7 April 1831

My Lord,

Since I last wrote to your Lordship I have had a survey & estimate made of the outbuildings etc which a residence at Crendon absolutely demands: & I find that about £115 or £120 would cover the expense.

I propose with your Lordship's concurrence to sell a close of one acre (belonging to the Living) situated in the Midst of a Gentleman's property [1] and the two other pieces of land to the amount of one acre & a half, at a very great distance from the Church & my allotment [2] : the value of which land laid out upon the premises alluded to would make the House of residence very decent & respectable & just in keeping with the value of the Living. If, therefore your Lordship will take the earliest possible steps to effect &

11

designate a proceeding, I shall look upon it as a personal favour, & use every exertion to be in residence next year.

> I have the honour to be your Lordship's faithful & obedient servant,
>
> Thomas Hayton

L.A.O. Cor. B 5/3/21/1

1. A small close in the middle of Lord Churchill's property.
2. Two small closes at Lower End.

[19] To Bishop Kaye

Thursday morning April 1831

My Lord,

I am perfectly ready to acknowledge the truth & propriety of your Lordship's observations, and to plead guilty of being out of order, though actuated by the best intentions for the furtherance of the Temporal and spiritual advantage of my Parish. Since the memory of man no clergyman ever lived in the Glebe House at Crendon — the premises attached to the Living were bought expressly for the Occupier of the land: such being the case, it is not unnatural for me to act without your Lordship's permission.

The Governors of Queen Anne's Bounty have no money in their hands belonging to the Living. To specify before them the population of the Parish, to exhibit the proofs of what I have expended, & at the same time, to pledge myself to the earliest possible residence, might possibly induce the Governors to grant me some assistance, inasmuch as the deed would be in thorough accordance with the spirit of the Act of Parliament [1].

Trusting your Lordship will use exertions on my behalf I have the honour of remaining,

> Your Lordship's very respectful & obedient servant,
>
> Thos. Hayton

Population of Crendon 1500
What I have expended on the Living £293.

L.A.O. Cor. B 5/3/21/1

1. Sir William Scott's Act of 1803, dealing with the non-residence of the clergy. 43 Geo. III c. 84.

[20] To Bishop Kaye

Haddenham 26 May 1832

My Lord,

I have at different times mentioned to your Lordship the great expenses which my Living of Long Crendon has caused me in my endeavour to improve it, & make the Glebe House habitable. By calculation I find that upwards of 2½ years Income has been expended upon it; & though I have rebuilt the cottage in the plainest style & at a most moderate cost, I find myself unable to render it decently suitable for a humble pastor. I wish, however, to make all possible exertions to effect this object; but, looking at my own monied engagements I find myself woefully constricted — may I, therefore, entreat your Lordship to lend me some trifling assistance to purchase some fixtures, grates etc., and I will be in residence by Michaelmas. Nothing but the extremest lack of means urges me to press this upon your Lordship; & aware as I am, how often a Bishop must be appealed to for his charity, & knowing at the same time, that the Bishopric of Lincoln is not a wealthy See — even five pounds would be very acceptable to me, & I should feel grateful to your Lordship for it.

At any rate I wish to live at Crendon, for, there lies my duty and I wish to perform it. There is a Tenant in the Glebe House; & I wish your Lordship to make an order for my going into residence by the first of September sooner should your Lordship wish, & a copy of such order to be transmitted to me or to one of the Churchwardens, so that no impediment may arise to obstruct my wishes.

Should your Lordship wish to know the exact details of my expenditure on the Living &* how much may still be required to accomplish the object alluded to, I will be happy to state all particulars.

Be pleased, my Lord to pardon me, for manifesting the qualities of an importunate & sturdy beggar, & to accept the assurances of my profound respect.

> I am my Lord, your Lordship's very faithful & obedient servant,
>
> Thos Hayton

*£50 or £60. There is House, garden, wash house & stable; I will more particularize should it be required.

[Minute by Bishop Kaye]

June 2nd 1832 £5 No. 23022 N. Stock

L.A.O. Cor. B 5/3/21/1

[21] To Bishop Kaye

Crendon, June 1832

My Lord,

I take an early opportunity of thanking your Lordship for the remittance which I have this morning received & of removing the erroneous impression under which your Lordship seems to be labouring. The order which I requested was not to remove the Tenant from the house (which he already is willing to give up to me) but for me to show to my Landlord your Lordship's wishes on this subject. This gentleman has been very kind to me and I was apprehensive he might think me ungrateful had I removed from his neighbourhood under my own spontaneity. — Had your Lordship sent me an order I should not have used it in an ordinary manner — my feelings are in diametric opposition to such proceedings; — nor would I have thrown the odium of such an act upon your Lordship — this would have been utterly abhorrent to me. I therefore as Tenant must make as good a case as I can.

One word allow me, on the other point. I declare to your Lordship most solemnly, that nothing but the hardness and urgency of necessity would have brought me to prefer such a request before your Lordship: After having been 14 years in the Church & labouring with triple duty and often times more, & having expended so much on my Living & then finding myself in poverty, & Mother Church so unkind in her returns, some excuse may be found for me, when I lose my philosophical temperament, & I am anxious to have my burden alleviated. I envy not your Lordship adorned with a mitre: I think you are one of the best of the order; but I am not blind to a system of favouritism which has been so long carried on both in Church & State, & which is now beginning to get spoken of without much rancour. We must set our houses in order or that will be done for us, & perhaps with a vengeance.

Pardon me, pardon me, my Lord, this is a subject on which I am apt to be warm: nevertheless, I look upon your Lordship with very great esteem and I feel grateful for your assistance.

> I have the honour to be my Lord, your Lordship's faithful & obedient servant,

> T. Hayton

P.S. I really do not remember anything in the 'Manner' of my letter, either disrespectful towards your Lordship, or unsuitable to the relation of life in which I stand; if there was, I should be heartily sorry for it. As to the 'Matter', though I have acknowledged that the object of the requested order did not appear on the face of it, yet, were your Lordship placed in my situation, & wishing to 'give none offence', there would appear nothing extraordinary. Neither my inclinations, nor any occasion, has led me to study the boundaries of a Bishop's power; an error, therefore, on this head may be pardonable, having heard also that such power, but not in your Lordship's person, has been exercised with authority. Nor could I for one moment wish to extract an answer from your Lordship marked with 'arbitrariness' & apply it in a way disgraceful to my own character, or at all reflecting on the character of my Diocesan. T.H.

L.A.O. Cor. B 5/3/21/1

[22] To Bishop Kaye

5 September 1832

My Lord,

The Tenant of my House at Crendon now demurs about giving it up to me at Michaelmas (although he was sent a regular notice to that effect) without some money compensation — on the ground that he has a right to occupy it till next mid-summer in order to take off his crop, & that he looks upon the House as merely a farm-house, no Clergyman having in remembrance lived in it. As I am not versed in these matters, perhaps your Lordship will be so kind as to give me advice on this point. I must leave my present house on the 29th & am consequently rather awkwardly placed. I would not wish to act in any way unbecoming or illiberal, but I will not gratify the wishes of a designing knave.

> I am my Lord, your Lordship's faithful & obedient servant,
>
> Thos Hayton

L.A.O. Cor. B 5/3/21/1

[23] To Bishop Kaye

Crendon, 4 April 1833

My Lord,

I have been induced by some of my friends to address your Lordship respecting the living of Radnage [1]. I do so in despair, in as much as I have not, I conceive (for I will be candid) at all times received at your Lordship's hand the most courteous treatment: to hope however against hope is no new doctrine.

I have no priestly pretensions to urge; I have no deep treaties of theology to recommend me; I disdain to sue for human testimonials of general conduct, or particular sanctity; and if I were to present your Lordship my published political opinions, they would not, I predict, receive the stamp of your Lordship's approbation; but I may venture, I trust, without impertinence to ask — has any man in your Lordship's Diocese during 15 years laboured more unremittingly with triple duty (& oftentimes more) for so poor a remuneration? Has anyone expended on so small a Living upwards of £500 to accomplish residence — without encumbering his successor? This I have done, & more; & I have gained by it rebuke & much sorrow. This thing, however, is done; and twenty years must elapse before in any likelihood I can repay the money lent to me by my friends: which leaves me barely £100 a year for my subsistence.

Your Lordship's depriving me of the Curacy of Chearsley ought also to be taken into consideration: besides this, if promises have any meaning (I do not allude to the promises of the Lord Chancellor [2]) the Living of Radnage would have now been mine. Thankful and proud of your Lordship's notice, I shall be patient under a refusal.

I have the honour to be my Lord with deep respect for your Lordship's talents & station

> Your very faithful & obedient servant,
>
> Thos Hayton

L.A.O. Cor. B 5/3/21/1

1. The living of Radnage had belonged to the Crown since the Dissolution. The presentation was in the hands of the Lord Chancellor. *V.C.H.* Vol. III p. 32.
2. Lord Brougham was Lord Chancellor in 1831.

Crendon, 8 October 1834

Gentlemen,

The overseers of the parish of *Long Crendon* have shown me their answers to your inquiries [1], as some of their answers do not appear sufficiently explicit, I think it's expedient as a landowner to make a remark or two thereon. This parish has for a long time been notorious for paying the wages of labour out of the poor rate, the evils which occur from this ruinous system I need not specify; suffice it to say that twenty one-shilling rates were levied last year, the amount of which is £3150 or thereabouts. Of this sum £1000 will clear *all* claims for relief, to which add £200 for labour, the remainder is an unnecessary exaction, creating jealousy and dissatisfaction loud and long. Four or five years ago a 8½ or 9 rates were levied, but this was due to independent and efficient overseers to obtain which I find, is a thing of no ordinary difficulty in consequence of so many playing the game of self interest. The affairs of this parish are conducted by what is *called* a Select Vestry [2] — but after no provision of any Act of Parliament whatsoever; indeed it is more like a private cabal (I will explain more fully should it be so desired). Were each individual who now takes his allotted number of men to pay them out of his own pocket and not 'from the Book' we would require very little rating except on the aged etc.

I am sorry to find that an attempt is made in a High Quarter in this county to ridicule and deprecate the 'New Bill' which in my humble opinion is one of the boldest and wisest measures of the century. It is purely English, it *organizes* the people on *their* own behalf, and seeks to enforce *their justice to one* another. The 54th clause [3] is the height of legislation — it grapples with the affair at once, and must be successful unless spoilt by ill advised conduct on the part of the Board.

I have the honour to be, Gentlemen, your obedient & humble servant,

Thos Hayton

Perhaps you will have the kindness to tell me whether a 40/- a year tenement would enable the occupier by paying rates to gain a settlement? If this is the case, we shall be inundated by paupers from adjoining parishes, unless these cottages are struck off the rent book. Or must the tenement be by a £10 rental as before. T.H.

Note for reply
. . . the situation and circumstances of the parish will at no distant time be carefully examined.

M.H. 12/9732

1. The Poor Law Commissioners in October 1834 sent a circular to all parish vestries.
2. A self-perpetuating body, recruiting its own members.
3. The Poor Law Amendment Act, 4.5. William IV c. 76, cl. 54. — 'It shall not be lawful for any overseer to give any further relief from the poor-rate than such as shall be ordered by the overseers'.

Crendon, 31 October 1834

Gentlemen,

The system of paying the wages of labour out of the poor-rate has at length been abolished, a consequence of which is that there is much animosity and considerable difficulty arising from this very temper respecting the best means of employing the surplus labour now entirely at a *standstill*. In fact, we are in a very awkward dilemma, totally at a loss how to employ the labour alluded to. There is no poor house, no spirit of public improvement, nothing whereon such labour can be profitably expended, and worst of all scarcely any cash forthcoming. I am requested by the overseers to write to you for advice. How are they to proceed? Is money to be given to the men, or sustenance alone? When may we expect your rules and regulations, and what is to be the *principle* of Union — incorporation? As an ardent friend to the new law, I earnestly request of you to let me have something in the shape of a decision. The *shadow* of *wavering* is good for the enemy, I know how the measures are beset with difficulties, but human passions & prejudices will make little allowance; & I have lived long enough to find out that there are many impediments marring parish discussions.

Do you recommend the allowance to continue in existence till your orders are issued? & when may we have these orders? I trust, Gentlemen, you do not flatter yourselves that this Bill will work out the benefits which it involves by its own energy and virtue — an inference which may be drawn in case of an unnecessary protracted delay. I need not again repeat, that any information (of course local) which I can give you is entirely at your convenience. In the mean time be pleased to give me an answer to this letter as speedily as may be convenient, in order that our labourers be employed and the minds of some of my parishioners may become more entire and reassured.

I have the honour to be, Gentlemen,

Thos Hayton

[Abstract of Draft Reply]
It would not be advisable to discontinue the system at once but every opportunity should be taken of promoting its gradual extinction — The Board feels very strongly the difficulty of making any suggestion without full information of local circumstances — allowances to be given to paupers in employment and to be given in bread alone.

M.H. 12/9732

[26] To the Commissioners of the New Poor Law

Crendon, 10 December 1834

Gentlemen,

I am sorry to push you at a quicker pace than may be convenient, but I can assure you that there is tiptoe expectation here to see a commissioner in this neighbourhood, inasmuch as there will be no more fertile field in England for the exertion of his powers and his talents. So far as regards this parish, we are all quiet at present — how long this may last is very problematical. The farmers have each taken a proportionate number of men; some we have put at stone digging; others are at spade husbandry without task work & consequently doing little good & no payments have yet been made in kind. We have a great struggle against the 'paying out of the Book' system — that fleshpot by so many so much longed after.

I have spoken to different persons respecting an incorporation of parishes; there seems to be a Loose & general wish to avoid unions of all description — the idea of sending from one parish to another the very worst characters not being much relished. I have endeavoured to shake this prejudice by the reasons adduced in the 'Remedial Measures' & among the most intelligent, I flatter myself not without some success.

The Town of Thame appears to be a fitting place for such an attempt. The Parishes of Long Crendon, Chilton, Chearsley, Winchendon, Cuddington, Haddenham, Kingsey, Towersey, Sydenham, Tetsworth, Moreton, Shabbington & Ickford — all lie in a circle from one to three miles from the centre of Thame. If this should be disliked, Crendon, having a large piece of parish ground with houses & barn adjoining, might be made the centre of a smaller union, say Chilton, Chearsley, Winchendon, and Shabbington.

I hope, Gentlemen, ere long to hear of some progress made in this matter, as we are all very anxious to elect Guardians, & bring our parish matters into something like shape & order.

I have the honour to be your respectful & obedient servant,

Thomas Hayton

M.H. 12/9732

[27] *From the* Bucks Herald

17 January 1835

A Hint to Dr Lee. We have been told of a parson (a friend of ours) who living not more than ten leagues from Long Crendon, preached an orthodox sermon on Sunday morning, and in the afternoon went canvassing his parishioners for Dashwood [1] and Lee [2].

1. G.H. Dashwood of West Wycombe.
2. Dr Lee of Hartwell, radical eccentric (1783—1866). The election was won by the Conservatives, Chandos, Praed and Young.

[28] *To the* Bucks Herald

24 January 1835

Sir,

You were often times amusingly sportive, and last week you were inclined to be so at the expense of truth. In giving a 'hint to Dr Lee' I cannot but recognise something more than a hint to myself, which compels me to inform you that a part of that paragraph was utterly false. The only house I visited on the Sunday alluded to, was the abode of a dying neighbour, whose conversation was much less earthy than the grovelling topic of politics. Certainly a person in the village called upon me in the evening and asked me for my vote for Dr Lee. I expressed to him my astonishment at his request: refused him an answer —— I am Sir, 'The Parson not ten leagues from Long Crendon' and with many failings.

> Yours respectfully,
>
> Thomas Hayton

[29] To the Poor Law Commissioners

Crendon, 7 February 1835

Gentlemen,

Lady Day is advancing apace & no tidings of a Commissioner [1]. Our system now is a strange one; for we have no vestry. The Overseer, who is a large *renter of land* only, because he could not have his own *select clique*, calls no meetings, but signs a rate; carries it to the magistrates who confirm it! even tho' they know it has no sanction from the vestry. No books have been seen for months, & consequently there is much dissatisfaction. We are waiting patiently for a Commissioner in order that some proper arrangements should be made.

I shall not be at home till the 13th but my churchwarden Mr *Edward Shrimpton* [2], who is a sensible man, will readily and plainly point out to the Commissioner the system on which we have been acting. There will be two tales but the commissioner must hear them both.

I hope that as little delay as possible will take place: for we have some excellent offers of emigration to Jamaica, but the labourers will not accept — under the delusion that the parish *must find* them labour & consequently wages. They will not be dissuaded of this error.

> I have the honour, Gentlemen, to be your obedient servant,
>
> T. Hayton

M.H. 12/9732

1. An Assistant Commissioner was sent to form a group of parishes into a Union.
2. Edward Shrimpton, needlemaker (1778—1863).

[30] To the Poor Law Commissioners

Crendon, 12 February 1835

Gentlemen,

Thank you for your attention to my letter of the 8th instant, but I must plainly tell you that yours of this morning was anything but satisfactory, especially as your Assistant Commissioner has been within 3 miles of this parish.

I wish most distinctly to know whether you sanction the suppression of vestries [1], and whether the overseer is to do as he pleases? The reason for asking this sanction arises from the circumstances of many families here wishing to emigrate to Jamaica, and who, having requested answer from the overseer, met with a refusal, on the ground that he, the overseer, had consulted with one or two of his brothers, rack-renters, who were unwilling to grant any help; when it is a known fact, that were the question put to the vote at a vestry, it would be carried on behalf of emigration [2].

This point is of importance, inasmuch as the minds of many are warm for the object — having lately heard from friends at New York reporting very favourably.

Surely, Gentlemen, the overseer should be taught his duty; & it appears to me, you should not be backward in rebuking him.

I have the honour to be,

Thos Hayton

[Answer on back of letter (extract)]
. . . the powers now exercised by Parish & by Elected Vestries . . . will in great measure be suppressed when the management of Poor Law affairs is placed in the Hands of a Board of Guardians.

M.H. 12/9732

1. Poor Law administration had been taken out of the jurisdiction of the Vestry.
2. Vestries encouraged their paupers to emigrate, thus saving on the poor-rate.

[31] To Christopher Hodgson

Crendon, 4 March 1835

Sir,

Perhaps you may remember that six or seven years ago the Governors of Queen Anne's Bounty granted the sum of £900 to the Living of Long Crendon, provided Lord Churchill (the patron of the Living) made a satisfactory Title to twenty acres of land about to be given by his Lordship for the augmentation of the Living. *The Title was not deemed satisfactory* — the objection laid down was its being *lifehold* property — Since that time an Act has passed for the 'abolition of fines & recoveries' [1], in which it is provided that *tenants for life with the next person in remainder may join* in effecting conveyance. Lord Churchill & his eldest son now 24 years of age are still anxious that the said 20 acres should be conveyed to the Living; the more so, as I have expended between £500 and £600 on the wretched dwelling which was there & am now resident parson — the first since the flood! The Living is very small: the duties very great: & if you would have the kindness to move for me; so as to be enabled to augment the value of the Living I should feel deeply obliged to you. I have written to Mr Dyneley on this subject; unless I could feel satisfied that the Title would be accepted, I should not like to give you or any one any trouble. The last attempt cost me £30!! so many windings were in the path of the Law.

> I am very respectfully yours,
>
> Thos. Hayton

Ch Com. F.1278

1. Act of Fines and Recoveries 3, 4, William IV c. 74.

[32] To Edward Gulson [1]

Long Crendon, 12 May 1835

Sir,

An annual sum of four pounds was left as a 'Charity' for apprenticing boys belonging to this parish [2]: such money, tho regularly taken by the parish officers has not been appropriated for these 15 years & upwards; and as we hold a vestry on Wednesday next to consider the best means of applying this 'fund', (which exists not as it has been sunk in the great gulf of parish rates) can you, will you be so kind as to give me any information how the Commissioners of Charities would act in the case of no appropriation?

Some wish that something should be said about the matter, others say, it is a shame, & some affirm that so much should be taken out of the rates & applied to emigration. Will you direct or recommend in this matter?

> Yours very respectfully,
>
> Thos Hayton

N.B. Last week there were 75 men & boys entirely out of employ.

M.H. 12/9732

1. Edward Gulson, Assistant Poor Law Commissioner.
2. Hart's Charity founded 1664. An annual sum of £4.2s.1d. was received by the churchwardens for apprenticing boys.

[33] Testimonial from Hayton for Richard Lee, Licentiate of the Apothecary's Company

Haddenham, 1835

My Lords & Gentlemen,

This is to certify that Mr Richard Lee surgeon [1], of the parish of

Haddenham has been personally known to me for these last 16 years; & as to his conduct & abilities, I believe them to be unexceptional [*sic*].

I have the honour to be your obedient humble servant,

Thomas Hayton

M.H. 12/9732

1. Richard Lee (1805—1882), 5th son of Timothy Tripp Lee, Vicar of Thame.

[34] To the Poor Law Commissioners

Crendon, 4 March 1836

Gentlemen,

Will you condescend to answer the question below submitted to you; which, although it may not fall directly within the lines of your public duties, will tend to allay much jarring & squabbling at our parish meetings.

In this parish of Long Crendon, Bucks, we have no select Vestry, nor other similar body constituted under any local act — it is what is called an open vestry: will you be so good as to inform me whether decision of any particular question must be by a *show of hands* or by the graduated scale of voting beyond the £25 ratal?

As our annual officers are about to be chosen & the question is much in dispute, & as the magisterial authorities differ, I hope you will at your earliest convenience have the kindness to send me your opinion.

I have the honour to be Gentlemen, your obedient servant,

Thos Hayton

Minute from the Commissioners
. . . the modes of voting by the Select Vestry Act and Parish Act are not applicable to the ordinary business transacted in an open vestry.

Mr Nichols
Mr Frankland Lewis [1]

[Poor Law Commissioners]

M.H. 12/9732

1. George Nichols (1781—1865). Thomas Frankland Lewis (1780—1855). Poor Law Commissioners. 'Their letters were first sorted out by clerks, the Assistant Commissioners either dealing with them on their own authority, or else submitting them to a Board, which consisted of the three Commissioners, it being apparently assumed that two formed a quorum'. B. and S. Webb, *English Poor Law History. The Last Hundred Years*, Vol. I, Part 2, p. 110.

Crendon, [undated]
[Received 6 August 1836]

Gentlemen,

You have already been informed, that the Board of Guardians [1] at Thame have noted £160 per annum for a Master & Matron to the Workhouse union. Being a member of that Board, I am confident that the decision was made upon very slender & insufficient information, & that the Board, upon further inquiry, would be inclined to follow the example of their neighbours & reduce the sum to £120 *at the farthest.* As, however, it might seem a little unlike business to rescind a resolution so lately passed I trust, Gentlemen, you will seriously consider this & not be inclined to sanction what seems to me & others a very extravagant stipend.

The Aylesbury Union, with a population far greater than that of Thame, have engaged a most able & efficient Master & also Matron for the sum of £100 per annum. & I should feel personally obliged, if you would condescend to state to me the terms given for the like purpose in other Unions of a like population to this.

If the Machinery for this New Poor Law is to be so expensive, this Union will not receive any thing like the benefit anticipated. In this parish of Long Crendon, we now pay *more* for medical charges by £20 annually than when we could ourselves procure such services [2].

I hope you will do me the favour to consider this. It is odious to curtail a Governor located & giving satisfaction. What should be done, must be done quickly — the Election for the Governor is fixed for the 17th of the month.

> I have the honour to be, Gentlemen, your very obedient servant,
>
> Thos Hayton

M.H. 12/9732

1. Crendon became part of the Thame Union in August 1835. Fifty three guardians were elected by the thirty five parishes.
2. Hayton became a guardian in April 1836, and asked for a return of the number of paupers attended by the medical officers of the Union (O.R.O. Thame Union Minute Book V/i/1).

Letters of Thomas Hayton Galley 28 — AB

[36] To the Commissioners of the New Poor Law Amendment Act
Crendon, 7 August 1836

Gentlemen,

I beg to thank you for your ready attention to my letter of the 5th instant respecting the salary for the Governor & Matron to the Workhouse at Thame. I do not think we should give more than our neighbours & I purpose to propose £100 per annum for both the services alluded to; — will you be, therefore, so good as to furnish me with the names of certain Unions about 15 to 20,000 in population where the salary is such or near such as I have stated? This will be a better argument than any thing I can adduce & I am sure to be listened to with more attention. Your early reply will be esteemed a favour.

Gentlemen, your very respectful & obedient servant,

Thos Hayton

[Answer on back of letter]
The Commissioners are not prepared to sanction a higher salary than £120 per annum.

M.H. 12/9732

[37 To the Poor Law Commissioners

Crendon, [undated]
[Received 13 August 1836]

Private
Gentlemen,

In all likelihood you will receive by this post from the Clerk of the Board of Guardians of Thame, *again requesting* your sanction to the payment of £160 per annum to the Master and Matron of the Workhouse, or perhaps something couched in stronger language. Yesterday at the Board five out of seven voted for this proceeding. I urged the propriety of adopting your decision, or of calling of the whole body of the Guardians together (for we have no less than 53) and discuss the question afresh (which question I beg to remark was never discussed at all) — *this* was overruled, and the upshot was the letter you will receive. I hope Gentlemen, you will think to your decision, as I am confident that in the course of a year such an *extravagant* sum will be deeply repented of. Implicit confidence was reposed in one or two individuals, who did not bring any information on the subject, — either as to the nature of the service; or to the wages in other districts, except that of Abingdon, which I do not consider to be any criterion. You certainly would have conferred on me a personal favour by giving me the names of certain Unions from 15,000 to 20,000 in population, and the wages given to the Master and Matron, as thereby I conceive much point would be given to the argument.

I am, Gentlemen, your obedient servant,

Thos Hayton

N.B. If you forward the enclosed notes to Mr Gulson & Mr Hill [1] you will oblige me. They are skilled in matters in reference to the Poor Law Amendment Act.

M.H. 12/9732

1. Richard Hill, Barrister-at-law and Assistant Poor Law Commissioner for Oxfordshire.

[38] To the Commissioners of the Poor Law Amendment Act
Crendon, 16 September 1836

Gentlemen,

The new Registry Act [1] absolutely appoints the Clerk of an Union the superintendent Registrar — a clause in Mr Chadwick's circular [2] says 'subject to the approval of the Poor Law Commissioners'. Will you be so good as to reconnect this?

The 29th section of the Registry Act says 'In case of an Union the said several sums shall be charged to the account of the Parishes in which such births and deaths respectively, shall have occurred'. Are such charges to be admitted as 'Establishment Charges' [3]? If so this parish of Crendon will pay the expenses of Registration for other parishes as she now does in her Medical department. Does the payment for the first 20 entries of births etc. refer to each parish respectively, or to the whole of the district collectively?

Your early attention to the letter will much oblige

your obedient servant,

Thos Hayton

[Note on letter]
Mr Chadwick [4] The writer is right & we are wrong.

[Answer (abstract)]
The payment is for the whole District collectively, but nevertheless the charge for each entry will be debited to the parish where the event takes place.

M.H. 12/9732

1. Births and Deaths Registration Act 6, 7, William IV c. 80.
2. Circulars were sent by the Poor Law Commissioners to all Boards of Guardians.
3. The Thame Union's establishment charges consisted of payments for the upkeep of the workhouse, plus medical charges, wages, etc.
4. Afterwards Sir Edwin Chadwick, K.C.B. (1800—1890). Served on the Poor Law Commission Inquiry; Secretary to the Poor Law Commissioners 1834—1847.

[39] To Bishop Kaye

Crendon, 5 December 1836

My Lord,

The Patron of the Living of Crendon is inclined to give £200 towards the augmentation of it. Will your Lordship have the goodness to inform me what sum the Governors of Queen Anne's Bounty would *in all probability* be inclined to advance in furtherance of this object? Your Lordship, I believe is aware how liberally I have expended here, & what ardous duties fall upon me, to say nothing of the battles of Dissent I have engaged in; & if your Lordship would advocate my cause with the Governors, I should feel very obliged to you. Accept, my Lord, the assurance of my unfeigned esteem and

I remain your Lordship's faithful & obedient servant,

Thomas Hayton

L.A.O. Cor. B 5/3/21/1

[40] Editorial in Aylesbury News

31 December 1836

Mr W. Hopcroft [1], the Baptist Minister has answered the derisive letter entitled 'Voluntaryism' written by the rector of the parish. By the language and slang phrases of which we should suppose the author to have been educated at Billingsgate. Although Mr Hopcraft has not had the advantage of a classical education, he displays a much better knowledge of the scriptures, and the spirit which ought to be shown by a Christian minister, than his antagonist. We intend noting this little work in its proper place next week [3].

1. William Hopcroft, Minister of Long Crendon Baptist Chapel 1822—1845.
2. *Voluntaryism: (that curse on good government) disproved from Scripture and Experience; in a letter to the inhabitants of Long Crendon,* By Thomas Hayton. (Bodl. 130 g 214).
3. *The Voluntary Principle: The Religion of the Bible and a Blessing in the World: Contrasted with a letter to the Inhabitants of Long Crendon entitled* Voluntaryism. (Bodl. 130 g 215).

[41] To the Aylesbury News

Crendon, 3 January 1837

Sir,

I feel honoured by your notice of my pamphlet, and your little abuse of me: it was better than an advertisement which I never wished, and never courted. As you are a 'liberal' man and no doubt an advocate of fair play, perhaps, in adverting to Mr Hopcroft's pamphlet, you will notice also my arguments which Mr H. has taken care not to do. I know they are unassailable and will stand the test of truth. This controversy has been forced upon me. I was challenged to the field, and my motto is 'Lay on Macduff etc'. I have not received the best treatment at the hands of the dissenters; and, were I to tell you the 'whole of the matter' you would not be surprised at a little harsh language which I may have indulged in — language which in cooler moments I might have altered: in short the letter was written at a time of considerable excitement and was never meant to exceed the bounds of the neighbourhood. Besides this, my maxim has ever been not to allow differences, either in religion or politics, to degenerate into personal vindictiveness nor did I expect it in discussing the incidental question of a church establishment. This line has been broken through by Mr Hopcroft; and my reply now ready for the press embraces topics not very sweet to prejudiced ears. I do not deprecate abuse or scurrility, as long as the arguments remain unshaken. As an old political brother, who can now conscientiously support neither Whig nor Tory, I have 'on the voluntary principle' ventured to say thus much in reference to the Billingsgate you christened me with.

I am yours etc.,

Thomas Hayton

[42] To Dean H. Hobart [1]

Crendon [June] 1837

Reverend Sir,

There is an old dilapidated Court Room in Long Crendon [2], said to belong to the Lords of the Manor, viz The Dean & Canons of Windsor, All Souls College & The Duke of Buckingham. This room is only used once annually from 3—4 hours. The windows, or rather I should say receptacles for windows have merely a wooden shutter, moveable to obtain light, and in all other respects the room has a sorry appearance. My object in writing to you is this; to solicit your consent that this room should be a Sunday School in conjunction with the National Society, and of course to be used at any time for Court purposes. May I venture also to prefer another request which I hope will be deemed reasonable under the circumstances I will mention? The village of Crendon contains about 1500 souls. I am the first resident clergy-man 'since the flood' and have expended £100 upon the Living, tho' the living is under £200 a year. There are two dissenting chapels in the place, under which many of the children have been trained. I have resided here for 5 years. When I first came the Sunday School had 27 scholars, now it has upwards of 100 and more to come, but then I cannot carry out the system to say nothing of many other objections. Now this said Court House adjoins the Church-yard, & would with about £20 expense make an excellent place for the purpose. If I could raise a sum of money to the amount of £10—£12, perhaps the National Society would grant something & make up the deficiency. May I therefore say, how very gratified I should be, if you as Dean would use your influence with the Chapter in order to help me in this matter? All Souls has frequently helped me by donations for the School & for the poor, & the names underneath will show the amount of Annual Subscriptions which are expended by paying the teachers. The importance which I attach to this subject & the peculiar circumstances attending it, arising from an uphill battle of Dissent. The few resident supporters, will I hope plead my case for troubling you on this subject.

I have the honour to be, Reverend Sir, your very obedient servant,

Thos Hayton

Lord Churchill	£2.2s.0d.
Lord Chandos [3]	£2.2s.0d.
Mr Stone [4]	£1.1s.0d.
Mr Reynolds [5]	10s.
Mr Crook [6]	5s.

27

Mr Wainwright [7]   2s.6d.
Mr Shrimpton [8]   5s.
Mr Hanson [9]   5s.
Mr Jackman [10]   2s.6d.

The other demands, books etc are made up by myself.

Windsor

1. The Revd Henry Lewis Hobart D.D., Dean of Windsor 1816–1846; youngest son of George, 3rd Earl of Buckingham.
2. The Court House is now owned by the National Trust.
3. Richard Plantagenet-Temple-Nugent-Brydges-Chandos-Grenville (1797–1861), son of the 1st Duke of Buckingham.
4. John Stone (1790–1862), tenant of the Dean and Canons of Windsor.
5. Henry Reynolds (1774–1839), farmer, owner of Notley.
6. William Crook, farmer of Lower End.
7. George Wainwright, butcher and farmer.
8. Edward Shrimpton, needlemaker and churchwarden.
9. William Hanson, farmer and grocer.
10. Mr Jackman, farmer and horsedealer.

[43] To the Committee of the National Society [1]

Crendon, 16 January 1837

Gentlemen,

I beg to say in addition to the 'return' that my Sunday School would greatly increase if I had assistance in Procuring a *proper place* for education. There is an old Court House in a dilapidated state used only *once* in the year by the Lords of the Manor, which would be an excellent place for the purpose, provided I could get any funds for fitting up etc. The Lords of the Manor would grant such liberty provided the room was still available for their purpose once in the year, & they would never interfere with the business of a Sunday School. Besides, the room is within 50 yards of the Church. The dissenters use every exertion to wean away the Scholars, which have increased from 27 to their present number since I resided here — being the first resident Minister here on record. The Living is very small; & my yearly funds for the School, arising from gratuitous contributions, are very constricted. The cost of fitting up etc might be £20; & perhaps I could raise a contribution of £5 or £6. If you could assist me, I do assure you it would be of essential service both to the rising generation & to the Church.

The Lending Library is much used both by Church people and dissenters; & I am exceedingly grateful to the Society for it. I hope I shall be able to enlarge it shortly.

I am, Gentlemen, your obedient servant,

Thomas Hayton

N. Soc., Crendon file

1. The National Society, founded 1811 for the Education of the Poor in the Principles of the Established Church.

18 February 1837

THE VOLUNTARY PRINCIPLE, THE RELIGION OF THE BIBLE, AND A
BLESSING IN THE WORLD, CONTRASTED WITH A LETTER TO THE
INHABITANTS OF LONG CRENDON, entitled 'VOLUNTARYISM'. By
W. HOPCROFT — Bradford, Thame.

In this little pamphlet will be found a plain and straightforward defence
of the voluntary principle, in reply to one written by the incumbent of the
parish, who took the opportunity, a church-rate being there refused, to abuse
the Dissenters in a manner that we are sure all Liberal Churchmen will dis-
claim any sympathy with, and consider it a production fit only for that age
when abuse was taken for argument, and ribaldry for satire.

We give the following list of phrases which this Christian minister
applies to his Dissenting brethren, as specimens of the language and temper
with which *Voluntaryism* is written:— Men of corrupt minds. Prating puppies.
Whining jargon, or hacknied phrase. Cloven foot of dissent. Fanatical brains.
Drill-sergeants of dissent. Philistines. Whimsical and obscure men. Gullers.
Smooth-faced gentry with tender consciences. Sucking doves of meekness.
Patentee Gospel expounders. Radical crew. Worshippers of Lord Brougham.
Virulent mob-courting republicans. Levelling Dissenters. Ranters. Jumpers.
Muggletonians. Arithmetical legerdemain thimble-riggers. Moon-struck bigots.
Devilish and malignant motives. Voluntary mania. Vagaries of discontented
men. Sousing in the tank. Poor deluded hearers. Appearances of piety and
holiness. Wolves by nature. Ministers of Satan, &c. Curse of God resting upon
them.

In the pamphlet under our consideration, no such language is indulged
in: the author, after calmly and temperately exposing the abusive and
intolerant spirit of his antagonist, gives a history of the rise and progress of
religion at Long Crendon; in which he shows that, in spite of all the opposition
and persecution with which it has been met a far different feeling is entertained on this subject than was expressed in the year 1799, when the voluntary
principle was first introduced in that parish.

The author then goes through the usual and well-known arguments
(founded on scripture, reason, and church-history) in favour of the voluntary
principle; and proves the unreasonableness of the connexion between a
spiritual church and a temporal state. We have only room for one extract:—

'The design of the writer of *Voluntaryism* is to shew that some national
established Church is agreeable to scripture, common sense, and experience.
If so, would not some directions be found in scriptures concerning the constitution and support of such church? Would not Jesus Christ have directed
his apostles to have formed such churches? It is evident the Saviour never
designed it should be so; neither did the apostles ever attempt to establish
one, nor call on any Monarch to assist in such a procedure; nor lament the
want of one such church. The writer of the letter knows that the word of
God has neither precept nor example for a national church. He says we must
not look for any command of the sort; then we tell him, Dissenters cannot be

mistaken in denying national establishments of religion to be agreeable to scripture, common sense, and experience.'

J.R.G. [1]

1. John Rolls Gibbs (1815–1846), son of John Gibbs, editor of the *Aylesbury News.*

[45] *To Bishop Kaye*

Crendon, 25 March 1837

My Lord,

The enclosed paper requires your Lordship's signature, provided the object meets with your Lordship's approval, of which however I have no doubt.

I am located amongst dissenters, but I fear not, nay I may say that the Church has increases in its followers, and as for the Church rate question, we can beat our opponents ten to one, out of 3000 acres in the parish only 27 acres belong to a dissenter, but unfortunately we have no resident gentleman, so that at times much of the Temporal, as well as spiritual matters falls upon the clergyman.

If the Society will help me to carry the object of the enclosed paper into effect, I confidently anticipate great accession of numerical strength to the Church Party. Your Lordship's strong recommendation will greatly oblige and please me.

Believe me my Lord with the profoundest respect,

your Lordship's faithful and obedient servant,

Thomas Hayton

L.A.O. Cor. B 5/3/21/1

[46] *To the Reverend J.C. Wigram* [1]

1 April 1837

Reverend Sir,

I received safely the forms of application etc which you were so good as to send me. I have transmitted to the Bishop of Lincoln, one of the forms, stating the gross expense of the fitting up of the old Court Room here, & other matters bearing on the subject, so that I hope on Wednesday next my case will be brought forward, & attract the notice & benificence of the Board. The Living of Long Crendon is a very poor one; & I have expended upon it £100 upwards, & really I cannot do every thing myself. I have resided here only three years; & I have no doubt but the fitting up of the room in question would be a means of still further increasing my Sunday School which I found with 27 scholars but numbers now 115.

30

The Lords of the Manor have most willingly assented & no doubt would give any pledge to the Society of the rooms not being alienated for any other purpose: indeed I can see no possible contingency of affairs which could possibly require it; and I have only to say, that if you will add any thing that may further this very desirable object, I shall feel personally obliged; for I am now teaching the children close adjoining the altar table in the Church & down the aisles, which is very inconvenient, troublesome, & very improper.

I shall feel exceedingly anxious to hear the decision of the Society.

> I have the honour to be, Reverend Sir, your very obedient & faithful servant,
>
> Thos Hayton

P.S. A rough sketch of what the room requires and *separately* specified in the *Form of application*

Taking down partitions — putting up & repairing the floor	£4.0s.0d.
18 seats with backs — 10 feet long each	£6.6s.6d.
Two desks & seats for Teachers	£2.0s.0d.
Two book cases	£2.0s.0d.
Two writing desks for children — 12 feet long each	£2.0s.0d.
Six windows — shutters & glass (complete) £8	£8.0s.0d.
	£24.6s.0d.

N.B. There is virtually no day school in the place; & the Baptists want themselves greatly to wean away my Scholars: but with assistance I *shall* prevail.

N. Soc. Crendon file.

1. Revd J.C. Wigram, Secretary to the National Society, The Sanctuary, Westminster.

[47] To the Commissioners of the Poor Law Amendment Act
Crendon, 5 April 1837

Gentlemen,

Our overseers are at a complete standstill in reference to the point of 'ratal' & they can get no information *how they are to act*. Will you have the goodness to inform me, whether they must make a rate on the old valuation — a very unequal one indeed — or proceed forthwith to a new valuation? There will be much variance on the point of choosing a valuer, if one be elected at the vestry, will that be valid? Our vestries are conducted by a show of hands & is that to be adhered to? As considerable time must elapse before the rate is ready, will you be so kind as to give me any information on the subject; & I myself will thank you very kindly.

> I am your obedient servant,
>
> Thos Hayton

M.H. 12/9733

6 May 1837

Sir,

I beg to inform you that the National Society has contributed £15 towards the fitting up of the old Court Room here for a National School; & that the Duke of Buckingham & All Souls College have transmitted to me their assent to appropriate the old Room for the purpose alluded to.

I shall begin the works immediately; & I think that the best way will be to forward to me directly by post the contribution which the Chapter of Windsor was pleased to vote & of which you gave me notice on the 14th of January.

I have the honour to be your obedient servant,

Thos Hayton

Windsor

[49] To the Chapter Clerk [1]

Crendon, 15 May 1837

Sir,

It is now upwards of a week since I wrote to you respecting the contribution of the Dean & Canons of Windsor towards the repairing of the old court room etc at Crendon. Not having heard from you, I am somewhat apprehensive of the miscarriage of the letter or letters. At the time I wrote the enclosed paper had not returned from the Duke of Buckingham [. . . torn . . .] hope you will have the kindness to present it to the Dean or his official agent for registration: it will be merely kept by me in order that the room may not be used for purposes alien to the object. Your early reply will oblige.

I have the honour to be your obedient servant,

Thos Hayton

Windsor

1. William de St Croix, Chapter Clerk until 1843. Previously he had held a position of trust with the Royal Family.

[50] To Dean H.L. Hobart

Crendon, 22 May 1837

Reverend Sir,

I received a letter from Mr de St Croix dated the 24th of January last, stating that the Chapter had voted £5 towards the establishing of a school in this place & repairing the old Court Room, & wishing to know how the money should be remitted. To this I replied by saying that, when my application to the National Society was concluded I would write to inform him on the subject. A fortnight ago, I did so — mentioning the sum viz £15 which the National Society has voted for this purpose; & requesting him, at his earliest opportunity, to transmit the £5 enclosed to me, as I am anxious that the works should be completed as expeditiously as possible, as the teaching of children in the Church is found to be very inconvenient indeed. To this I have received no answer. On Monday last I wrote again enclosing the signature of the Duke of Buckingham & the Warden of All Souls College to a paper (which I had not on the previous Monday received from the respective parties) signifying their assent to the undertaking. To this letter also I have received no reply. Under these circumstances I feel myself compelled to trouble you on the subject, by assuring you how deeply obliged I should be, if you would condescend to make some enquiry about the matter. It was on the strength of the Chapter's subscription, & I may say, my own, that the Society made the grant; and I should be extremely sorry were this opportunity to be neglected of carrying into effect so desirable an object, both as it refers to the Old Court Room itself, & the prospering of the Sunday School.

> I have the honour to be, Reverend Sir, your very respectful servant,
>
> Thos Hayton

Windsor

[51] *To the Poor Law Commissioners*

Crendon, 26 May 1837

Gentlemen,

The following case I submit for your consideration, & not, I hope for your approval. It is abstractly the case of the wives of labourers committed to jail on suspicion of petty thefts, whether they — the wives on application for relief, should be uniformly ordered into the workhouse.

Richard Holliman [1] of this parish of *Long Crendon* is now confined in *Aylesbury jail*, waiting his trial for having some potatoes on his premises, supposed not to have been his own. He has a wife and three small children under 7 years of age; she, the wife, is a woman of good character, & steady, industrious habits; & the Board of Guardians at *Thame* relieved her *out of the workhouse* two weeks, but a fortnight ago ordered her into the House, agreeably with a standing rule in reference to persons so situate. This rule, I, as guardian, never could approve being carried rigorously into effect, inasmuch as it frequently bore unnecessarily harsh upon a poor female: & this woman alluded to has been undergoing the severest privations rather than fall in with an order, which I cannot but consider Unenglish & against the spirit of the Poor Law. Starvation, however is before her, if she does not enter the Workhouse; & doing this she must necessarily give up her Cottage, have her little goods scattered among alien hands, or sold, her garden planted with cabbages is pillaged & should her husband be acquitted, they will be homeless almost castaways. These are the obvious consequences of sending her into the workhouse. I will not pretend to work upon your feelings by describing to you

33

how agonizingly reluctant she is to be compelled to enter the 'Prison House' as she calls it, for no fault of hers, & a *supposed one* of her husband's; neither will I hinge the matter upon the question of Economy, which decidedly is favourable to her receiving some assistance *out* of the house, & perfectly in accordance with the wishes of the Guardians of Crendon; but I put it to you as men, I put it to you as Christians, whether she is to undergo all the privations of heart-burnings mostly because a majority of Guardians at a weekly Board may unbendingly adhere to a rule which carries with it the Spirit of Revenge & punishment rather than that of a wholesome operation towards the *necessary relief* of her & starvation wherever it presents itself. I write this not in any underhand way, I told the Guardians of Crendon I should do so; & the Board of Thame also is apprized of it; and if you, Gentlemen, will only fairly consider the case, I am sure you will not sanction that which I conceive to be cruel in the extreme.

> I have the honour to be, Gentlemen, your very respectful & obedient servant,
>
> Thos Hayton

N.B. The poor woman only wishes for 6/9 per week to keep 4 persons! nay she will contentedly struggle with less till her husband is released.

[Answer from the Poor Law Commissioners written on the back of the letter.]
                                                                31 May 1837

Sir,

The P.L.C. have to ack. the receipt of your letter of the 26th inst. stating the case of Richard Holliman . . . on this subject the Commissioners have to inform you that they are at all times extremely reluctant to interfere with the legal proceedings of a Board of Guardians . . . The Commissioners feel since that the direction insisted upon in your letter has not escaped the notice of the Guardians and as the Regulations impinged by the measures of such, and repeated deliberation on the circumstances of the case . . . the Commissioners are not disposed to alter their decisions.

> *[signed]* Richard Hall
> 29th May

M.H. 12/9733

1. Richard Holliman was found guilty and sentenced to six months hard labour at the House of Correction, Aylesbury.

[52] To the Poor Law Commissioners
                                                        Crendon, 27 May 1837

Gentlemen,

In my letter of yesterday to you I said that the wife of Richard Holliman had received for a fortnight from the Board at Thame 6/9 (for herself & three children) per week — the figures should have been 5/9.

Try it on the way of Economy; in the House, the parish will be charged between 10/— to 12/— per week; & she would gladly accept 5/— & make shifts, as the saying is. There is also another female in an adjoining parish in the same predicament, the parishioners of which wish her to receive an allowance *out of the house;* but no — Board or rather a section of the Board adheres to this, I must say, oppressive rule. I do entreat you to step in & save the Law from being defaced by an order almost universally condemned. Let the economy of the thing have weight; for I can assure you the machinery of the New Bill is bringing a greater expense on many parishes than formerly, tho' it gives a more uniform & correct administration.

I shall be happy to hear from you on this subject, as the poor woman's cottage & garden will be lost to her, if she goes to the Workhouse, & to the Workhouse she must go; for private charity, on which she has been living this fortnight, must have an end.

> I have the honour to be, Gentlemen, your very obedient servant,
>
> Thos. Hayton

M.H. 12/9733

[53] To the Poor Law Commissioners

Crendon, 5 June 1837

Gentlemen,

On my return home I found your answer of the 31st inst, & if I were disposed to cavil, that letter affords me ample material. If it be true, that language was invented to mystify human ideas, or evade direct replies, most surely your letter is an illustration of the doctrine. The first sentence is an exparte statement, foreign to the object of my letter, the second pretends to give me information such as I did not want, nor ever disputed; the third is meant to be an inference, after the manner of Tenterden Steeple [1], & quite at variance with matter of fact, to say nothing of an implied contradiction in it. I did not wish you to interfere with *legal* proceedings of the Thame Board; neither did I reflect upon the want of knowledge in that Board; — my question merely was, 'Did you sanction the virtual negation of liberty to a female because her husband was suspected of petty theft? & do you think it manly, legal, humane or Christian to immure her for no fault, cause her Cottage to be taken away from her, & the summer produce of her garden to be spoilated?' This you have not attempted to justify on any *principle* of relief, neither can you. Besides, it was the Mode of relief alluded to, & not to what you are pleased to call a *principle.* You say, no regulation is infringed by treating the poor woman thus. That is very true — it is your own regulation urged upon the Board by one of your Assistant Commissioners, who in case of Bastardy asserts that nothing in the shape of punishment or revenge is to be sanctioned, & to be made to feel a heavier pressure of degradation; & this forsooth, is called a *principle of relief.* Carry out this principle at once by the introduction

35

of the thumb screw & the Gibbet; abandon a regulation which it is impossible to reconcile with English law, Christian institutes, or the common feelings of humanity.

I am, Gentlemen, your servant,

Thomas Hayton

M.H. 12/9733

1. The proverb 'Tenterden Steeple is the cause of Goodwin Sands' refers to the fact that any reason is better than none (Eric Partridge, *Dictionary of Slang*, vol. ii).

[54] To the Chapter Clerk [1]

Crendon, 9 June 1837

Sir,

I beg to acknowledge the receipt of your letter this morning, enclosing a donation of five pounds.

I am truly sorry if I have given you the least uneasiness on the point of my having written to the Dean. The fact was as you imagine — *I had written to the Dean & my letter must have been at Windsor a day or two before you wrote*. Not hearing from you, I fancied you were from home either on pleasure or business; & having formally addressed the Dean, I thought it best under the supposed circumstances of your absence to address him again, particularly as I felt great interest in the furtherance of the object I had in view, & aware of the slender materials I had to work upon.

I really am perfectly ignorant of the real nature of your engagement with the Chapter. I conceived you were in the character of Bursar, so that I thought my addressing you was perfectly in order.

You may remember that I enclosed a paper for you, with the signature of the Duke of Buckingham & the Warden of All Souls College; that paper perhaps you may have an opportunity of returning to me, either by Frank or a simple letter; for which I shall be obliged. Allow me again to say I did not mean to impute any negligence to you; & that you will allow that stated 'supposition' to have its weight.

I am your obedient servant,

Thos Hayton

Perhaps if you would present the paper to Mr Cust [2] he might forward it to me at his convenience & opportunity.

Windsor

1. The Chapter Clerk kept the Register of the Chapter Acts. He also rode with the Steward to keep Court and to ingross the Court Rolls.
2. Hon. Henry Cockayne Cust, (1913–1861), son of Lord Brownlow. Canon of Windsor.

Crendon, 26 June 1837

Reverend Sir,

Since the receipt of your letter of the 12th April announcing to me the *conditional* grant of £15 in aid of the furtherance of my Sunday School undertaking, I beg to inform you that the works are nearly finished and that they are in strict agreement with the condition, viz, that the (fittings up) can hereafter be moved if needful into any other school room. I beg also to certify that the three Lords of the Manor have given me their hearty assent, & also some assistance and that there will be no existing debt after the payment of the grant. There is one point to which I pray leave to draw your attention. I would feel greatly assisted and obliged if the Society could afford me a few slates and books. After the kind grant already alluded too, I perhaps ought not to prefer such a request. I can only say that straightened funds compel me to do so. If you could in any way further this matter, believe me I should be exceedingly grateful.

From yours very respectfully,

Thos Hayton

N. Soc. Crendon file

[56] To the Collegiate Chapter of Windsor

Crendon, 4 July 1837

Sir,

I beg you will present my sincere thanks to the Collegiate Chapter of Windsor for their kind acquiescence to my request & for the proffered assistance of five pounds to carry the object of the National School into effect. As soon as other arrangements are completed, I will write again & inform you of the proceedings & how the money may be remitted.

I have the honour to be your very obedient servant,

Thos Hayton

Windsor

[57] To Bishop Kaye

Crendon, 25 July 1837

My Lord,

I have lately joined my Sunday School at Long Crendon to the National Society, and have fitted up an old Court Room (for the children formerly were taught in the Church) for its accommodation. The number of scholars has increased from 80 to 132; and if your Lordship would be so kind as to

37

recommend this case to the Society for Promoting Christian Knowledge, I should feel greatly obliged, as the funds are very low & the School has not many supporters, save those of slender property. I also will write to one of the Secretaries forthwith, stating the matter.

Mr Wigram gives me great hope of success.

I have the honour to be, My Lord, your Lordship's faithful & obedient servant,

Thomas Hayton

L.A.O. Cor. B 5/3/21/1

[58] To the Aylesbury News

21 October 1837

THE REV. GEO. CHETWODE [1], HIGH PRIEST OF CHILTON, AND REV. MR. PEACEFUL [2], PRIMITIVE METHODIST.

The latter individual is a located preacher in this district, commonly called a ranter, a very innocent and harmless man, holding doctrines which no churchman need be ashamed of, though the discipline in worship is rather foolish and absurd. Mr Peaceful has drawn about him a little congregation at Ashendon, and is about to license a house there for public worship. Neither is the Marquis of Chandos against this proceeding, so long as the hour of worship interferes not with that of the Established Church. This redounds to the credit of the Marquis, who has, at no time, sanctioned any persecution, or thrown in the way any annoying impediments. But widely different is the treatment which Mr Peaceful has met with in the village of Chilton. There, from the garden of a rev. gentleman, have rotten eggs and missiles been hurled by the gardener, butler, and gamekeeper, when Mr Peaceful and some pious inhabitants were pouring forth their orisons to heaven. Not satisfied with this, these 'unclean birds' have issued from their cage; followed the harmless preacher through the village; let loose their unhallowed tongues upon him, whilst the keeper held by the hinder legs a dog over his back, howling and yelping with pain. Indeed, the behaviour of these scamps is such, that the preacher has ceased for a time to enter the village, lest these maddened dogs devour him. We cannot say that the Reverend George, the pink of all politeness, encourages and sanctions such proceedings of his servants, though many are inclined to believe so; oh, no! he can twirl up his eyes in sanctimonious mood, after the most approved fashion — a fac-simile of Liston — he who one day prays, that magistrates may have 'grace to execute justice and maintain truth', and the next whips a poor creature off to Aylesbury gaol for six months, for looking into a hedge where a snare was set — he who shows himself a Whig at Lord Hatherton's [3], and a Tory at Wotton, and who scowls hatefully on all who worship him not — he, who weekly petitions for all 'in danger to be succoured, helped, and comforted, and that the oppressed should be defended' — he, above all men, would nor could never throw the smile of his approbation over conduct so base and brutal. We would, however, warn this High Priest, whose conduct in many instances has been most unbecoming his station. He knows well how he has treated some individuals who dare think for themselves, and have the English spirit in them to give utterance

38

to their thoughts; and we can tell him that they will never quail before him, though the whole House of Wotton, and all the magistracy, are linked together with him in his attempts to bully and overawe those who will 'never bend the knee to Baal, and whose lips will never kiss Him'. It would be infinitely better if this meek divine would attend to his parishioners at Ashton at other times besides St. Michael and the Lady, and not leave them so much to hirelings. Perhaps then the church-rate might be carried at that place; but no, no, he is too wily for that — he can be King, Priest, and Law-giver at Chilton — at Ashton, from which he draws £1,500 a-year, he would sink to the common level of a parish priest, and that of a very ordinary stamp. Less of law and more of divinity would recommend him more strongly to our notice. Z.

*A person named Edwards, now at Aylesbury, can testify to this.

1. Revd. George Chetwode, second son of Sir John Chetwode, 4th Baronet. Perpetual Curate of Chilton from 1829 to 1870.
2. William Peaceful, Primitive Methodist, he held a mission in the Thame area, and was maltreated in several villages.
3. Edward John Littleton (1791—1863), 1st Baron Hatherton. (M.E.B.).

[59] To Bishop Kaye

Crendon, 19 December 1837

My Lord,

Having been informed that your Lordship has appointed the Revd. George Chetwode of Chilton, a Rural Dean, — will your Lordship have the kindness to inform me, whether Long Crendon is included in his District & what are the powers with which he is invested? I ask this as a matter of Courtesy whilst I assure your Lordship of my most deferential respect both to your person & your Office.

> I have the honour to be, my Lord, your Lordship's faithful & obedient servant,
>
> Thos Hayton

L.A.O. Cor. B 5/3/21/1

[60] Bishop Kaye to Hayton

W.M. 24 December 1837

Reverend Sir,

Mr Chetwode and Mr Alford of Aston Sandford are the Rural Deans for the Deanery of Waddesdon: but your Ministries of Long Crendon and Lower Winchendon are placed under the supervision of Mr Alford. The duty of the rural Dean with reference to Incumbents is fully to inspect the Parsonage House and Premises and to report upon the state of these to the Bishop and Archdeacon.

L.A.O. Cor. B 5/3/21/1

20 January 1838

When will the hectoring Chandos cease to make himself ridiculous, and when will you farmers, cease to believe in him? When he is fairly shelved in the House of Lords, and you find yourselves wheedled, duped, and forgotten — unless you occasionally may be reminded that his scion of nobility — his now chrysalis offspring, — will, when out of his leading-strings, be recommended to your notice as a fit and proper person to represent in Parliament the interests of the county! Wonderful magic! astonishing beyond measure, that a man should be born a legislator — that he should understand by intuition constitutional law! It may be on the principle that 'like begets like'; so that if the son follow the steps of his father, we shall only say that the Grenvilles have degenerated — that there is no soundness in them — from the head to the sole of the foot there is but one mass of cloddish obtuseness. We have not, however, yet done with the father. His Christmas pantomimes are good things in their way, and we shall make as much of them as we can. At Buckingham his Lordship not even alluded to you farmers; he told you what fine fellows the Conservatives were; and that, if they fairly got hold of the State ship, how they would tow you all into something better than a Mahommedan paradise — how your crops would grow without tillage, and your cattle graze in luxuriant meadows, where no winter would blight their greenness. He boasted of being a disinterested person in the carrying of his political caperings. Did any of you believe him? In former days did he not sigh to become Governor of the West India Islands, to try his hand upon the blacks before he attempted to subjugate the whole county? Had the Admiralty Office no charms for him, when post-captains courted him, and taught him the difference between the bow-sprit and mizen mast, and jib-boom and the union jack? His friends say that he might have held this office, had he not so foolishly adhered to the abolition of the Malt Tax; but — 'tis all false: no Ministry could even have been so demented as to have placed such a country booby over the naval power of England, unless they wished to make us a laughing-stock to the world. And, with all his professions of purity and disinterestedness, do you really think he has no ambitious dreams of becoming the Lord Lieutenant of the county, and distributing to his minions the patronage resulting therefrom? Whilst we have a Liberal Ministry, this would be a dream indeed; with the English Thugs in power, he is the very man for them — to support and carry on their thievish, cruel and tyrannical practices. For the future, interpret all his professions of purity by the rule of contrary; you will thus arrive at the feelings of his heart, and discover with what guile he smoothes you and cajoles you to his purposes, which at all times, tend to protect arbitrary power and advance his private interests.

His Lordship was mighty fierce in reference to Canada — talking of bringing the country over the Atlantic and 'laying it down at her Majesty's feet' — himself the very Quixote to attempt such a performance! And did you mark his boast how he would drag the Ministry to the bar of the House of Commons to answer for their colonial conduct, and for the blood of the slain? Had you seen him the other week in the House, as we did, cower and skulk under the glance and defiance which Lord John Russell hurled at him, challenging him to the contest, and daring him to carry the threat to execution, — oh! how would the contrast of his crowing, Dorking-like, on his own dunghill at Buckingham and of this dastardly exhibition of himself, have sickened and undeceived you! No more would you have hurrahed the Plantagenet at his feasts, unless your souls were as earthy and debased as his own — no more would you have relied on this railing Thersites, this political Shinner, who bullies and curses at a distance the appointed Ministers of the Queen. Whatever may be the issue of the present contest with Canada, we have no doubt but the time will come, when she will throw off the domination of the Mother Country, and erect herself into an independent power. What Junius said of the Americans in former days we are inclined to think applicable at present:— They left their native land in search of freedom, and found it in a desert. Though divided in forms of policy and religion, there is one point in which they all agree — they equally detest the pageantry of a King and the supercilious hypocrisy of a Bishop.

This subject will lead us shortly to some remarks on our foreign trade, and by consequence to the corn laws — that scare-crow which Chandos occasionally holds up to terrify you, and respecting which he betrays a most lamentable ignorance. Nothing can be more ridiculous than to propose to augment the wealth of nations, and to increase the amount of money, by forcing a scarcity of corn, which his Lordship and such like advocates deem a benefit to the farmer, though it be in the face of the most undoubted evidence to the contrary, and against the laws both of nature and Providence. Z.

B.R.O. P.R./134/1/8

[62] To the Poor Law Commissioners

Crendon, [undated]
Received 20 July 1838

Gentlemen,

The new valuation and ratal tables made for this parish by Mr Webbs of Burford has been laid before the parishioners, who last night at a vestry called for the purpose of considering the equality of justice, almost unanimously were of opinion, that it was a most unequal and unfair rate and that some plan should be devised to alter and amend it in order, if possible to give satisfaction to the rate-payers. Thirty-nine individuals were present at the Meeting — 37 of which expressed in no measured terms their condemnation of a rate replete with much flagrant errors. Two of the thirty-nine were *verbally* satisfied because they were *lowly rated*. The amount of ratal of the 37 is upwards of £105 in the shilling rate; that of the two satisfied £10.2s.7d. These two however, practically admitted the injustice of the rate, in as much as when a Committee (of 14) was named for the purpose of amending & virtually making a new rate, they objected not to be included in that number. At the request of the Vestry, I beg leave to ask you whether you will sanction our proceedings. We do not think that strangers to such a large parish as this, where the land varies so very materially, will ever give satisfaction; & when I inform you, that fourteen practical men, including the Guardians of the parish are in that Committee & anxious to do justice to all parties, I do not think you will throw any obstacles in our way, especially when I tell you that the Overseers, since Lady Day, have been only collecting on *account*, are now almost at a standstill, that if something is not speedily done to effect a good & equal & just rate, very great confusion will arrive — followed in all likelihood with disputes, pleas & demurrers of all kinds. It is proposed that the Com-

41

mittee should enter on their labour forthwith, provided you approve of the plan suggested — Your earliest possible reply would oblige

> your faithful & obedient servant,
>
> Thos Hayton

Crendon Parsonage

As Chairman of that Committee I will feel personally obliged to you if you would send me any papers, printed directions — or give me any advice which might tend to facilitate & expedite the matter & put it on a fair principle. If you would inform me how to calculate or distinguish the *gross estimated* Rental from the rateable value, I should thank you as I cannot discover the principle in the new rate, I mean whether it is a percentage or otherwise; or *how* otherwise.

M.H. 12/9733

[63] To the Poor Law Commissioners

Crendon, 24 July 1838

Gentlemen,

You will greatly oblige me by a reply to my letter of Thursday last, respecting the rate which you have made for this parish. The rate is universally condemned; & the overseers refuse to collect upon such a blundering & unjust scale. The vestry wish to know whether you would approve of their attempting to make a fair & equitable rate, *agreeable* to the recent act.

> I have the honour to be, Gentlemen,
>
> Thos Hayton

M.H. 12/9733

[64] To the Poor Law Commissioners

Crendon, [undated]

Gentlemen,

At a meeting of the Guardians of the Thame Union to consider the propriety of dividing the districts for the more efficient administration of Medical Relief, it was proposed by the Chairman that the South District should be divided into two, & that the person taking the Western division should establish a *dispensary* at Lewknor for the accommodation of the poor — that place being more central than the residence of the present Medical Officer, which residence is at Stokenchurch! This proposition was carried unanimously.

It was likewise proposed by another Guardian, that the North District should in the same manner be divided, as it was equally large, both in population & acreage — which proposition was rejected by a majority of five.

On what grounds the Guardians came to this Conclusion we pretend not to say, tho' the district be now virtually divided into three, Mr Lupton jun. [1] having the whole sub-letting, on one part to a Mr Knight [2], another to a Mr Smith & himself retaining a third portion — this being practical & acted upon.

All the Guardians expressed themselves perfectly satisfied with the skill and attention of Mr Smith & Mr Knight, & yet these two persons are virtually excluded from tendering, in consequence of what we conceive to be some undue preference to a young man of about three & twenty years of age & that young man not even a householder!! The Necessary Consequence of this is that he can distress at any time his seniors!! As a proof of the above statement, we deduce the following, that last year Mr Lupton's tender was £35, that of a Mr Ayres £15 [3] — Testimonials being equal in every respect; and an additional expense of between £5 and £6 was incurred by the Board in the teeth of the written contract, for the purchase of Barclay's ointment for the cure of the itch!

Under these circumstances we hope you will not think it unreasonable if we request at your hand the presence of an Assistant Commissioner on Wednesday the 18th Instant when the tenders for the Medical Officers will be received.

We beg also to say that Mr Parker is already apprised of the unusual bearing of the case, which truly demands investigation.

We have the honour to be, Gentlemen,

yours very truly & faithfully,

Thomas Hayton
Charles Stone [4]
Frederick Lee [5]

Guardians

Received Dec. 7th 1839

M.H. 12/9733

1. Sackvill Lupton, (1813—1856), surgeon. Son of Harry Lupton.
2. T. Knight, surgeon of Brill.
3. Philip Burnard Ayres, M.D., surgeon of Thame.
4. Charles Stone of the Prebendal, Thame. Retired London haberdasher; Poor Law Guardian.
5. Revd. Frederick Lee; third son of T.T. Lee, vicar of Thame; unlicensed curate; Poor Law Guardian.

[65] *To the Poor Law Commissioners*

Crendon, 27 February 1840

Gentlemen,

A long conversation took place yesterday before Mr Parker [1] on the Thame Board of Guardians regarding the nature of qualifications for guardians [2]. As much doubt was expressed on the subject, bearing on the election of two, or three of the Guardians I am inclined to lay before you the nature of my qualifications, earnestly requesting you at your earliest convenience to express an opinion on validity, I am the more anxious for this opinion, as I am informed that my recent support of Mr Parker's proposition for Medical officers, in that Union have given great offence to a certain party — so much that I have even met with insult as the consequence.

I am the incumbent of the Living of Long Crendon and Winchendon in this county (Bucks) to which are attached nearly 200 acres of land. I reside in the Vicarage House here, and have in my own occupation 8 acres of Glebe, letting out the remainder to different tenants. The annual *value* of the Vicarage house, Orchard, Barn etc together with the acres is about £35 (nay I would let the whole for more) the whole is rated under £20 per annum. I also rent 35 acres of land in this parish belonging to a college of Oxford, and I am rated at nearly £30 for this, but I *underlet* the *arable* and greater portion of this, the tenant agreeing half-yearly to re-pay me the rates advanced. My name therefore stands in the book for nearly £50 per annum, for which rates I am responsible. It is because of this underletting, because I have no team horses, nor carry corn to market, nor ostentatiously appear (save on the rate book as beneficial occupier) that head of the Union supposed me not to be qualified, you will therefore personally oblige me by your opinion on that point, as soon as you conveniently can, as I have been requested to allow myself to be put in nomination for Guardian, which thing I would not permit myself until I was assured of my qualifications.

I have the honour to be Gentlemen, your obedient servant,

Thos Hayton

I think it proper to inform you that the ratal of this parish (agreed upon at a parish vestry) is barely two thirds of the real value; so that a double wrong is inflicted, first in the way of barring a qualification, & 2nd in the lessening of the number of votes. Moreover this ratal at two thirds of the real value, is more advantageous to the largest and best farms, & a virtual plunder on those of smaller value & extent. Surely this is worthy of your attention, when four one shilling rates might make the annual expenditure, instead as now six & a half rates.

[*Abstract of Answer from the Commissioners*]

Refer to Mr Parker.

M.H. 12/9734

1. Mr Parker, the Assistant Commissioner for Oxfordshire.
2. The qualification for a Guardian was fixed at an occupancy of £25 per annum (S. & B. Webb, *English Poor-Law History*, Part 2, Vol. I, p. 120).

[66] To the Poor Law Commissioners

Crendon, 6 March 1840

Gentlemen,

Will you have the kindness to reply to my letter of the 27th Feburary last, requesting qualifications for Guardians.

I have refused two or three Invitations to be a Guardian, until I have an opinion on the point submitted to you I must continue to do so. I do not, I assure you ask this opinion for any gratification that I can possibly receive for what is a very thankless office.

> I have the honour to be, Gentlemen, your obedient servant,

> Thos Hayton

M.H. 12/9734

[67] *From the* Aylesbury News

22 February 1840

AN ALLEGED CASE OF ASSAULT
LUPTON, Surgeon v HAYTON, clerk.

On Friday, the 14th inst., at a special petty session of the magistrates at Ashendon [1], Mr Lupton, surgeon [2], of Thame, preferred a complaint against the Rev. T. Hayton, of Crendon, for having shaken his whip at him.

It appeared that Mr Lupton waylaid Mr Hayton on his return to Crendon from Thame on the 6th of the present month, in order to give vent to some angry feelings lurking in his breast. As the matter is not finally adjudicated, we forbear going into particulars. The leading points seemed to be, that angry words had passed between them, and Mr Lupton had holden up his stick and told Mr Hayton his coat protected him. It was alleged by Mr Lupton, but not proved, (for Lupton's own witness broke down), that Mr Hayton in return shook his whip at him, called him a nasty snake, and told him to fancy himself horsewhipped. Within a few hours after this occurrence, Reynolds [3], a co-partner with Lupton in surgery and hate, called upon Mr Hayton, in company with a Mr Holloway, a solicitor in Thame. Mr Hayton refused to see them. Their business was to entrap Mr Hayton into the preliminaries of a duel, as the blackguard language of Reynolds at the gate evidently proved. Soon after this, a letter arrived from Reynolds, which Mr Hayton returned unopened, saying that he wished for no communications with him. These galled doctors, thus foiled, had recourse to the petty sessions at Ashendon, being determined to defame and injure, if possible. The magistrates assembled were the Rev. G. Chetwode, Rev. J.S. Baron [4], and John Stone, Esq.

Mr Hayton objected to the last-named individual sitting as a judge on the matter. The grounds of the protest were these: that Mr Stone was his personal enemy, always seeking an occasion of quarrel against him, and giving currency to the most malicious misrepresentations; that within a few hours before Mr Stone's appearance on the bench, he had been proclaiming to the workmen on the high road that Mr Hayton had sent him a challenge – an infamous falsehood delivered to Stone by a gossiping, tale-bearing doctor, whose four and five hours' medical visits have become disgusting to Stone himself; and, above all, that Mr Stone's confidential servant had been very active in running about for evidence against Mr Hayton, and even threatening three months' imprisonment to one individual if she would not make out a case against him.

Mr Stone denied any knowledge of his servant's so acting, and expressed very readily his willingness to have nothing to do with the case, but unfortunately let out, evidently to Chetwode's chagrin, that he would not have come near if Mr Chetwode had not requested him!

No objection was taken to the other magistrates, although (and we have it on undoubted authority) Mr Chetwode's remark the previous day to a gentleman was 'that the Radical sway was increasing at the Thame Board of Guardians, and he must attend the Ashendon case'. The inference is plain: 'I must give Lupton a lift — I must give my old frient and Radical brother a kick'. However, nothing was fairer and more impartial than Mr Baron's conduct.

After patiently hearing for five hours the whole case, the magistrates would not give any decision, and sent Mr Lupton for his remedy to the quarter session.

Thus has the Doctor been beaten on his own ground — within a stone's throw of Wotton House [5].

At present we will make no further comment on the business, except we think Mr Hayton ought to have been the complainant. If the magistrates could have decided against Mr Hayton, no doubt they would; but it would have been too great a triumph for him, and — 'Lupton was their friend'.

When the proper time comes, we shall be able to draw up this quarrel to the last general election for the county, when that brute edict of the present Duke of Buckingham was issued — 'Every political enemy must be a personal one'; and to a recent election of medical officers for the Thame Union, when Lupton's Tory party received a signal defeat.

1. The Petty Sessions were held at the Red Lion Inn at Ashendon.
2. Henry Lupton (1785—1861), son of Sackvill Lupton, surgeon of Thame. Author of *History of Thame and its Hamlets* (1860).
3. Henry Wells Reynolds, step-son and partner of Henry Lupton.
4. Revd. J.S. Baron, curate of Brill.
5. Wotton House, the home of Lord Chandos.

[68] *From the* Bucks Herald

22 February 1840

ASHENDON PETTY SESSIONS.
Magistrates Present — Rev. G. Chetwode and Rev. J. Baron.

Yesterday week the Rev. Thomas Hayton, vicar of Long Crendon, was summoned before the Bench at Ashendon, for an assault on H. Lupton, Esq., of Thame.

Mr Lupton on being sworn, said on Thursday the 6th instant, he was proceeding to the village of Long Crendon, but perceiving the Rev. Mr Hayton, was coming behind him, waited till he came up, and then said to him, "You are well aware, Sir, I did not seek this meeting from any pleasure I could derive from it, neither would I shun it from its bitterness, for I was determined to tell you my feelings of the base conduct you have pursued towards a man who was your best and staunchest friend." Mr Hayton said, "What do you mean, explain yourself?" Mr Lupton told him "There was no necessity for explanation, he had but to refer to his own conscience for it." He replied, "He had the greatest reason to complain." Mr L. told him he had nothing more to say, excepting that he would never under any circumstances again hold communication with him, and then rode on towards Long Crendon, and saw Mr John Stone on the road leading to Chearsley, and stopped to speak with him, and told him what had passed between himself and Mr Hayton. Mr Hayton passed a few minutes afterwards, and Mr Lupton rode towards Long Crendon; overtook Mr Hayton, whose horse was then walking; the moment Mr Lupton passed, Mr Hayton put his horse into a faster pace and rode up to his side, who directly pulled up to a foot pace; Mr H. did the same, and Mr Lupton cantered on, when Mr Hayton put his horse into a rapid pace, and rode again up to his side, splashing him all over. He asked Mr Hayton if he "meant to insult him;" he said, "I insult you, you are a damnation snake — you, in conjunction with that damned old villain that is dead, Kipling, of Chilton, wrote a letter in the paper against me." Mr Lupton said to him, "then you are 'Rusticus?'" Mr Hayton replied "you are a damned liar and a villain." Mr Lupton told him "not to bully him and take advantage of his cloth." Mr Hayton said, "we will soon settle that if you will get down, in five minutes I will give you the d——st thrashing you ever had in your life." Mr L. said, "I am not going to make such a blackguard of myself, or disgrace myself in any such way." Mr Hayton said, "if you mean anything else I will accommodate you, at any time or at any place, here or out of the country." To which Mr Lupton replied, "very well." Mr Hayton then shook his whip and said he would attack Mr Lupton with it, and he might defend himself with his stick, and he menaced Mr L. by shaking it in his face, and told him to consider himself horse-whipped. Mr L. said, "why don't you strike?" Mr H. replied, "you will take advantage of me." Mr L. said, "if you strike me directly I will not." Mr Hayton continued to follow him up the hill into the parish, and abused him all the way; there were one or two persons standing by the side of the road, and Mr Lupton said, "now I have you before witnesses, and in your own parish, I tell you you are the liar, and not me; I believe your conscience is pretty much seared, but the time will come when you will bitterly repent the conduct you have pursued towards me this day," and Mr Hayton then rode towards his home and Mr Lupton towards Chilton.

Mr Lupton, in his cross-examination by Mr Hayton, said — I certainly did not wait in the road to pick a quarrel with Mr Hayton, the base conduct he has pursued towards me has been in libelling me and my wife some years ago, and he confessed that he had libelled us in the presence of Mr Costello, a surgeon in London. I never held any stick up to Mr Hayton, and did not say your coat protects you. I do not recollect Mr Hayton saying to me that if I go up into Long Crendon he would pull off that coat and accommodate me, for that he thought he could thrash two such doctors as me. Mr Hayton said to me, "I suppose you mean pistols." I replied, "I do not mean to disgrace myself in the way you propose." I did not offer, at any time, to strike him with my stick. In answer to Mr Hayton's conversation with me charging me and the late Mr Kipling with writing a letter in the newspapers against him, I said, then you are "Rusticus." I did not say to Mr Hayton, I wish you would

47

hit me. I did not hear Mr Hayton say he would not take advantage of me if I acceded to his wishes.

Mr Lupton called one witness and Mr Hayton two, but as their evidence is of little consequence we omit it. The Bench bound the Rev. Mr Hayton over to appear and answer the charge at the approaching sessions.

[69] From the Aylesbury News

29 February 1840

LUPTON v. HAYTON
'One tale's good till another's told.'

It was not our intention to have noticed, until the proper time, the pretended case of assault lately heard at the Petty Sessions at Ashendon; but as Ryde [1] has thought proper to 'loose his tinkler jaw', and give a false gloss to the matter, we think it right and just that Mr Hayton's statement of the matter should be heard, and the substance of the evidence of both the witnesses made known (which Ryde says is of little consequence, but we think otherwise).

Since Mr Lupton's medical tender was thrown out at the Thame Board of Guardians, three or four of those Guardians have incurred the mighty displeasure of this Knight of the Lancet. Against the Rev. F. Lee Mr Lupton first let off his spite; and Mr Hayton was informed that he next was to be attacked. That Mr Hayton wished to avoid all altercation with Mr Lupton was plainly proved; that Mr Lupton way-laid Mr Hayton is admitted. When Lupton came galloping up to Mr Hayton, after the first interview, (and this shows an 'animus' in Lupton to renew the quarrel) Mr Hayton's horse struck into a canter, which any high-spirited beast will do, particularly when the hounds are near. This Mr Lupton complained of, and pathetically added before the Magistrates, 'that Mr Hayton splashed him', though he was riding on a full-sized horse and Mr Hayton on a pony. Mr Lupton then held up his stick at Mr Hayton, and told him that his coat protected him. (Mr Lupton denied this on his cross-examination, but his own witness swore to the truth of it.) Mr Hayton's reply was, 'It would be no difficult matter to thrash two such Doctors as you. If you think my coat protects me, you have got a stout stick, and I a very slender whip — if you chose to attack me, I will defend myself'. Mr Lupton then replied, 'No, I will have it another way'. 'You mean pistols, I suppose'? said Mr Hayton, 'but that is only the resource and the subterfuge of a coward; circumstanced as I am, you know I cannot accept your offer. If we were on the continent, you dared not thus insult me'. 'I wish you would attack me now', said Lupton. 'No, you would take advantage of me', was Mr Hayton's reply. Mr Hayton was then asked if he were 'Rusticus' [2], which led to some remarks on the treacherous conduct of the late vicar of Oakley (who, on his death-bed, however, deposed of the honourable and self-sacrificing conduct of Mr Hayton towards him), and of Mr Lupton's double dealing thereon. On Mr Hayton's denying that he was 'Rusticus', Mr Lupton called him a liar, and repeated his assertion, with a variety of other abuse, all of which there are now witnesses ready to depose to.

On Mr Lupton's cross-examination, he seemed to forget everything but his own laboured, vamped-up, deposition. He swore he met no one during this occurrence; and yet Markham, his own witness, was passed within a couple of yards, who deposed that he saw Mr Lupton with his stick up, and heard him tell Mr Hayton that his coat protected him; and within 120 yards of Markham was there another individual (here again the Doctor's sight and memory failed him,) on the road, who neither saw Mr Hayton's hand raised up towards Mr Lupton nor the whip shaken at him in any way whatever; and yet this same witness remarked them both for upwards of 500 yards, having a full commanding view of the road during the whole occurrence. When they passed this witness, he heard Mr Lupton ask Mr Hayton 'to hit him', and heard Mr Hayton's reply, 'No, you would take advantage of me'. And all this Mr Lupton swore he neither saw, nor did it take place! What a medical 'Majocci' this is! Can such a 'non mi ricordo' be found in the whole pharmacopeia of puff and pride! The last witness' evidence was confirmed by Mr Edward Shrimpton, who had viewed the road, and who averred that if anything like what Mr Lupton had deposed did take place, it must have been seen by the witness. To all this however (which Ryde says is of no consequence) it unfortunately happens that another witness will be forthcoming, who saw the transaction from beginning to end, and will fully acquit Mr Hayton of the assault imputed to him, and will turn the abusive language entirely to the credit of Mr Lupton.

We have authority to state that Mr Hayton never in his life, either by word or deed, spoke or wrote any thing disrespectful of Mr or Mrs Lupton. Some 13 years ago, Mr Lupton called upon Mr Hayton to act as his second in a duel which he wished to fight with a gentleman now in Thame, for having written, as Mr Lupton said, an anonymous letter, defamatory of Mrs Lupton. From such a purpose Mr Hayton dissuaded him. We really advise Mr Lupton not to refer to matters which time possibly might heal, and which to him must be anything but pleasing if they are ferreted into light again.

The inhabitants of Thame can see clearly through the flimsy veil which the Doctor would draw over his peevishness and jealousy; and his endeavours to suppress the rising fame of the young medical men in that town, will, we assure him, be only gall and bitterness to him, whilst the dynasty of Harry IX. and 'the Lord Mayor elect', is fast, very fast, waning into obscurity.

1. Ryde, Editor of the *Bucks Herald*.
2. 'Rusticus' was the author of a series of letters attacking the Revd. John Kipling, Vicar of Oakley.

[70] The Record of the Court
Easter Sessions

31 March—7 April 1840

Thomas Hayton for an assault a true bill

Pleaded Not Guilty

Recognizances   Thomas Hayton   £50
                     Edward Shrimpton   £50

No evidence offered. Acquitted.

B.R.O. Quarter Sessions Records.

Aston Sandford, 24 April 1840

My Lord,

I regret that, having been from home when your Letter arrived, I did not receive it until to-day.

Your Lordship is correct in your impression of an Assault having been committed by Mr Hayton of Long Crendon. The person on whom it was committed, a respectable Apothecary of Thame, summoned Mr Hayton before the Magistrates, who thought it a case of sufficient importance to be reserved for the determination of the Quarter Sessions. But as the Sessions are past, & I have heard nothing further of the case, I conclude that the Parties have privately arranged it. I will make enquiries in order to ascertain this fact, & will inform your Lordship of the result.

The assault was committed last February; & the circumstances of it were generally reported to have been of an aggravated description. Much remark was excited by it at the time reflecting on Mr Hayton's conduct. Indeed one of the Magistrates before whom it was heard, informed me it was a sad instance of violence, & immoral language.

I am, my Lord, your Lordship's obedient servant,

H.G. Alford

L.A.O. Cor. B. 5/3/21/1

1. H.G. Alford, rector of Aston Sandford 1836 to 1850. Father of the celebrated H.G. Alford, dean of Canterbury.

[72] Mr Alford to Bishop Kaye

Aston Sandford, 29 April 1840

My Lord,

Upon Enquiry I find that Mr Hayton's assault case was not brought into court, but was referred, & upon his consenting to make an apology the prosecution was dropped.

I am, my Lord, your Lordship's obedient servant,

H.G. Alford

L.A.O. Cor. B. 5/3/21/1

[73] From the Aylesbury News

11 April 1840

This was an indictment for assault with the particulars of which our readers are already well acquainted. Mr Roberts appeared for the complainant & Mr Taylor for the defendant.

Upon Mr Roberts proceeding to open the case, Sir T.D. Aubrey [1] stated that the Court strongly recommended the parties to settle the matter without proceeding to trial. After a consultation of about half an hour, Mr Taylor stated on behalf of his client that he retracted all the expressions he had used calculated to injure the feelings of Mr Lupton, & wished that gentleman to consider them as if they had never been used. Mr Roberts made the same statement on behalf of Mr Lupton towards Mr Hayton, & thus the matter was settled as far as the public were concerned.

The case was afterwards referred to the Rev. Mr Small [2], who decided upon leaving the case as he found it. He could not see sufficient reason, either for imposing anything like a fine on the defendant, or calling on him for any apology more than had already been made by both parties.

1. Sir T.D. Aubrey (1781–1856). Chairman of Buckinghamshire Quarter Sessions; nephew of Sir John Aubrey of Boarstall, from whom he inherited the title and estate.
2. The Revd. Henry Alexander Small, J.P., rector of Haversham 1827–1856.

[74] From the Thame Union Minute Book

27 January 1841

A letter from the Rev. Thomas Hayton addressed to the Board complaining of the neglect to give notice to the Guardians of special meetings, or sending such notices after the event. Of the Chaplain for neglecting to visit the able bodied men's ward. Of the Master of the workhouse for overbearing conduct and being totally inaccessible. The Schoolmaster for being in attendance only half of his time. Of the Porter for negligence and referring to the case of Richard Holliman's Child. Of the Soup and Gruel being miserably thin and the suet puddings tough. Of an idiot pauper named Par being deprived of an extra allowance for food which had reduced him to a pitiable and Emaciated Spectacle and hastening him to his grave. And of the visiting Committee neglecting their duty and also a statement made to the Guardian of Long Crendon by Richard Holliman relative to the neglect of his child in an illness, delivered by Mr Humphrey.

O.R.O. V/i/3

[75] From the Aylesbury News

2 February 1841

Gentlemen,

It was no quixotic tilting on my part that induced me last week to lay before you certain charges touching matters at the workhouse. Those charges were brought to my very door, and urged with a fervency and earnestness sufficient to make a person less credulous than myself believe in their general truth and correctness; and, I do assure you, I was glad to find that, upon investigation, the most important, perhaps, of those allegations could not be satisfactorily substantiated. There are, however, one or two points to which I beg leave to draw your attention. The clerk informs me "that you do not think it *expedient* for the chaplain to visit the able-bodied ward, unless requested by any of the men so to do". Here I am quite at issue with you. It appears to me *essentially necessary* that his ministrations should be carried to the able-bodied men, as a duty involved in the very office of chaplain. I remember well the arguments made use of in discussing the propriety of having such an officer at all; — that Christian instruction was a thing which ought to be *urged* upon man; that an aggressive movement should be made on the fortress of his wickedness; that it was not a matter of indifference whether he received such instruction or not; that the supply here should always exceed the demand; — and this line of argument is reckoned very powerful in behalf of an established church. But you, gentlemen, by this resolution, have admitted what is called the *voluntary principle;* you are verily guilty of a practical inconsistency in having elected a chaplain on the compulsory principle, and making his services to depend upon the voluntary. If it be *expedient* that spiritual advice to the able-bodied be only given on demand, why depart from your rule in reference to the aged and infirm, unless you think these latter the only fitting recipients for ghostly counsel and heavenly consolation? If Christian instruction be at all important, it is all important — whether it refer to the old or young, the healthy or the infirm. Or, perhaps you deem one hour on a Sunday sufficient to cheer a man on his way to heaven, and to aid his moral improvement. Have you not had lately a practical illustration of the inefficiency of such scanty ministrations, when, out of nearly 400 inmates, only four aged individuals could be found willing to partake of the holiest of sacraments? Surely, gentlemen, if you will only consider the temper of mind in which young and sturdy fellows are compelled to seek a shelter in your dwelling, and the effect of evil counsel on those who are not wholly contaminated, you must allow that for the chaplain to speak a word of kindness seasonably to these men, to sympathize with them in their misfortune, and inculate familiarly the duties of conduct and obedience — even under a law admitted to be severe in its enactments — would have a far more beneficial tendency than answering their complaints by displaying the arm of power or the frown of a sullen authority; the governor, then, might be under no alarm, either for the safety of his person or the establishment. And at the present time it seems the more requisite for the Chaplain to bring all the weight of Christian admonition to bear on the soured and refractory dispositions of the inmates, especially when the "visiting committee" have so notoriously neglected their duties; in reference to which complaint you have not even ventured the slightest palliation or excuse. In many institutions of the like nature a week-day service, together with personal visitings, have been required of the chaplain by the guardians; and such services, I conceive, are but due to the inmates and the rate-payers. I would humbly ask, "how is it possible for the chaplain conscientiously to answer the printed queries of the commissioners touching the moral improvement of those inmates, unless he have some personal knowledge of them"? This resolution of your's virtually bars all access to such knowledge. During the last year your medical officer visited the workhouse upwards of 400 times, for which he received the net payment (say) of £10; you vote your chaplain a clear yearly salary of £10 for little more than one weekly attendance! The rate-payers are not satisfied with this disparity; they feel bitterly the expensive machinery required to carry out this Poor-law Amendment Act; they will either have money's worth for their money or demand a reduction of the scale of payment among some of the officers of the establishment. Be consistent, then; make not a mockery of this important and holy office to which I have alluded; purge away this leaven of *expediency*, it is but the doctrine of infidelity — "be just and fear not"; either counpel your chaplain to perform those duties which the circumstances of the case so imperatively require or carry out your principle and abolish at once and altogether the office of chaplain itself.

> I have the honour to be, gentlemen, Your obedient servant,
>
> Thomas Hayton

[Reply to the letter of the 2nd inst.]
Thame Union to the Reverend T. Hayton

5 February 1841

Sir,

I am directed by the guardians to acknowledge the receipt of your letter of the 2nd instant, which was read at the board on Wednesday; and to inform you that the guardians see no reason to alter the opinion they had before expressed.

> I have the honour to be, sir, Your most obedient servant,
>
> John Hollier
> Clerk

[Rejoinder to the above]
To the Thame Board of Guardians

Crendon, 8 February 1841

Gentlemen,

I feel deeply sensible of the value of your important reply: I shall, therefore, be very plain with you. You do not *wish* your chaplain to enter the ward for able-bodied men, lest he should bring you information of an unpalatable nature, and therefore impose trouble upon you — you prefer hearing a gentle, one-sided report of those who "prophecy smooth things". This is a part of the utilitarian philosophy of Commissioner Parker, which (tell it not in Gath!), is sanctioned and approved of by your reverend vice-chairman! But, you shall not escape. How comes it to pass, gentlemen, that the men in the workhouse, both old and young, are actually in a state of contumacy and insurrection; that the locks are broken off the doors daily; that the governor is assailed with hissings and hootings; and that curses are uttered both loud and deep? I charitably presume the fault is in the system — not in the governor. How was it that, last week, you refused to admit into your presence a pauper of unblemished character, who wished only to prefer a very reasonable request in reference to the welfare of his child? And how is it that, during this inclement season, the females with young children are kept shivering in the cold and cheerless wards from breakfast till dinner time? It would be more creditable to you to order the fires to be lighted earlier — to dedicate a little more time to the internal affairs of the workhouse — and see that justice is done to the poor; otherwise, I shall begin to think there are persons now in existence like those mentioned by the prophet *Amos* (chap. ii.), who would sell "the bodies of the poor for silver, and their souls for a pair of shoes".

I have the honour to be, gentlemen, Your obedient servant,

T. Hayton

*Whatever the poor law may have done elsewhere, the sum of money raised for the relief of the poor in Crendon is more by £200 yearly than it was under the old law, and such outlay is gradually increasing. There is a superfluity of labour; thence the wages of it are miserably low. It is no longer a question on what the wages of labout depend — they certainly depend not on the price of corn.

[76] John Stone to the Dean and Canons

Crendon, 5 February 1841

Sir,

I am requested by the Thame Board of Guardians to ask permission of the Dean & Canons of Windsor for the poor of this parish to be vaccinated in the Court Room [1].

The Clergyman (Mr Hayton) uses it only as a Sunday School room, but has forbidden the use of it for the purposes I mention, simply I believe for the sake of opposition.

I remain, Sir, your obedient servant,

John Stone

[Minute by Chapter Clerk]
Feb. 8th Wrote to Mr Hayton requesting him to inform me whether there is any objections to the room being used in the manner proposed.
Feb. 13th Whether the room under the Court House or the 'place of payment' might be used instead for the purpose.

Windsor.

1. This activity was in consequence of an Act for Extending the Practice of Vaccination, 4-5 Victoria c.32. It was not compulsory until 1851.

[77] To the Chapter Clerk

Crendon, 11 February 1841

Sir,

I am glad to have an opportunity of writing to you respecting the Court Room at Long Crendon.

You perhaps may remember when I wrote to the Dean & Canons respecting my having it for a school room, their *express condition* was, that I would allow it for no other purpose; & when the National Society gave £20 to repair it to such condition, was communicated to & accepted by them. This struck me as a powerful reason why I should refuse permission for its use as a vaccinating house, especially as the demand was made almost as a right. If however, the Lords of the Manor wish it so to be used, of course I comply. But there are other circumstances which ought to be considered — the use is not for the parish of Crendon alone, there are two or three other parishes which are to be accommodated; & this is not once or twice, but to continue every fortnight for two years upwards! I have been at great expense & trouble in keeping the place at all decent, & I know that all the trouble of cleaning after them will devolve upon my servant & without the least renumeration. Mr Hollier, the Clerk of the Court, has promised for years some assistance merely to keep the tiling in order. and one pound I must lay out for this immediately. The room formerly had no glass windows in it; I have procured very nice sash windows. These are sure to suffer. However if the Lords wish it, I will comply.

I should also add that the relieving officer informs me that he has offered his *place of payment* in the village for the purpose, & would suit very well. There is also an empty room *below* the School room which with little expense might be made suitable for the purpose, which if the Lords of the Manor saw would never allow to be left in the sorry condition it is. The fact is all the *under rooms* are in the most wretched, shuttered condition, scarcely fit for pigs to abide in — a disgrace to the village [1]; & if the Lords of the Manor would order the doors, windows etc to be walled up & white washed, a service would be rendered to the village, especially as the Court Room only receives damage from such habitations & the Lords no profit.

Any further enquiries on this subject I will be happy to answer.

I have the honour to be your very obedient servant,

Thos Hayton

Windsor

1. These rooms had been used for housing the poor until the Poor Law Amendment Act of 1834.

[78] To the Commissioners of the Poor Law Amendment Act
Crendon, [received 5 March] 1842

Gentlemen,

The enclosed is a copy of a petition from the ratepayers of Long Crendon to the Thame Board of Guardians, presented and supported by the Guardians of the same parish, by whom I have been requested to transmit the same to you with a brief statement of the case.

Five weeks ago, a person of the name of *William Dodwell* [1] of this parish, with his sickly wife applied for relief to the Board; the trade of the man was a shoemaker, and for many years he has been unable to earn his own living, his sight having failed him, and his age being upwards of 65 years. His character is good, having for many years been entrusted with making out rates and collecting them, and having been respectably allied. It was supposed as a *matter of course* that he would get 'out door relief' but the workhouse was offered him, where he is now located [2]. The parishioners and rate-payers (only two having refused their signatures to the petition, & these only small contributors) deem this to be a stretch of powers, unjust and without a precedent in the Union, & against the fair interpretation and spirit of the Poor Law Amendment Act, and yet in the face of a small cabal at the Board, contrives to detain the aged couple in the workhouse, on the sole ground that the man had *brothers* wealthy enough to keep him. True, he has brothers in the parish, rack-renter farmers 'well to-do in the world' [3] as the saying is, but each has a large family of 9 or 10 children, & they have for many years partially assisted him, but now are disinclined any longer to do so. As the law cannot force them to this act, & as they are determined not to be forced, it is thought downright cruelty to make the destitute brother a sufferer (& he does suffer extremely) for their refusal to maintain him. I wish to give no colouring to this subject, nor has it been taken up on any party or factious grounds. The parishioners at large sympathize with this aged & respectable couple, thus forced to herd with characters foreign to their habits and dispositions; and regret at the same time that they should be driven to appeal to you as a tribunal which I have always deemed absolutely requisite to restrain the caprice & tyranny of petty local caballing jurisdiction.

> I have the honour to be, Gentlemen, your respectable & obedient servant,
>
> Thos Hayton
> Incumbent of Long Crendon

I refer you to Captain Hamilton, the Chairman of the Board now in Town, by whom this subject is well known [4].

A petition is enclosed with 81 signatures of rate-payers, and headed by the names of the Churchwarden [5].

Draft reply from Mr Power, Assistant Commissioner [6]
If the proprietors and occupiers of land are permitted to thrust their nearest relations on the poor rate, and the workhouse test is not to be applied to such cases on the alleged ground of 'cruelty' to the parties proposed to be maintained, it is usually to be expected that the elderly relations of labouring men receiving weekly wages of from 8s to 12s weekly should not be put on the outdoor relief lists. The names of James, David, and Benjamin Dodwell are subscribers to the memorial of rate-payers, and the whole affair of rescue to be grossly unprincipled.

M.H. 12/9734

1. William Dodwell: see Dodwell family tree.
2. One of the main objects of the Poor Law Act was the abolition of 'out door relief'.
3. 'Rack Rent': an adjustable rent as opposed to a customary rent.
4. Charles John Baillie Hamilton (1800–1865), grandson of the 6th Earl of Addington. Married Lady Caroline Bertie and lived at Thame Park. M.P. for Aylesbury 1839 to 1847.
5. The signatures include all the parish with the exception of the six offending Dodwell brothers, John Stone, and the Baptist Minister, William Hopcroft.
6. Mr Power, afterwards Sir Alfred Power (1805–1888); Factory Commissioner 1833; Assistant Commissioner 1834 to 1843; barrister-at-law of the Middle Temple (*M.E.B.*).

[79] From the Aylesbury News

26 March 1842

Considerable excitement has taken place here on the subject of Guardians for the parish for the coming year. The place returns two Guardians to the Thame Union, and the four following gentlemen have been nominated:— Rev. Thos Hayton [1], Mr Edward Shrimpton, Mr John Hollis, and Mr Robert Dodwell, all of this place. The bustle of a village election has set the inhabitants on the *qui vive,* the nominators being anxious for the success of their respective candidates. The well-known care displayed by the reverend candidate makes his return almost a certainty.

1. Hayton was Poor Law Guardian from April 1835—37, April 1839—40, April 1842—43.

[80] To the Poor Law Commissioners

Crendon, 8 April 1842

Gentlemen,

I yesterday moved for & obtained a copy of the Clerk's letter to you from the Thame Board of Guardians in re Wm Dodwell of the parish of Crendon; which letter I hesitate not to denounce (as I did yesterday at the Board) as an *ex parte* statement, not borne out by the facts of the case. As to their being owners of property — one has a rood of ground, another 6 acres & a third 18!!! They are certainly rack-renters of 700: the eldest [1] for many years kept his father & mother & has now 2 grandchildren dependent on him, together with 7 of his own. The other brothers each 10 or 11 children. As to the eldest refusing to listen to the proposition of the younger as to their keeping their brother, I am requested to say, it is all entirely false from beginning to end; that he never shrouded himself under the Law of the case; that there are family reasons which need not be opened up to justify his conduct, which might have been surmounted had he been treated with courtesy. In my opinion, after calmly looking at the case, it was a battle of selfishness between the Squire of the parish [2] & the renters alluded to.

In self-justification in this matter, I have thought it proper to say this much.

I am, Gentlemen, your obedient servant,

Thos Hayton

[Minuted]
To Mr Power with former papers
Mr Hayton says 'this is a battle of selfishness between the squire & the 3 brothers — renters of 700 acres', Mr Hayton seems however to have taken a distinguished part in the battle himself on side of the renters.
R. Power 16 April 1842

M.H. 12/9734

1. John Dodwell, tenant of Lord Churchill.
2. John Stone, tenant of the Dean and Canons of Windsor.

Crendon, 25 June 1842

Gentlemen,

Your letter to the Vice-Chairman of the Thame Board of Guardians [1] respecting some changes made by the Clerk in his legal Character, was duly read last week at the Board and much difference of opinion arose respecting it. As the Board was only thinly attended, I moved that the Guardians be especially summoned on Wednesday week to re-consider & finally dispose of the matter; will you, therefore, have the goodness, simply to say, whether your answers to the Vice-Chairman's letter has both a retrospective & pro-spective view. It was doubted whether the recently issued orders respecting the duties etc. of the Clerk applied to Actions at Law begun two years back; & that tho' the Clerk's salary was raised from £60 to £100 in order to meet all *ordinary legal charges*, still the *whole* of his Bill, & not the disbursements only (as specified in rule No. 2) were rightfully his — I am aware it is rather unpleasant to dispute with the Clerk on this subject; but as the Income committee objected to the Charges, the subject forced itself upon the attention of the Guardians.

Your early reply will much oblige, Gentlemen,

your obedient servant,

Thomas Hayton

M.H. 12/9734

1. John Hollier, solicitor, Clerk to the Thame Union.

[82] *Revd. R.P. Smith* [1] *to Bishop Kaye*

Long Compton, 16 September 1843

My Lord,

Your Lordship having allowed the Revd. T. Hayton to nominate me to the curacies of Long Crendon & Lower Winchendon, Buckinghamshire, I beg leave to put forward my letters or ordin: & a testimonial from the Vicar of Long Compton whose Church I have been serving during the Long Vacation. Immediately on my College meeting I will forward to your Lordship a Testimonial from the Master & Fellows of Pembroke.

I remain, My Lord, your Lordship's obedient servant,

R.P. Smith M.A.

L.A.O. Cor. B 5/3/21/1

1. Revd. R.P. Smith, (1819–1895) later Regius Professor of Divinity, Oxford. Incumbent of Ewelme.

21 October 1843

CHURCH DISCIPLINE
(From a Correspondent)

Some months ago, a commission of inquiry, under the Church Discipline Act [1], was issued out by the Bishop of Lincoln, in reference to a reported improper intimacy between a clergyman in the neighbourhood of Thame and one of his female parishioners — the ground of the allegation being, that the female had been taking supper at the parsonage, and was detained there till a late hour. After two days of investigation, of the most searching and inquisitional character — worthy only of the dark annals of the Star Chamber — when questions of the most impudent and impertinent nature were put — a *prima facie* case was reported by the commissioners. The minister declined to assent to the bishop's arbitration, giving 'the enemy' an opportunity of carrying the matter before the Court of Arches, where he had determined to defend himself, if required. After a delay of four months, and no sign of attack appearing, the clergyman agreed for the bishop to pronounce sentence; and last week the churchwardens of the parish received his lordship's decision, which triumphantly frees the parties from the alleged charge; nay, not only was the case not made out, but every part of the evidence against the clergyman entirely disproved. We are promised a digest of the evidence (which is very lengthy, in which the characters of the accusers will fully appear, together with the shameful agencies employed to establish, if possible, this cruel and revengeful proceeding. The complainant was a discarded parish clerk, who had been previously twice expelled from the Methodist connexion — once for a felonious act, and a second time for the most bare-faced lechery; this man was supported by an ex-beershop keeper, who had also in time past been dismissed from the Sunday school as a teacher in consequence of his sottish habits; and who, to show the purity of his principle, wrote twice to the bishop for *more* money for giving his evidence, although he had received from another source the wages* of iniquity. This brace of miscreants was hallooed on by a magistrate and his virtuous dame (not an Oxfordshire magistrate, for in that county there is none such); but by one who neither theoretically nor practically is acquainted with a Christian principle, whose name, heart, and head are all of the same solid material, and who, to gratify his hatred and revenge, cared not what vile instrumentality he made use of, or whose feelings were outraged. In short, there was a cursing Shimei, a traitorous Judas, a priestly embodiment of Caiaphas urging on the accursed *expediency* principle, and requiring only a mitred *Pilate* to make up the group and complete the nefarious design; but *such an one* was not found in the Bishop of Lincoln. His lordship cast aside all the dirty private communications which were sent to prejudice him, and pronounced on the evidence with the impartiality of a judge, and did honour to the high and divine attribute with which he was invested.

CAUTION — The Right Honorable the Lord Chief Baron of Brill and Boarstall [2], and William the Archbishop of Claydon [3] are quite anxious to be upon another commission of inquiry. Indeed, they think there should be one monthly, and particularly near their own homes, to check anti-rubrical teachings, anti-teetotal practices, and reported mes-alliances. They believe themselves exceedingly expert in the knowledge of *prima facie* cases; but more skilled are they by far, as many people think, in *secunda facie* cases, which in common parlance means, carrying two faces under one hat, whether it be a four-and-nine penny one or a "chapeau de billy-cock".

*The wife of the dismissed clerk has admitted that a parcel containing money was left at her house, to be divided between her husband and the person here alluded to. We understand that an indictment will be preferred at the next Quarter Session against these parties; and a presentment made at the Easter visitation of an individual who may think himself secure.

1. Church Discipline Act 3-4 Victoria c.86. The bishop could sanction a Committee of Inquiry which consisted of himself and three assessors.
2. Revd. J.S. Baron, vicar of Brill 1814 to 1866.
3. Revd. W.G. Freemantle (1807–1895), brother of 1st Baron Cottesloe; vicar of Steeple Claydon 1841 to 1868; evangelical (*M.E.B.*).

[84] To Bishop Kaye

St Heliers, Jersey, 22 November 1843

My Lord,

I infer from a letter of Mr Smith's that his testimonials are satisfactory to your Lordship; I therefore enclose his nomination to be my Curate at Crendon and Winchendon, which I trust your Lordship will sanction, as also the amount of stipend from the *special & peculiar circumstances* mentioned in an accompanying paper — the justice of which I hope will be readily acknowledged.

I have been absent from Crendon since the last Sunday in September, and will petition for a licence of non-residence during the next month, on the allowable grounds stated in the 1 & 2 Vict. C. 106 [1]. That licence, if granted I should hope might bear date from 1st January 1844, as I shall have only during the current year (I may say during 25 years) been virtually absent from the parishes 13 weeks.

Mr Smith, with his family, is now at Crendon residing at the Parsonage.

I have the honour to be, my Lord, your Lordship's obedient servant,

Thos Hayton

Postscript
Lest your Lordship may think I am the only one in the neighbourhood of Crendon of whom there has been & is now evil report — I will venture to subjoin a case or two. It may be distressing to your Lordship, & you may despise me for it; but remember a wronged man, in his outraged feelings, does not stand on conventional refinement. Of three rural deans, one not long ago kept Susan B—— at Oxford; another before his wife came to reside with him was frequently taking a female to Oxford in a post chaise, who was reported to be enceinte by him; a third, attentions to a married female in his village have been long talked of, & since my absence from Bucks an outbreak has occurred of which one of my parishioners thus writes 'If such a thing had occured at Crendon — what a stir would there have been! but one man may steal a horse without notice, whilst another looking over a gate at it must be dragged before justice'. A Doctor of Divinity — I have each of these state-

60

ments on indisputable authority — only a year or two ago, lived for seven years in an Hotel in London under the name of Captain with a female, whom he left there to pay the cost; this said Doctor regularly speculates in the Derby Sweeps at Evans [2] ! A parishioner of a neighbouring village avowed before me that the Incumbent was drunk in the pulpit on a Sunday — it was not Mr Willis [3] : no, no, his irregularities are the result of a disease, rather than an indulged taste. I could protract this list in 3 other cases; but these are melancholy enough; and if I am to be trampled under foot thro' the instrumentality of that bigot Freemantle, it will be owing to my clemency if each case is not dragged into light & notoriety.

L.A.O. Cor. B 5/3/21/1

1. Pluralities Act 1-2 Victoria c.106 — a licence of non-residence could be given on account of ill health.
2. Evans in Covent Garden was a music hall where smart people sat in their boxes, eating and drinking. (K. Chesney *The Victorian Underworld*, p. 310).
3. John Willis, vicar of Haddenham. He had been suspended for a year on account of drunkeness and immorality (*Wilberforce* No. 177).

[85] To Bishop Kaye

St Heliers, Jersey, 11 March 1844

My Lord,

Herewith I enclose a petition for non-residence — not, however, on the grounds I intended in petition. Mr Lee misunderstood me. I only told him, that your Lordship might *probably* require a certificate of the nature of Mrs Hayton's complaint etc. Under clause 44 I purposed to petition; for I decidedly think mine is a case of expediency (if ever there will be one) arising from ministerial, prudential considerations. It will require years to pass before the bitter party spirit & personal rancour may subside & my ministerial influence be regained. Besides, my deadly foe & his wife are jealous, implacable & revengeful, & delight in weakening my hands in every possible way, & subjecting me to annoyances. Were I compelled to reside at Crendon, I must return every object of residence, save the cold & reluctant performance of duty, expecting my 'life's life lied away' & virtually to be devoured; & therefore I throw myself upon your Lordship's protection, & decision of the grounds of application, thankful to escape residence by any means, tho' at the same time regretting the existence of either sickness or expediency.

For these few months I have enjoyed a quiet which for years I never experienced: this with its stillness, bids me to forsake 'troubled waters for a purer spring' & nothing but a sense of justice to others keeps me from surrendering the Living into the hands of the Patron.

I have been occasionally assisting a clerical friend here; & am now doing part of the duty at a proprietary Chapel, under the sanction of Dr Jeune [1] . This *Chapel has no cure of souls; no district attached to it, nor does it belong to any other Church or Chapel: The proprietors have always elected their Minister for 5 years. Their late Minister was dismissed rather uncourteously & therefore the Bishop of Winchester has claimed the right of licensing the Minister to the exclusion of the Proprietor's power in that respect, & the claim is admitted. As my ministrations seem to give satisfaction, I have been encouraged to offer myself as a candidate; but I should not feel myself justified in doing so without your Lordship's sanction & assurances of Countersignature to my Testimonials. Not being so supported, I would decline the matter altogether, retire into the wilds of Brittany where a shelter is offered us under the roof of a friend, & where I may possibly find peace and forgetfulness of the wrongs that I have endured.

> I have the honour to be, my Lord, your Lordship's obedient servant,
>
> Thos. Hayton

*would your Lordship condescend to inform me whether the acceptance of *such a Chapel* would cause my Living to be vacated. If I could promise the proprietors a continuance of my services, this would, I am told, be of great avail. I need scarcely add how effectual this would be to remove the incumbrances on the Living of Crendon, & therefore make by return there an object of pleasure rather than reluctance. T.H.

[*Draft reply of Bishop Kaye*]

> Riseholme [2] , Lincoln, March the ——

Reverend Sir,

I will direct Mr Smith to prepare your Licence of Non-residence: the state of Mrs Hayton's health being in your case a ground on which I can grant it. If the Chapel, of which you speak, has no cure of Souls, I do not think it comes under the description of a Benefice, as defined by the Plurality Act.

I shall not decline to countersign your Testimonial: but I shall feel it right to state to the Bishop of Winchester the circumstances under which you have left Long Crendon. Mr Vayne is not yet licensed; he has not returned the Communication which was issued to him some time ago.

L.A.O. Cor. B 5/3/21/1

1. Dr Francis Jeune (1806—1868), Dean of Jersey and rector of St Helier 1838 to 1843, vice-chancellor of Oxford 1858 to 1862, see D.N.B.
2. The Bishop's new Palace, two miles from Lincoln, built 1841, at the cost of £52,000.

[86] Revd. S. Langston [1] *to Bishop Kaye*

> St Heliers, Island of Jersey, 25 October 1844

My Lord,

A clergyman of your Lordship's Diocese, Rector or Vicar, it is said, of Long Crendon Bucks, & now resident here, has been offering his assistance to various clergymen of this Island.

A report has reached them myself among them, that this Mr Hayton has been removed from his Parish by your Lordship's Episcopal Censure for some misconduct & *that* of a gross character.

It happens that I have been proposing to avail myself of this gentleman's assistance in the duties of a large Episcopal Chapel in this Town of which I am the Minister Incumbent.

I should feel deeply obliged to your Lordship if you would inform me whether there is truth in this statement; the consequence to the cause of religion & to the interests of our Church of employing unfit Persons in the sacred office of divine worship will, I hope, justify this application to your Lordship.

yours with much respect,

S. Langston

[*Minute by Bishop Kaye*]
Told that Mr H. was non-resident under a Licence from me; and that a charge had been brought against him which after investigation was pronounced not to be proved.

L.A.O. Cor. B 5/3/21/1

1. The Rev. S. Langston was officiating minister of St James' Chapel, St James's Street, St Heliers from 1843 to 1846.

[*87*] *To Bishop Kaye*

St Heliers, Jersey, 25 March 1845

My Lord,

In consequence of your Lordship's letter I beg leave to spare your Lordship and the Bishop of Winchester any trouble on my account. I have declined all ministrations here, & we shall leave as soon as possible. I should have asked your Lordship's countersignature as a *right*, which from your Lordship's expression would have been granted with reluctance. With one hand you presented me with a rose — in the other was a dagger; and without wishing to give offence (which never in my life did I purposely give to any one) I will venture on the liberty of thought and speech which neither persecution nor torture shall make me relinquish. I cannot of course understand the duties and responsibilities of a prelate; but to report an imputed sin of a Christian brother to another Bishop, does appear to me in ill accordance with Pauline or Christian teaching. Your Lordship *could not* make a true and fair statement of the *circumstances* under which I left Crendon simply because you are not in possession of the materials to do so: this being the case, in all probability the circumstances would be looked upon as *Causes*. Pecuniary Embarassment owing to a thankless (perhaps thoughtless yet with a good object) sacrifice of money on Church property, domestic affliction, & rascally treatment at the hand of a Brute are the real cause of my absence — the last, however, without the former would have no power with me.

I know that your Lordship is prejudiced against me — I *know* those who have done anything in their power to rivet the prejudice — This feeling,

63

by such a communication alluded to, would, I conceive be transferred to the Bishop of Winchester; I should be looked upon as a suspected person, a kind of wolf; and, imagining myself under Episcopal Espionage and Vampirism, my feelings would become galled & my ministration marred. It would be a refinement in cruelty, *ni fallor* in common, vulgar parlance, 'Establishing a raw' & scouring the victim's wound to prevent its healing. A Prelate, in olden times thus writes on the subject 'Christian love will cover a multitude of sins; and reproof should be in secret. The publication of a miscarriage, instead of reforming the offender, may possibly make him desperate or impudent, either to despond under the burden of his infamy, or to harden his forehead like a flint; neither of which are like to conduce anything to the purposes of virtue, or to promote the person's recovery. — The end of every reproof (admonition) is remedy; but *to shame a man is revenge;* & such a one as the bitterest adversary in the world cannot act a sharper or more remorseless; for it is a piece of human barbarity to afflict a man but in order to his consequent good; & to be ripping up old sores & reminding an amended person of imputed miscarriages which perhaps stand cancelled in heaven, & even blotted out of the Book of God's remembrance, is like the breaking open of graves, to take out bones and putrefaction, & argues an unchristian, inhuman, & wolfish disposition'. God forbid I should impute such a disposition to your Lordship! but, do I deserve to be hunted as a wild beast, & branded as tho' I had been a convicted criminal? I have wished to avoid the appearance of evil — for the scandal to die away, & that I might be under no necessity of any further un-pleasant communications with your Lordship; but you will not allow me, you strike me at every turn, which a reference to facts during these last few years could amply prove; & yet never in my life, did I utter a disrespectful word of your Lordship, or display even the shadow of resistance to your authority. And now — but words are vain — only let me retire from wrongs & insults; I will exercise no ministerial functions, nor expend any Ecclesiastical proceeds; my wants are few & He who has never deserted me will not now allow me to perish. The grave may make me amends, tho' 'of human wrong great Nemesis never yet lost the unbalanced scale'. A time may come when the shade which has been attempted foully & illegally to be cast upon my character may be removed; & I hope when we meet at the bar of Judgement your Lordship may be 'justified in your saying and clear when you are judged'.

I know I am in your Lordship's hand; & assuring your Lordship of my ready acquiescence in all your commands.

> I have the honour to be, my Lord, your Lordship's obedient servant,
>
> Thos. Hayton

L.A.O. Cor. B 5/3/21/1

[88] *Bishop Kaye* [1] *to Bishop Samuel Wilberforce* [2]

[undated] [1846]

I was under the necessity of issuing a Commission of Enquiry into the charge of immorality against Mr Hayton: there was no legal evidence sufficient to sustain it; but there was room for grave suspicion. He afterwards applied

for a Licence of non-residence on account of his wife's health, and I was too
ready to grant it [3].

Bodl. M.S. Oxf. Dioc. papers, d. 550 page 159

1. A report from Bishop Kaye when he handed over Buckinghamshire to Bishop Wilberforce in 1845.
2. A letter from Wilberforce to Hayton is printed in Wilberforce, No. 84.
3. Thomas Hayton left Crendon in September 1843 and returned in March 1846.

[89] From the Bucks Advertiser

17 July 1847

DINNER AT THE SPREAD EAGLE HOTEL —
UPROARIOUS PROCEEDINGS

On Tuesday last, Mr Disraeli, as announced upon placards, met a
number of the electors of Bucks around the dinner-table at the Spread Eagle
Hotel, for the purpose of making an exposition of his sentiments. A large
number sat down to a good dinner; and afterwards, the doors being thrown
open, the room became excessively crowded in every corner. Mr J.K. Shrimpton
was called to the chair [1]. On his right and left sat W.L. Stone, Esq. [2],
J. Stone, Esq., Mr Paine [3], Revds. Messrs Stevens [4] and Partridge [5], &c.
Mr Hedges [6] was the vice-chairman.

The loyal toasts came first in order, and were given and received without
any commotion — Next came 'The Bishop and Clergy'.

The Revd. Mr Stevens rose to reply. He was glad to find that the public
were ready to support the authority of the clergy, and none more so than the
old nobility, gentry, and yeomanry of England. The clergy, he hoped, would
maintain their sacred character by their good deeds. (A sarcastic voice — 'As
they are accustomed'.) Many opinions prevailed in the present day respecting
the position of the clergy with the state (*hear, hear*). It was true they were
connected with the state; but they did not derive their power of authority
from the state — they were the ambassadors of Him to whom all power was
given in earth and heaven (loud cheers). They depended upon their commission from His authority, that commission which enabled the first preachers
of Christianity to overthrow Paganism, even without the aid of the state. For
three centuries Christianity was assailed by the Pagans. (A voice — 'And is
now trampled down by the clergy'.) However, even a Pagan emperor was at
last compelled to bow to its merits; to confess its merits, and to make it the
religion of his empire (applause). In the time of Constantine the clergy were
upheld by the state.

The Revd. Hayton immediately rose, and said that having heard the
remarks which his rev. brother had just made, he could not allow them to
pass without saying that it would not do for him to subscribe to all he had
uttered (*cheers*). He looked upon the main union between church and state as
an old established truth, consistent with reason, and not contradicted by
Scripture, and borne out by the policy of every country except America,
which should not be taken into the reckoning, (loud cries of ('Why not'?)
particularly when one-fifth of its population were slaves. To instruct the
people appeared to him to be one of the most pre-eminent duties of a govern-

ment, in order to prevent crime, and keep people out of the workhouse and the gaol. The experience of both barbarous, Pagan, and Christian nations showed that the alliance between church and state was a kind of bond for the preservation of the law. With respect to the bishops — (a voice, 'They have too much', and great commotion, the Chairman and others declaring that such expressions were out of order.) 'I accept the challenge (continued the rev. gentleman), and I tell that individual that the bishops have too much' (great uproar — hooting, yelling, groaning, &c.) He had yet to learn that a political government was of the essence of episcopacy. (cheers, and hooting, groaning &c.). If the clergy were not to get into the House of Commons, he saw no use for sending the Bishops into the House of Lords. Certainly the curates at all events should not be allowed to lie under the grasping policy of the bishop (loud cheers). And if certain acts of parliament were passed, the incumbents would be so too. If the bishops want to go to the House of Lords, let them not go there to look after their grinding purposes (cheers). God forbid he should say anything against the bishops which he did not feel warranted saying; but the Bishop of Oxford, he would remark, was a wag in his way (tremendous uproar, the loud cries of 'Shame, shame, go on, go on'.) Yes, the Bishop of Oxford was building dormitories at Cuddesden [7], and he hoped he would build refractories (sic) there too (loud laughter). I repeat he is certainly very waggish (renewed uproar), for in a speech of his I read the other day, he talked of the hospitality of the bishops, and of their charitable disposition (immense laughter). Now, if ever a bitter sarcasm was used towards any man, that was it. He had been acquainted with bishops, and he had heard of many — but to talk of their hospitality! (Loud laughter). Why, he had never seen the shine of their plate of the — (great uproar, drowning the sentence). He wanted to see the emoluments of episcopacy equalised, in order that the working clergy might be paid for their services (cheers). Mr Disraeli was called a nominee — he (Mr H.) wanted to know whether a nominee from Buckingham was not as good as one from High Wycombe (great cheering). The best men who entered parliament were nominees; and he was just about to say that Mr Disraeli had raised the hope of the country — at all events he meant the country. For what was the fact? Why, they had had eleven dummies for the county heretofore (loud laughter). And what had they done? Had they done anything? Yes, they had. They had added 25 per cent to the poor-rates of Haddenham, Cuddesden, and Brill (loud cheers). He next eulogised Mr Disraeli for taking Lord Bolingbroke as his model, and called upon him to raise his voice against the new removal act, and proceeded to show that the hon. candidate's scheme of custom-house duties would never do for England. There was a kind of thing which Mr Disraeli called protection; but this struck the farmer upon the left cheek (laughter). Did the malt-tax protect them? (Immense applause). The farmer had to pay £5.10s out of every acre of barley for this tax; and would Mr Disraeli repeal it? He wanted this question answered; and after apologising for speaking so long, he resumed his seat.

1. John Kirby Shrimpton (1809—1889) farmer, of Upper Farm, Easington; tenant of the old post windmill, Crendon.
2. William Lowndes Stone of Brightwell; acted as Disraeli's election agent.
3. Mr Paine of Aylesbury.
4. Revd. W. Stevens, vicar of Bledlow.
5. Revd. E.W. Partridge, vicar of Horsendon; a personal friend of Disraeli.
6. Mr Hedges of Scotsgrove House, Thame.
7. It had been agreed to spend £6819 on Cuddesdon, and in March 1847 Wilberforce's Palace had cost £1836 more than was estimated (Best, p. 366).

24 July 1847

Sir,

Will you have the kindness to insert the following remarks in your next paper — they are the very sentiments and words I made use of, as nearly as I can possibly remember? I ask this simply as a matter of justice; because some one of elevated sentiments, and noble and disinterested conduct, stole away to Cuddesdon, and told the Bishop of Oxford that I had made a low, ribald, and disgusting attack upon the bishops in general, and upon his lordship in particular. I dare say this individual thought himself a true son of the Church, though not a very bright follower of the spotless Nazarene who went about doing good instead of mischief. Let your readers judge whether they be the words of truth and soberness.

After some preliminary remarks, I observed, 'As to the alliance of Church and State, I had ever looked upon that as an established principle, sanctioned in the Old Testament, not forbidden in the New, most consonant with reason, and fully borne out by the experience of mankind, unless we take America for our pattern; but that nation should never be brought forward to illustrate an argument in our ancient civilization, in as much as she has no history attached to her, except it be a very awkward fact, that one-fifth of her population are slaves! Rulers, I conceive, are bound to promote the eternal as well as the temporal interests of the people whom God has committed to their charge; and if it be their office to advance the prosperity and the freedom of the nation, religion is the only foundation on which that prosperity and freedom can rest. Whether in Pagan or in Christian nations, religion is a strong bond of social and political union, which aids the efficiency of the law. Indeed laws, without a moral influence to fortify their observance, are a vain consideration; they only assert great principles, they only tell us what is right, they give no power to perform the right; but bring Christianity to bear upon their actions, and we have an orderly and a moral people, for religion is more effectual to check pauperism than the workhouse, and to prevent crime than the gaol. 'Righteousness exalteth a nation, and in righteousness shall thy throne be established'. Now, the national church establishment has undertaken this great, and serious, and important office of instructing the people and she should take the lead with clean hands and pure conduct, and I trust that we, here ministers, will all of us labour diligently and effectually in our high calling, and never lose hold of the affections of the people. (A cry was here raised, 'The Bishops have too much'.) 'I am of the same opinion with that individual; and I should be happy to see the episcopal revenues a little more equalized, and that the working clergy should be better paid. Episcopacy is fairly deducible from the New Testament; but I will candidly admit that its present position is somewhat anti-apostolical. I should like to see no necessity for their having seats in the House of Lords. I have yet to learn that government is the essence of episcopacy, which one might suppose was the case, judging from certain acts of parliament. The clergy are debarred access, without a shadow of reason, to the House of Commons:— why then should people be so anxious to have the bishops in the Lords? They have power enough already for all useful purposes. There was a bill now before their lordship's house of a harsh, grinding [a], and unconstitutional nature, which, if passed into a law, would throw into the hands of the bishops an entire power, not only over curates, but over every incumbent in the country. I had read lately that the hospitality of the bishops was a great item of their expenditure, and that the Bishop of Oxford had come to their rescue. His lordship was there said "to be a wag in his way" [b] (meaning that his lordship was quizzing); and that some of the bishops that heard him had taken it as a bitter sarcasm against their body' — (here an individual [c] cried 'Shame'; I told him to hear the remainder). 'God forbid' (I exclaimed) 'that I should speak evil of dignitaries; nor am I doing so — I am only stating what I read. I cannot myself speak experimentally of their lordship's hospitality. Though I have been under four bishops, I never saw the glitter of their plate, nor was regaled by the odour of their viands. I hear, however that there are dormitories building at Cuddesden, and I hope his lordship will not forget the refectory (not refractories); but that the chimney will smoke in true baronial style of hospitality'.

These were my sentiments — these were my words, except in two unimportant places. The latter sentences I spoke jocosely; I meant them as a joke, and I believe they were universally taken as a joke. I had no idea either of casting a reproach upon the Bishop of Oxford or bringing the bishops into contempt. We are living, however, in shifting times; and the bishops must not think themselves hemmed around by unapproachable divinity; whatever abuses or gross inequalities there may be in the episcopal establishment will not escape exposure and denouncement. Let the commissioners of Queen Anne's bounty lay claim forthwith to the full value of the first fruits and tenths of every bishopric and benefice above a stated amount of annual income. Commute this sum by act of parliament for a fixed annual amount, and distribute yearly amongst the poor benefices or in the provision for new churches and the revenues of the church would be rendered much more serviceable than they are. He is the best friend of the Established Church who seeks to render her services as efficient as possible; not he who, from a principle of conservatism, would destroy what he loves because he would not mend it. In the words of Dr Arnold, 'I look upon both the aristocracy and the church as positive blessings, and capable of doing good that can be done by no other means'. I love and would maintain both, not as a concession or a promise, but precisely with the same zeal that I would reform both, and enlarge the privileges and elevate the condition of the mass of the community.

I remain, Mr Editor, Yours respectfully,

Thomas Hayton

Long Crendon, July 19th, 1847

a I used the word 'grinding' to this act of parliament. On the Thursday following, thanks to the lay lords, much of the severity was extracted from this bill. The *Express* paper says, some of the bishops are very angry at this; at any rate, the Bishop of London has withdrawn the bill for this session. If it appears again, it is to be hoped that it will contain nothing of the spirit of the *chasse aux crimes* in it — that spirit of the Roman Courts under the Caesars.
b See the Twency-first Letter on Church Reform in the *Sunday Times,* where these very words are used, with some very unpalatable remarks.
c The individual alluded to cried, 'Shame', but like another great man would not wait for an answer — ,*abiit, evasit, erupit:* in vulgar parlance — 'he bolted'. He was seen in a bookseller's shop at Thame soon after, saying that the Bishops were attacked and the Church would fall! He was afterwards in Worminghall-Lane reading Ignatius Loyola — as a fit and suitable book to teach the young idea how to shoot. When a traitor is in the camp, Dr Arnold recommends a very summary process, which I certainly do not recommend to the Bishop, lest the word 'shame' should be duly merited.

[At the bottom of the page in the parish register, Thomas Hayton wrote:—]
The above occurred at a great political meeting at Thame where Disraeli was. Misrepresentations were made to the Bishop by a glazing sycophant. The Bishop felt aggrieved. I waited upon him & explained; and his Lordship was satisfied. T.H.

B.R.O. P.R.134/1/8

[91] From the Bucks Advertiser

6 October 1849

This place has happily been preserved from the prevailing epidemic, no cases of cholera having occurred, Wednesday the 26 ult. was duly observed as a day of fasting, humiliation, prayer and thanksgiving [1]. All business was suspended and the farmers' servants were set free from their labours, without being subject to a pecuniary loss. In the morning the Church was filled with serious and attentive hearers, and in the afternoon it was crowded, every seat being occupied, and forms being placed in the aisles, for the accommodation of the worshippers. The Vicar, the Rev. Thomas Hayton, whom to mention as a preacher is to praise, preached two truly eloquent and impressive discourses. In the morning from Joel the 2nd, 13th and 14th verses, and in the afternoon from Amos the 4th and 12th — may the fruit be seen after many days. Abused mercy turns to fury. The brightest sky may speedily be overcast with clouds.

1. The Government was in the habit of ordering 'National days of Prayer' either of thanksgiving or humiliation, as in plague. (Owen Chadwick, *The Victorian Church*, Part 1, page 491).

[92] From the Oxford Chronicle

30 March 1850

Case at Ashendon Petty Sessions

Nathan Beckett, Joseph Lester, Joseph Warner, Joseph Biggs, James Harper and Robert Harris, were brought up for having on Sunday, March 3rd, wilfully disturbed and annoyed the congregation in a Baptist Chapel [1] at Crendon. This case was adjourned from the last meeting. Mr H. Griffiths, attorney, appeared for the prosecution & called John Hobcroft & Thomas Shrimpton, who deposed they were in the chapel at that time & heard the noise the boys made which disturbed the congregation. For the defence, witnesses were called, who deposed they did not hear any language from the boys, or anything to annoy the congregation. The Rev. Mr Hayton of Crendon, who was in court appeared to be greatly interested on the part of the defence, who it appears were Sunday School Scholars. The magistrates considered the case had not been made out as being wilfully done, no one having checked the boys at the time complained of and they therefore should dismiss the case.

1. From 1828 to 1853 the Baptist services were held in a chapel on the Chearsley Road abutting on Burt's Lane.

69

[Abridged] 15 February 1851

On Thursday, Feb 6th, a vestry was held at the Eight Bells public-house [1], it being adjourned from the church in that place, on account of the church being too cold.

The Rev. Thomas Hayton, the vicar on taking the chair rose, and said it was customary for the chairman on such occasions to make some observations on the business which brought them together, and as he apprehended an opposition to the rate [2], he had prepared a written address which he would read to them. He commenced by recommending peace and good feeling among the parishioners, and hoped that those opposed to church rates, would not on this occasion disturb the peace of the parish by resisting the rate. Church-rates, he said were an ancient tax on property, and had existed upwards of eleven hundred years, and it was scarcely honest for dissenters to plead conscience in opposition to a tax, which they were legally bound to pay in consequence of the property which they held . . . They might with as much justice, plead conscience as a justification for refusing to pay the poor-rate, or road rates, or to pay for the repair of a certain bridge in the parish because they never used that bridge or never walked on that road. The Rev. gentleman then went on to assert that the present church establishment was of most ancient date, and existed long before the Roman Catholic religion was known to this country. After going on in this strain for a considerable time, he concluded by reminding the dissenters that their religion and the churchman's were essentially the same, and that it behoved them to unite in resisting the common enemy, the Pope, who was making inroads in this country and on their common religion.

The Churchwardens were then called upon to produce their estimates. There was one sum put down at £4 for visitation expenses &c. Here Mr Barry, of Chilton [3], who is a rate-payer in this parish, demanded the items of that amount, when it appeared the visitation fees were £1.10s; Churchwardens expenses £2; and the Rev. T. Hayton's expenses 10s. John Stone Esq then in a very conciliatory speech proposed a rate of 1½d in the pound. He admitted that it was a hardship for dissenters to be compelled to pay for a church from which they received no benefit, but it was the law, and they must submit. Mr H. Reynolds seconded the proposition.

Mr Barry rose to oppose the rate, and at considerable length went on to show the Rev. chairman's argument . . . He then proposed that the vestry be adjourned till this day twelve months.

Mr James Dodwell seconded the amendment and said (with considerable interruption from the chairman) that the present church establishment was not the ancient thing the chairman asserted, that it only dated its history from the time of Henry the Eighth . . . They could do very well without a compulsory rate, having a yearly income of £16 for this purpose, and if they wanted more they might obtain it by voluntary subscription.

The Rev. T. Hayton said 'I am willing to allow that the dissenters have a grievance in regard to church rates and that he has a right to complain; but he must remember that it is the law. . . May I beg of Mr Barry to withdraw the amendment? Mr Barry assured the chairman it was perfectly legal to put the amendment. He would not withdraw it. He begged of him to put it to the meeting and to use his influence with the ratepayers to carry it.

The chairman refused, and put the original motion, which was carried, some of the dissenters not voting. The meeting then dispersed.

It is said that the rate will not be enforced, as the notice in calling the meeting was not a legal one.

1. The inn nearest the Church. Its long upper room was often used for parish meetings.
2. Church rates were abolished in 1868.
3. Thomas Barry of Chilton Grounds Farm. He rented land near Crendon windmill.

[94] *From* Jackson's Oxford Journal

7 February 1852

A public Meeting was held at the Spread Eagle in Thame for the joint purpose of adopting a petition to Parliament for the repeal of the Maynooth Endowment Act [1], and the formation of a Protestant Alliance in Thame . . . The Rev. J. Prosser [2] was in the chair . . . the third resolution was moved by the Rev. Thomas Hayton of Crendon and seconded by the Rev. W.D. Littlejohn of Sydenham:

'That it appears desirable for the temporal and spiritual interests of this Kingdom that all classes of Protestants should combine in the formation of an alliance for the defence of the Scriptural doctrines for the Reformation and the principles of civil and religious liberty against the encroachment of Popery'.

1. This Act provided education for the Roman Catholic Irish clergy. In 1846 they were granted an annual permanent endowment of £25,000 plus a building grant of £30,000.
2. Revd. James Prosser, vicar of Thame; evangelical; theological writer.

[95] *To Lord Palmerston*

Crendon, 18 February 1853

My Lord,

I have this day been at the Ashendon Petty Sessions touching the conviction of George Munday for a petty assault, & tendered before the Magistrates certain declarations totally exculpating Munday. I also took one witness who *volunteered* to go. On hearing his evidence, however, the Magistrates thought there were certain discrepancies which could not be reconciled without the other two witnesses who were kept back — one by the influence of his Master, the other, the delinquent, by that of his parents.

I have been promised a copy of the deposition, which I will forward to you, together with the declarations (which the Magistrates thought they could not accept). Agreeably to the advice of the Magistrates, trusting that you will see that Munday is an innocent person, may I request *some form of declaration* most stringent & solemn which will be readily subscribed not only by the witnesses, but by the delinquent himself & if there be any other mode or form requisite by which the petition on behalf of Munday could be made the more admissible I will feel extremely obliged.

> I am, my Lord, Your Lordship's faithful and obedient servant,
>
> Thos Hayton

[*Minuted Rec. 19 Feb. 1853*]
Inform him that no particular form of Declaration is required by the Secy of State. H.W.

H.O. 18/353

[96] To the Right Honourable The Lord Palmerston

Crendon, 22 February 1853

My Lord,

Herewith I enclose, agreeably with the suggestion of the Magistrates at Ashendon, a copy of the depositions together with declarations most solemnly taken touching the assault of which George Munday had been convicted.

All the parties and the locality are well known to me, as well as the *springs of action;* & nothing but the firmest assurance of Munday's innocence could have induced me to request with all possible earnestness the exercise of your Lordship's power in this favour.

It is well known, nay, it is the woman's own confession made to the Mother of Munday, that 'she was not sure whether it was George or not', and that 'she never would have thought about a summons had she not been *urged* to it'; and so to her not seeing *Biggs* or Sawyer or Warner, it is accounted for by their being a little up the lane; the other parts of her statement about being frightened, hurt &c — it is all a pure fiction.

As to Johnstone's statement, I have visited the House, had all the points stated to me, & I am ready to depose most solemnly that it was utterly impossible for him to see almost any transaction out of his door, or outside of the house, his window being 4 feet from the level of the pavement and only 2 feet high with two rows of bottle and other materials in it.

I leave with your Lordship the statements of Hinton, Sawyer, Warner & Biggs. — There is a slight discrepancy between the statement of Hinton and Warner as to the words spoken by Elizabeth Ing; but this is accounted for by the deafness of Warner whom I have known from a child, & who was at a greater distance from her than of other of the parties.

I had the Boy Biggs before me, when he candidly acknowledged *that he & he only* was the person who touched Elizabeth Ing & that Munday is perfectly innocent. The truth is, that the case was hastily heard by the Magistrates, one of whom told me that it should have been adjourned; and Mr Bernard one of the 'signing' Magistrates told me on Sunday that your

72

Lordship's mediation in behalf of Munday would be acceptable, and this I was to intimate to your Lordship. I hope and trust therefore that your Lordship will allow, without any formal petition on my part, truth & justice to triumph over malice & perjury & keep from imprisonment a young man whose character has hitherto been unimpeached, and whose great desire is to deport himself as a good soldier & a Christian. I have the honour to be, my Lord,

> Your Lordship's faithful & obedient servant,
>
> Thomas Hayton

[*Minuted*]
The Secretary of State ought not to be called upon to try over again a trivial case of assault like this — the magistrates believed the witnesses *upon their oath* — these statements are mere declarations. (H.W.)

H.O. 18/353

Note
[Enclosed with this letter were three 'solemn Declarations' made in Thomas Hayton's presence by three witnesses, testifying to the innocence of Munday.]

[97] To the Right Honourable the Viscount Palmerston
Crendon, 25 February 1853

My Lord,

On Tuesday evening last I forwarded to the Home Office a copy of the Depositions and Declarations touching the conviction of George Munday — a parishioner of mine — for a petty assault. Knowing the punctuality of the Home Office and not having received a reply to my petition, I fear that either the papers have not been received, or I have been *informal* in my application. I will admit that I am more in the habit of *putting up* than in *drawing up* Petitions, & therefore, I may have failed therein; but as charity in above rubrics, so I hope that truth & justice will over-rule force.

On *Monday next* the young man will be committed to prison, unless your Lordship protects him from what will be a flagrantly unjust punishment.

> I have the honour to be, My Lord, your Lordship's faithful & obedient servant,
>
> Thomas Hayton

[*Minuted*]
Say that I cannot set aside on statements not on oath, a sentence pronounced by a Competent authority after Examinations of witnesses who were examined on their oath. P. 27/2-53
Ansd. 28 Feb. 1853

H.O. 18/353

Crendon, 27 February 1853

My Lord,

Permit me, my Lord, to apologize for troubling your Lordship again, but having received a letter this morning from the Editor of a local paper, enclosing me a letter proposing to subvert the testimony of Joseph Biggs in the case of George Munday & throwing discredit on the characters of Robert Hinton, Joseph Sawyer & Joseph Warner; & thinking it possible that such a document may have reached the Home Office, I take the earliest opportunity of replying to it.

The following is the statement alluded to 'I, Joseph Biggs make the following statement — George Munday first pushed me against Elizabeth Ing. I never touched her in any other way. George Munday might have insulted her after I went away. Mr Hayton has since sent for me to his house, & told me to say it was me that hit the lantern — that would get George Munday off. He would pay me for it. He, Mr Hayton, also told me to make a cross on a bit of paper but I do not know that it contained — he never read it to me

X the mark of Joseph Biggs

Witness Thomas Cross '

The above I pronounce to be a bare & malicious fabrication. I *never sent* for Biggs; he *was never at* my house. *I never* told him I would pay for his saying anything; but I requested Munday to bring all his witnesses, Biggs amongst the rest, to the public school room, & I would hear what they had to say; and when Biggs came in I warned him in the presence of all of them to speak nothing but the truth, & he owned at once that he was the person who assaulted Elizabeth Ing & that Munday had nothing to do with it. I read the statement over to him word by word in the presence of Munday, Sawyer, Warner, & Hinton before he signed it.

The letter (which I ought to remark the Editor declined to publish in consequence of its personalities & the internal evidence of its falsity) went on to denounce the above named young men as *pests of the village, street annoyers* &c., &c. I here most solemnly declare to your Lordship that my servant *Hinton* has been with me 6 years & I never had reason to dispute his word nor did I ever hear a complaint against him from any quarter. *Munday* is a servant of my Churchwarden who says he is one of the best & civilest servants he ever had and as to *Warner* & *Sawyer* they are equally unblameable & modest lads — never having been before a magistrate nor ever spoken to by a constable!!! To this I testify with the utmost assurance of its truth.

The name of the writer of the letter is *John Dudley* [1] — a *constable* & a *publican* & hunts for cases to bring to his house. His own Landlord told me that he would not believe him on his oath; & even last week at Ashendon in a case of affiliation his own maid servant swore that he encouraged her to prostitution in his own house. The name of Thomas Cross [2] is that of a Beer house keeper of shameful notoriety.

I have this day spoken to Mr Bernard [3] — the Magistrate to whom I alluded — & he advises a prosecution against the Constable Dudley & has sent

74

word to him not to touch Munday till your Lordship's decision is announced. I have the honour to be, my Lord,

> Your Lordship's faithful servant,
>
> Thos Hayton

H.O. 18/353

1. John Dudley (Wesleyan), landlord of the Churchill Arms, afterwards registrar and postmaster.
2. Thomas Cross, landlord of the Rising Sun at Easington.
3. Thomas Tyringham Bernard (1791—1883), fourth son of Sir Scrope Bernard, M.P. for Aylesbury 1857 to 1868; succeeded to the estates at Lower Winchendon in 1876.

[99] From the Bucks Advertiser

12 March 1853

The Rev. T. Hayton appeared before the Bench again respecting the case of George Munday who was convicted of an assault some time back, and was to pay a fine and cost of 12/6 or six months imprisonment. As the Rev. gentlemen did not like the decision of the magistrates, he had to apply to the Secretary of State on the subject, and he has now informed the magistrates he has received a letter from Lord Palmerston that there was nothing to induce him to alter the decision of the Bench at Ashendon. The money was paid.

[100] To the Dean of Windsor [1]

Crendon, 31 October 1853

Dear Sir,

Two or three years ago I addressed you with reference to a day school in this place [2], but as I did not hear from you the matter fell to the ground. The Dissenters here have built a large chapel and make every profitable demonstration to supply the 'screw' mentally and physically. The Church people have been aroused and a desire has been expressed to me that there should be an evening service during the winter, but the great hindrance is the *lighting* of the *Church*. For this I cannot call upon the dissenters and as I casually mentioned this three weeks ago, an occasional worshipper left with the Churchwarden a sovereign for the furtherance of the very desirable object. The congregation being very poor, I am compelled to turn to the *owners* of property in this place, who have responded to my appeal very satisfactorily. Lord Churchill [3] offers £2; All Souls College has also promised me; Messrs Kirby Beard [4], needle factors have given £2 but still we are much under the mark — the estimated cost of lighting a large Church will be nearly £15 — on a modest scale. Therefore you will in your official capacity plead for us before the College Authorities for a donation, let me hear at your *earliest*

75

convenience (for we have Sunday Evening service in the crowded Court Room) you will very much oblige

> yours very respectfully,
>
> Thomas Hayton

Windsor

1. Hon. George Neville (1789–1854), Master of Magdalene College, Cambridge 1813 to 1853; dean of Windsor 1846 to 1854; third son of 2nd Baron Braybrooke; co-discoverer of Pepys' Diary (*D.N.B.*)
2. See No. 77.
3. Francis George Spencer, 2nd Baron Churchill; born 1802 and inherited the estate in 1845.
4. Kirby Beard, needle-manufacturers from Redditch. (Their Crendon needle-mill ran from 1849 to 1862).

[101] To Mr Batcheldor [1]

Crendon, 5 November 1853

Mr Batcheldor,

Mr Hollier of Thame told me the other day that, if I addressed a letter to you, you would no doubt be kind enough to present it to the College.

If you will do so with the enclosed, it will oblige

> yours very truly,
>
> Thos Hayton

Windsor

1. Thomas Batcheldor, conveyancer. 5 Upper Cloisters, The Castle, Windsor.

To the Authorities and Members of Windsor College
[Enclosed with the last letter]

Gentlemen,

I wrote to the Dean of the College who informs me that he has sent my communication to you, nevertheless I think it right to add, that my congregation is very poor, and the rack renting farmers are of the name of *Dodwell* — a perfect clan of bitter dissenters amounting in numbers to upwards of 250 with dependants & to whom the 'screw' is applied morally & physically — in the first by depreciating our sacraments, & the second by taking advantage through dealing or servitude.

They have lately erected an enticing new chapel & are about to light it at an expense of £18—20. This has aroused the Church people to ask me to hold an Evening Service in the winter; & tho' from the smallness of the Living I am compelled to hold an adjoining Incumbency & have already 2 duties in winter & three in summer I am ready to meet their wishes, provided we can light the Church properly, we have estimated the cost & find that we shall be able to do it at about £14—15.

This I cannot raise here, therefore I am compelled to request the owners of property for their assistance.

Lord Churchill subscribes £2
An occasional leaver £1
A friend & myself £2

All Souls College has recommended payment from the Warden, who almost yearly remembers the poor through me, & two or three others have promised small sums: If therefore Gentlemen, you will be kind enough to take this into your consideration & aid as much as you can, I & my congregation will feel deeply obliged to you.

I have never solicited you to assist the poor in winter, tho' I have resided here since 1818; but you have been kind enough to help me repair the Court Room (belonging to the Lords of the Manor) which I have made at upwards of £70 cost a very comfortable place. As early a reply as possible to this as you possibly can give, would much oblige me as we are now on the Sunday Evening meeting in the said Court Room, somewhat inconveniently & uneconomically.

I have the honour to be yours very respectfully,

Thomas Hayton
Incumbent

Windsor

[102] *From Mr Batcheldor to Hayton*
Cloisters, Windsor Castle, 9 November 1853

Rev. Sir,

Your application for a subscription towards lighting the Crendon Church has been laid before the Chapter of the Dean & Canons of Windsor, & I am directed to inform you that the Chapter feel their Lessees and the inhabitants of Crendon should assist you in attaining your object, and they regret that the many calls on them for Aid in Parishes where they have estates, oblige them to decline the application.

I am respectfully your very obedient servant,

Thomas Batcheldor

Windsor

Crendon, 2 December 1853

Gentlemen,

The following letter I was about to transmit you to-day irrespective of your circular of this morning. 'Being a Trustee under a recent document of what is called the Sir John Dormer's Charity of 10/– weekly to be paid to the poor Inhabitants of the parish of Long Crendon in the County of Bucks, & having protested against the management & application of such money conceiving such application of the funds not to be agreeable to the Will of Sir John Dormer both in substance & form, I beg to request your advice on the matter, especially with the present Act, & to the furtherance of this. I will voluntarily bring the Trust Deeds for your inspection, & answer any question you may think fit to put to me. I have the honour to be etc. etc.'

I have for months ceased to act as Trustee because I do not conceive that a Labourer, hale & hearty, receiving 11/– a week is a person contemplated by Sir John Dormer, neither do I think that the Surveyor of the Roads should pay 5/– to 7/– a week for labour & make up fair wages from the charity to the exclusion of the old & infirm whom the late Commissioners in about 1830 especially recommended. Nay, to such an extent has this gone, that one Trustee found fault because *one farm* did not receive *its share*. There are other points of administration which I want to bring to your Notice, as well as the recent Trust deed, the validity of which I have some doubt. Should I be in Town next week, would it be convenient for me to wait upon you & where?

I am, Gentlemen, your obedient servant,

Thomas Hayton

Charity Com.

Crendon, 6 February 1854

Gentlemen,

Herewith I send you answers to the questions sent to me — illness prevented me sending them earlier.

I did not object to my name being put in the Trust Deed of 1848; but I now wish to withdraw from my responsibility in the matter. There are two or three names in the Deed which ought never to have been there, for more reasons than one.

I differ with the Trustees on the construction of the words *'poor Inhabitants'*. I can not think that every *hale farm labourer* was contemplated by the Donor as a fair recipient or to be looked upon as a pauper, otherwise he would not have been required at 3 o'clock each Saturday at the time of Evening prayer to attend Church, or that the Overseers should have anything to do with him. In case of illness I would admit the claim: nor do I think the word 'Inhabitant' is to be narrowed to those only *legally settled* — etc —

settled frequently by *Trick,* when others who lived here 10, 20, 40 years were passed over. There is not much of the Samaritan principle here.

Saturday is the day named in the Deeds when the Trustees are to meet & the persons to receive the benefaction & I am ready to read prayers at 3 o'clock agreeable with the will; or if you take the *spirit* of the thing the money might be given on the Sunday & the Trustees arrange their Meetings as they may; but I think it fair to use Saturdays to carry out a *part* of the will & that for a particular object, without having the Meetings on that day as specified, especially as the words are 'for the uses, intents & purposes' & 'in such manner as is expressed, limited & declared'.

Should you wish to see the Deeds, I will bring them next month to town or send them by some friend, I have no personal feeling or partiality to serve in this matter. I am not connected in any way, by affinity or otherwise, as some parties . . . [torn] . . .

I am, gentlemen . . . [torn] . . .

Charity Com.

To the Charity Commissioners

Crendon, 6 February 1854

Sir John Dormer's Charity; Parish of Long Crendon, County of Bucks.

In the year 1821 when I first became Incumbent of this parish, my attention was drawn to the above Charity by an anonymous letter, enquiring what has become of Sir John Dormer's Charity etc etc. I made enquiries of different farmers about the Deeds etc no one 'knowing anything about it' but they knew very well that certain monies were taken by the overseer & carried to the parish account. For years I tried in vain to get the poor what were known to be their rights; & it was not till the Commissioner of Charities of 1830 came to Aylesbury, that any Deed was forthcoming. The original one was produced, & the one of 1793 came to light & those persons who had been in the habit of taking the Charity money pretended 'there was another deed appointing them as Trustees but that deed could not be found' — nor has it been found till this day. It was admitted before the Commissioners that one individual held upwards of £60, & that another person had never accounted for one year's income. Promises were made that proper accounts should be kept (but this was not done until 1848) & the monies were to be distributed to the widows & worked-out old men at the Church after *divine service* on *Sunday Afternoons* each week, as being most agreeable to the *Spirit* of the Donor's request, the words of the Deed being 'for & towards the relief of *ten poor inhabitants of* Crendon to be paid weekly at the parish Church *there every Saturday* at about the time of Evening prayer, with the advice of the Minister & Churchwardens or the more part of them'. There being no Evening service on Saturday, the payment of the money on *Sundays* was sanctioned by the Commissioners of that day, thinking it preservative of the rights of the Church of England — This custom prevailed for some years; but a leading farmer & dissenter maintained that his *labourers* had an equal right to the Charity. In vain did I oppose, I remonstrated & it was met by noise & bullying; each farmer saw his own interest in it! & it is a well known fact that wages were squared accordingly & those miserably paid by the Surveyor were put forward as the legitimate claimants, & in order to change the day of payment from Sunday to Saturday a regular attack was made upon me. In two years all the *farmers' labourers* of *whatever description* were paid in *rotation,* a monthly charity of four shillings. I could not but denounce such a system as this, & lately I have been so disgusted after the remark of one Trustee that such a farm — naming — had not received a fair share, that I have retired almost altogether from attendance at any Meeting. I now therefore request your interpretation & opinion on this Charity, as such administration of it I conceive to be adverse to the will of Sir John Dormer & disparaging to the rights of the Church of England.

signed Thomas Hayton
Vicar of Long Crendon

Further particulars
The £30 of the charity is thus specified in the deed.
£26 to be paid to *ten poor Inhabitants.*
40/— to be retained for 3 years to defray the cost of a dinner when the Court Leet is held by Sir John Dormer or his heirs [1].
5/— more to be retained for 3 years — as a fee to the Clerk for his services on that day.
15/— per an. to be paid to some one to keep the monument in the Church erected to the memory of Sir John Dormer, & 20/— more every year to be paid & employed towards the repair of the said Tomb and Aisle erected in the Church. Neither the Aisle nor Monument . . . [torn] . . . The aisle became so bad that it was *lately repaired* by money advanced [2], which money is now being repaid by Interest of some parish stone-pits' money [3], the Monument or tomb however, has had nothing done to it, tho' broken in many places & defaced. The cost of repairing it will be about £20, How this is to be done, Gentlemen, you will suggest.

I expect to be in Town next month, & will leave the Deeds with you, if necessary. There are other little Charities, to which no Trustees have ever been appointed; & the documents are in the hands of Mr Henry Reynolds, Notley Abbey Farm, Long Crendon.

Charity Com.

Answers 811/54/3c

1. Trustees: John Stone Esquire of 2, Sussex Gardens, Hyde Park, but resident in Thame, not Long Crendon, when the last deed of 1848 was made. He is a considerable landowner in the parish of Long Crendon. Henry Reynolds [4] of Notley Abbey, farmer; heir apparent to the Estate of Notley — neither of these have lately attended any Meeting of the Trustees.
Joseph Dodwell, farmer & dissenter ⎫
Robert Dodwell, farmer & dissenter ⎬ take an active part
George Gibson, collar-maker & dissenter [5] ⎭
Edward Shrimpton, needlemaker

George Wainwright, Butcher, never attends
John Kirby Shrimpton, seldom attends.
William Hanson, farmer, attends regularly & pays 8/— weekly to such as are chosen.
A Mr Crook & a Mr Brangwin have died since 1848.
Thomas Hayton, Vicar, very seldom attends — not believing that the Charity is distributed according to the mind of the Donor, & knowing it to be done contrary to the advice of the last Commissioners of Charities.

2. The appointment of the above named Trustees was made in 1848 by a Mr William Syms [6], the heir-in-law of a Mr James Syms, the last surviving Trustee of a Deed, bearing date Oct 5th 1793, the Trustees in that Deed, not having appointed Trustees as directed by the indenture of Sir John Dormer. Mr William Syms is a Baker, living at Aston Rowant in the county of Oxford. In fact the Trustees may be said to have appointed themselves.

3. There are three extant Trust Deeds: the original one bearing date May 1st 1619, sworn 2nd May 1620, a second dated Oct 5th 1793 & the last in 1848, all of them in the possession of the Vicar of the parish.

4. On every Saturday about 5 o'clock four appointed Trustees distribute to eight persons, one shilling each or rather to deputies or little children sent by the persons chosen to receive the Charity *monthly* for four sucessive weeks. This is done sometimes at the home of the distributor — generally at the Church Gate. The recipients are selected by three of four of the farmers present.

5. Question see separate paper.

Thomas Hayton, curate
Feb 6th 1854

Charity Com.

1. The three lords of the manor took it in turns to pay for the court dinner, held on the Thursday of Whit week.
2. The aisle was repaired in 1850. £16.10s advanced by the trustees and £19.1s.3d by Mr Stone. See 'Dormer Account Book', p. 10.
3. The stone-pits were run by the parish vestry.
4. Henry Reynolds, son and heir of the late Henry Reynolds of Notley, farmer.
5. George Gibson, collar-maker, had a house and shop in the Square.
6. William Syms, born 1797. His sister married Robert Dodwell and his daughter married Edward Shrimpton.

[105] Charity Commissioners to Hayton
[Abstract]

10 June 1854

We are of the opinion that William Syms as the heir of the then last surviving Trustee, had no legal power to appoint new Trustees of this Charity, that the present Trustees are not entitled to retain the office by virtue of their appointment under the Deed of 29th January 1848.

Charity Com.

Crendon, 18 June 1854

Gentlemen,

If there were any truth in leading articles it would appear you are not invested with sufficient power to carry out the intentions of the Legislature, that the power you have is only 'permissive'.

If therefore I am to go before the Charity Commissioners for the appointment of new Trustees & a new scheme in the matter of Sir John Dormer's Charity on my own responsibility & costs, & probably may have to contend the matter with those who call themselves trustees, I must decidedly decline doing so for obvious reasons: but if the Charity itself must pay the costs & I can be an evidence in your hands for the attainment of a proper administration of the Charity, I am ready to do so — All that I have asserted & much more I depose to than what I have brought forward, I am willing to prove, nay, I can almost prove that Sir John Dormer's Charity has been used for years as a nest egg for needy farmers (as you may see from the printed returns) who without capital, since I can remember, are now in very flourishing circumstances.

The solicitor will *back* his deed of 1848, & two or three of the Trustees will, I know support him.

Under these circumstances, I would not be justified without your express sanction & support in bringing myself into bitter collision with men already sore at the option you have given touching the Deed.

I am Gentlemen, yours very respectfully,

Thomas Hayton

Charity Com.

[107] To the Charity Commissioners

Crendon, 27 June 1854

Gentlemen,

Your letter of the 20th Inst. I duly received touching Sir John Dormer's Charity. I read the letter to different parties, & fixed it on the Church Door on Sunday last. In order to aid the churchwardens & myself in making an application, will you be kind enough to reply to the following queries.

1. May a less *number* than *twelve* be appointed? It is rather difficult in a country village to get 12 independent men who would act without reference to connection & party bias.

2. As we look upon the Charity as one especially belonging to the Church & desire the scheme to deviate as little as possible from the original purposes and intentions of the Founder ought we to appoint as Trustees men who are *not Churchmen*?

This is a point we wish particularly to hear your opinion upon. There is a family here large & influential, all to a man fell & bitter dissenters, who have uniformly grasped at the Charity at every opening. On the last Enquiry, one of them had £68 belonging to it in his possession; & after the express sanction of the Commissioners to distribute it to the poor widows & others infirm from labour & age, the weekly amount, the leading man amongst them introduced the payment of the farm labourers, which has been incorrectly, we conceive, carried on for many years more or less — each farmer of course being anxious to support his wages given by a monthly four shillings from the Charity — it is, therefore, our request on the 46 Clause of the present Act, & urged thereto by past experiences, testifying that dissentient elements have diverted & abused the Charity from its legitimate objects.

3. Will you also define for us the term 'poor inhabitant' & whether a labourer in full health & pay was contemplated by Sir John Dormer.

4. Whether any more money should be paid till the new scheme is sanctioned? I have told the churchwarden that I thought he was not justified in paying any more money, after your decision: & I conceive that the repair of Sir John's Monument in the Church is a just requirement, there being no reserved funds for that object, the money left for that purpose having been otherwise expended in the course of six months, some money would accrue for the repair of the Monument; nothing has been done to it since its erection.

6. Should the Trustees be *inhabitant & householder — resident in the parish*?

7. Might we select one to be a Trustee the heir to a considerable Estate (340 acres) living with an aged Mother whose life interest in the Estate & who is in reality the owner of it (while she lives but cannot *will it*) but the Individual is 40 years of age & manages the farm etc.?

Your earliest reply to this communication will much oblige

yours very respectfully,

Thomas Hayton

N.B. I do not wish any longer to be a Trustee — all I have ever desired is to see fair play for Sir John Dormer which I hope a new scheme will secure.

Charity Com.

[108] To the Charity Commissioners

4 July 1854

Gentlemen,

Immediately after posting my letter of yesterday, the Churchwardens informed me that the solicitor (a Mr Hollier of Thame) who drew up the Deed of 1848 appointing Trustees to the above Charity (& which Deed you have pronounced invalid) had advised the remaining Trustees 'not to be thrown overboard so easily' & he asserts that you, Gentlemen, have no power to set aside that Document. Whether this be so or not, I cannot pretend to say & I therefore under the circumstances have thought it my duty to inform you of this — also to say that the Trustees (so calling themselves) held a *private* meeting on the subject — were very savage & appointed a Mr Joseph

Dodwell the great dessenting leader (who from his bullying propensities no gentlemen can meet) to communicate with you & reason you out of it, & not allow me one single recommendation on the matter.

I know three or four of these persons are very jealous in their business — all I want is fair play for Sir John Dormer & those whom he wanted to remember in his work.

I will send you an honest list of fit persons to be Trustees when you have been kind enough to reply to my queries.

I am, Gentlemen, yours respectfully,

Thos Hayton

Charity Com.

[109] *To the Charity Commissioners*

Crendon, 3 August 1854

Gentlemen,

I am well aware that your hands are full of work, & that we must not be very pressing in matters of inferior moment. I merely write now to say, that I think of being from home for 3 to 4 months in the autumn, & therefore I should like to know whether the matter of Sir John Dormer's Charity would be ready for the Court shortly; & whether it might not stand over till next year; or what might be your advice on the subject.

I have given notice to the acting Trustee Mr William Hanson, my churchwarden, that I shall claim for the charity all money due from Midsummer last to be applied to the repairing of the monument & other purposes as specified by you, the Commissioners, and I have also requested the Agent of the Estate (Mr Meere, solicitor, Bagshot Heath) out of which the rent charges proceed [1] to stay payments till you have decided the matter. I think it's right also to inform you that all communications from this place by Messrs Dodwell* and Reynolds are the efforts of their solicitor who drew up the Deed of 1848, and I am told that the principle of selection was *affinity* to defunct trustees. In 4 instances out of the 12 this was so, but now *two* of these are dead, *one* has left the neighbourhood, and the 4th is not a householder, and three are merely the tools of Messrs Dodwell etc.

I hesitate to say that their anxiety to become Trustees is only, if possible to make it a *labour* question, & take advantage at the Board of Guardians of any supplemental aid to the paupers. I hope, however, the new scheme will defeat their purposes.

I am, Gentlemen, respectfully yours,

Thomas Hayton

*As to their being the *most respectable men* in the village this is perfectly gratuitous; they are *not* so either as to competency or morals.

Charity Com.

1. The original rent charge of £30 yearly was on Chilling Farm, Brill. Owing to Land Tax it had decreased to £23.6s.0d.

[110] To the Charity Commission

Crendon, 10 August 1854

Gentlemen,

From the tenor of your yesterday letter, I think you are labouring under some misconception in reference to the other charities of this parish.

In reality, there are *no Trustees* to any charity in this place, except those which fall under the *specific* direction of the churchwardens, & in one case, viz. Greening Charity for the apprenticing of boys, with the churchwardens & overseers.

Westbrooke Charity [1] — amounting to 10/— yearly — is duly paid to the Churchwardens who distribute the money at the Church on the appointed days of Christmas & *St John the Baptist:* and, as to the rent issuing out of what is called churchland, it is laid out by the churchwardens for the repair of the Church on strictly legitimate principles. Having just seen the Churchwardens, I am requested to say that they object to throw open to *other Trustees* the management of the Westbrooke Charity of 10/— yearly, and as to the *Church land* [2] I myself claim an interest in this, & believe (if it could be discovered) that part of it is for the Minister; I therefore, with the churchwardens protest against the including of that rent with the Sir John Dormer charity, as well as that of the Westbrooke's charity the propriety & the justice of which I trust will be apparent to you.

Your views on these two points at your earliest convenience will oblige.

The Baptist Minister of this place had left him by a Mr Howlett [3] ten pounds yearly, which money has been alienated for some time past: Should not this be an object of Inquiry? Also £200 was left by a Mr John Dodwell towards the building of the Baptist Chapel — Should not the executors give an account of this?

Thanking you for your courtesy in case of absence,

I remain, Gentlemen, yours respectfully,

Thomas Hayton
Vicar

Charity Com.

1. Thomas Westbrooke of Horsepath (by a will dated 1630) left land worth £15 to the poor of Crendon.
2. Churchlands left for the repair of the Church. Source unknown.
3. Thomas Howlett, founder of the Crendon Chapel. In his will he left £10 yearly to the Chapel, but the bequest was declared null and void under the Mortmain Act of Geo II c.36, as he died within a year of making it.

[111] To the Charity Commissioners

Crendon, 2 January 1855

Gentlemen,

The Churchwardens called upon me last night & reported from Mr Dodwell your recommendations as to the small charities of the Parish. At last they seem willing to begin; & as soon as possible. I shall be ready to hear from you.

Every allegation I made in reference to the administration of Sir John Dormer's Charity I am ready to substantiate whatever the smoothing down made by Mr Dodwell may be.

Allow me, however, to remark that the parish Charity of 12 acres was embodied in the Act of Parliament for the Inclosure of our Common Fields in 1827, & the *Award* specifies distinctly the Trustees, viz. Minister, Churchwardens & Overseers: I therefore presume that no new Trustees can be required for that: & the *One* which is peculiarly left for the *Churchwardens* for *the time being.*

Your reply will much oblige, yours respectfully,

Thomas Hayton

Charity Com.

[112] To the Charity Commissioners

Crendon, 20 January 1855

Gentlemen,

In accordance with your wishes of your letter of the 15 Inst I forward you the extracts required from the Parish Award; & the earliest reply to the first — the allotment for the poor — will oblige, as we are very anxious, if justified, to distribute during the cold weather the fuel to the poor.

Placed as I am in the midst of so many dissenters (for the Dodwells are a legion) I am naturally jealous of their interference which has always been of a selfish & exclusive character.

I am Gentlemen, yours very respectfully,

Thos Hayton

Charity Com.

[113] To the Charity Commissioners

Crendon, 5 February 1855

Gentlemen,

I think it right to inform you that the overseers, Churchwardens and myself met and agreed to distribute the proceeds from the 12 acres of land in

86

fuel to the poor, the inclemency of the season and other reasons urging us to do so, to say nothing of our honest conviction that we acted right in doing so — this Charity never having been disbursed.

My Churchwarden, Mr Hanson, informs me that a meeting may be called by the surveyors of the Parish touching the drainage etc, when a petition will be drawn up and then signed praying you to adopt the old *Trustees* under the new arrangements, so eager do they appear to get their hand on the spoil. I do trust you will not be led away by one-sided representations. *Joseph Dodwell* is the great dissenting leader and lords it over the parish, so much so that few of the most respectable will attend any meeting or vestries. As for myself, I have long ceased to do so from the blackguardism of the said Dodwell who was twice found guilty of brawling at the Church and using language unfit for a pot-house, and should he become a Trustee, I never could attend — for other reasons which, if specified would astonish you. Besides he is only a rack-renter of 300 acres and has no property in the parish.

Henry Reynolds is not a *householder*, he only for his Mother manages the farm. *George Gibson* is a collar-maker, owner of 5—6 acres of land, which he lets to the poor at . . . [torn].

Edward Shrimpton, aged 78, rents about 15 acres, and has no property.

George Wainwright rents 15 acres and never acts: these three are completely under the finger of Dodwell & Reynolds, so that with the number of Dodwells as specified, they could appoint every recipient & the Church people would have no chance; 2 overseers and a parish Churchwarden they could return; so if Mr Dodwell should be trustee they would have 4 votes and influence 3 more — Robert Dodwell aged 70, with no property, and a rack renter with his son, of about 200 acres. Indeed the only two creditable and unobjectionable persons are Mr J.K. Shrimpton and Mr Hanson.

Since I wrote to you in August last, a *Mr Jacob Watson* [1] has come to occupy the best house in the village, and the best farm belonging to Mr Stone (who now lives in London) & he is a most fitting and respectable man of long standing in the neighbourhood & a man of property; & as such I recommend him to you.

Mr Richard West rents about 200 acres, is a steady respectable man. Mr William Crook, a proprietor of about 120 acres. His ancestors have been trustees.

If a Dodwell should be among them, decidedly *James Dodwell*, the Deacon of the Chapel, & a renter of about 200 acres with some property of his own, would be the most prudent choice.

There are one or two more quiet unbiased men who should be Trustees provided the number is to be increased. The anxiety displayed by some to become Trustees is of a very suspicious character.

It is reported that Dodwell etc. offered to repair the Monument without touching the funds; this is very specious; but as Minister I could not allow access to the Monument except thro' legitimate channels.

The Scheme as formerly proposed is a little objectionable, as to the annual number of recipients, and the age, viz. 60, should not exclude the bed-ridden and others infirm under that age — I hope every attention will be paid to guard the Charity from abuse, & as I have upwards of 30 years been fighting for this, I hope my suggestions will not be deemed impertinent.

I am Gentlemen, yours very faithfully,

Thos Hayton
Incumbent of Long Crendon

Charity Com.

1. Jacob Watson belonged to a well known Thame family. He rented the Manor Farm as a sub-tenant of the Dean and Canons of Windsor.

[114] To the Charity Commissioners

Crendon, 12 February 1855

Gentlemen,

I hasten to reply to your letter of the 9th last. In consequence of Mr Stone leaving the neighbourhood & a new disposition of property, I would respectfully submit to you the following alteration as to Trustees.

1. Mr Jacob Watson now living in Mr Stone's house with the best farm; a gentleman of property & well known, his family having resided in the neighbourhood for generations.

Mr John Kirby Shrimpton
Mr William Hanson — all respectable men who would act honestly & impartially
Mr Richard West

These I think, with the parish officers & Vicar would have been sufficient; but others wish it otherwise; & therefore instead of Mr James Dodwell I would substitute the name of Mr Joseph Hutt, farmer of upwards of 200 acres. Mr Hutt is a dissenter as well as Mr James Dodwell, but the latter is a tenant of mine, it may be thought he would be under influence, and as in the original application, I named Mr Matthew Shrimpton Junior, I would now substitute Mr *William Crook* as suggested by the Churchwardens.

This being eleven, for all purposes of business uses might be a number quite satisfactory, if not to others, I hope to you.

The Draft of the proposed Scheme may be deposited for inspection at the Register's Office here — Mr John Dudley; & to this effect I have spoken to him.

But allow me, Gentlemen, a remark or two on the Scheme; That a Book for receipts & expenditure & for minutes of each meeting be provided the names of the recipients of the Charities inserted therein; & that the Churchwardens be appointed jointly to receive & jointly to give a receipt for all monies received half yearly from the Estate out of which the rent charges issue to be deposited the same on receipt at the Savings Bank at Thame in their name on behalf of the Charity & that no money be drawn thence except with the sanction of the majority of the Trustees.

Not many years ago the Parish Churchwarden received one whole year's rent & applied it to his own use & never to this day was a shilling recovered. The man is now dead.

I have consulted with Magistrates, Laymen & clergy about this Charity, whether they thought it exclusively a Church one or not; uniformly have they been of opinion that it was; & inferred this from the *Spirit* of the original Document; that Sir John himself was a Churchman; had identified himself with the Church here by a *Monument*, by a *Sepulchre*, by a *Benefaction* — to be *given away at the Church* at the *Evening prayer*, to worshippers there. If you, Gentlemen, think this inference a fair one, by the construction of Law, legitimate & borne out by the 46 Clause of your Act, I would deferentially suggest also, that after the words 'five poor men & five poor women' be added 'members of the Established Church'. This would have a very pacifying effect on the many ultra dissenters amongst us who are as anxious to get hold of the spoil as vultures are of their prey & who themselves, after long experience, I find to be most exclusive in all their dealings & doings.

I have the honour to be, Gentlemen, your obedient servant,

Thomas Hayton
Vicar of Long Crendon

Charity Com.

[115] *To the Charity Commissioners*

Crendon, 12 March 1855

Gentlemen,

I am requested by the Churchwardens to ask you whether we are acting entirely under your opinion & advice in applying for new Trustees & a Scheme; & if consequently so acting, we shall be indemnified in accordance with the 16th Clause of the Charitable Trusts Act.

I am, Gentlemen, yours respectfully,

Thos Hayton

Charity Com.

[116] *To the Charity Commissioners*

Crendon, 27 March 1855

Gentlemen,

I forward to you as requested, the Scheme for Sir John Dormer's Charity, together with a Notice for an application to the County Court [1] signed by myself & the two Churchwardens.

I believe the Scheme is satisfactory. Two of the old Trustees in the document of 1848 drawn up by Mr Hollier of Thame still persist that they are Trustees; & very likely will urge Mr Hollier to [put] this before Mr Wing at the County Court [2].

Can Mr Wing, — the Judge of the Court , — entertain such a proposition, & has he the powers over you to settle it; but Country law is very perverse.

In a month from this date Mr Wing will be at Thame again, & any directions from you will be attended to by us.

I am, Gentlemen, yours very respectfully,

Thos Hayton
Vicar of Long Crendon

Charity Com.

1. County Courts were reconstituted in 1847. The Thame Courts were held in the Market Hall.
2. John William Wing (1813–1855); barrister Lincolns Inn; Judge of County Court Circuit 1847. (*M.E.B.*)

[117] Hayton to the Charity Commissioners
To Mr Vane [1]

Crendon, 3 May 1855

Dear Sir,

I hear that our 'great man' has been with you again. He is a man of suppressed manner & of glazing speech & I know him capable of any misrepresentation; if therefore you will have the kindness to inform me of his communications, if they *bear on the charities*, I should be obliged to you. He & two of them call themselves 'the parish' much on the same principle as the 'Three Tailors of Tooley Street'. When the Commissioners wrote to him & Reynolds, I was refused all access to the Communication, tho' I made public every letter I received. They, in fact, do not like that I should expose to the public doings and abstractions in their charities.

The result of his calling upon you last week was duly made known to the Solicitor of Thame, Mr Hollier, who says he will prove the document of 1848 to be good . . . [torn] . . . I do not wish to teaze the Charity Commissioners as I conceive they are . . . [torn] . . . to the decision & I doubt whether Mr Wing will entertain the question. If however you would offer me any suggestion or put me in possession of the Tactics of the enemy I should be extremely obliged.

Yours very faithfully,

Thos Hayton

P.S. The said Dodwell lived at Chilton once, but for his 'bullying' was noted to quit & Mr Chetwode does not regret it.

Charity Com.

1. Henry Morgan Vane (1808–1886); barrister-at-law, Inner Temple; Secretary to the Charity Commission 1853 to 1886 (*D.N.B.*)

10 March 1855

LONG CRENDON

The 'tender mercies' of a parish union are cruel. The miserable pittance assigned to men in their sickness, as noted down in the weekly list of that misnamed official, called relieving, which practically means 'starving', is made very apparent by numerous instances. Here is one! Not that we mean to say that the relieving-officer is answerable altogether for it, for he is merely a piece of mechanism in the hands of grinding guardians who check him at every point:— a kind of seal, the 'imprimatur' of which is given in a secret conclave of inquisitors. William Swain, aged 45, of the parish of Crendon, was the son of a soldier of the 56th Foot. At the age of 20 he enlisted into the 14th Light Dragoons — a fine upright young fellow, nearly six feet high. He served eleven years; and, from his activity and strength, was made what is called 'rough rider' — that is, had the care and the breaking of unruly horses. At a field-day, in Glasgow, he had one leg broken from the kick of his right-hand man's horse. At Longford, in Ireland, he had an arm broken, crushed by a horse; jaw-bones broken in three places by a kick, and the bridge of his nose broken; three ribs also broken by a crush, and head cut open by another kick; and in later years had his other leg broken by a large stone falling on him. From these varied wounds and bruises he was invalided on a pension of 6d a day for two years, which pension ceased about 12 years ago. Since that time he has lived in this village, married here, and now the father of five children, the eldest just ten years old. He has been working for the surveyor, in the stone-pit, at an average of 9s. per week; and from sheer exhaustion and cold, and a miserable diet, has been on the sick-list for these last five weeks; and the allowance granted him, as copied from the weekly return, is 'Swain and family, 8s.7½d!!' Let us now see how much per day his family have for their support, premising that two loaves — No. 1 of 'tender mercies' — are allowed for poultices for the poor fellow's neck. No. 2 of 'tender mercies' 1s.6d. for his boy, employed by the surveyor upon the road; — in other words, 2½d. a day weekly. Now for the family of six. Out of the 8s.7½d. deduct —

	s.	d.
Coals — 1½ cwt, during the cold weather — at		
1s.½d. per cwt....................	2	0
Candles, 3d., soap and soda, 2½d.		5½
Rent of cottage	1	0
	3	5½

Deduct from this 8s.7½d. and we have 5s.2d. left for existence (we cannot say subsistence), which, divided by his family of six, makes 10d. and a fraction, or little more than one penny and a farthing each daily. So much for 'tender mercies', relieving officers, and guardians of the poor! What a mockery! In the name of sacred justice, what a blasphemy! the poor fellow for four years has not been able to purchase one article of clothing for himself; and as he himself expressed it, 'the only clothes he had were those he stood in', and these only a parcel of rags. His case, last Sunday, was brought to the vicar of his parish before his congregation (for every source seemed closed up against him), and sufficient was collected for this 'wraith' of a soldier (who, a few years ago, gloried in his military uprightness and bearing) to buy him a smockfrock — this was his modest request — and his children a few articles. Still, his family and household are in the most wretched plight.

This mode of sympathising with the needy has given offence to certain officials, as being out of the usual routine! Surely the Balaklava system [1] must have had its origin in some Poor-law Union! Should any one, who may read this unvarnished statement of truth, be inclined to give the most trifling assistance, no doubt the minister and churchwardens would apply it to the poor soldier's needs and necessities. As for any application to a Board of Guardians, it would be perfectly useless — that board would be as 'deaf as Ailsa Crag'.

1. Hayton is referring to the lack of help for the sick and wounded after the Battle of Balaklava in October 1854.

[119] To the Charity Commissioners

Crendon, 5 June 1855

Gentlemen,

Mr Wing, the Judge of the County Court, is so unwell that he is about to go into Germany for 2 or 3 months, so that the case in reference to this matter is postponed till August or September.

Our dissenting village aghast. Hollier, a Solicitor of Thame (who has communicated with you), has so worked on the feelings of the Church-wardens, that they are sure, they say, that the matter must go into Chancery & involve them in a law suit. I have expended my eloquence almost in vain in endeavouring to show them that the County Court is the substitute for Chancery & that such a thing can not be; but you would gratify both myself & them & further the ends in view if you would be kind enough to *state explicitly* whether any other Court, *under any pretext* can have *cognizance of the Case*, because if this prejudice is not removed, I may be thrown to stand alone, as I did not secure other signatories to the Notice, which I easily could have done & would have done if it had not been suggested by the Church-wardens themselves that they did not think it necessary.

You must remember that in a country village, the minds of farmers are curious things to work upon or reason with.

I am, Gentlemen, yours respectfully,

Thos Hayton

Charity Com.

[120] 'Maria James' to the Poor Law Board

[undated]

Gentlemen,

I send you the enclosed admittance of fact, which if you have any regard for the poor, ought to be dealt with as they deserve. The child of James Cherry of Long Crendon is alluded to, the first coffin sent was returned, and the second coffin in which the child was put, was in the opinion of the carpenter who screwed it down, in the same condition as the one returned. His name is William Lovell, carpenter of Long Crendon. He says it was quite shameful, the forehead and the nose regularly bruised flat, & the Clerk of the parish says the dress of the dead was visible at the grave. It is a great scandal and an insult to the poor. The case was mentioned to the relieving officer, but no notice was taken of it, but only last week the child of James Turner of Long Crendon, was put in a coffin so shallow that the women were compelled to put pieces of lath to keep the wood from bruising the face, and when done the coffin would scarcely keep together. These are matters well known, and the Guardians take no notice of them. They treat the poor like a set of clogs. They hunger them living and insult the dead, and therefore I hope you will interfere and stop such things. The man who contracts for such coffins at 1/9 each when spoken to, says he would not do it except he used up some old slats and boards, useless for other purposes.

I am yours respectfully,

Maria James

[Minute by Grenville Piggott [1]]
Received June 16th 1855
As the writer of this letter has given no address, the Communication might be deemed anonymous. Indeed I have no doubt that the letter and the newspaper article proceed from the same pen; the Rev Thomas Hayton, brother to the Chaplain of the Union, spoke to me in the same sense as the writer of the letter a few days since having met me accidently — I told him that if such practices existed it was the duty of those who were cognizant of them to bring them to the notice of the Poor Law Board & that he might be certain that any facts addressed would be promptly dealt with. G.P.

M.H. 12/9738

1. George Grenville Pigott 1797—1865; eldest son of William Pigott of Doddershall; M.P. for St Mawes 1830; Assistant Poor Law Commissioner. (Robers Gibbs, *Worthies of Buckinghamshire*, p. 325).

[121] From the Bucks Chronicle

7 July 1855

THE DEAD TELL NO TALES

In the wilds of Brittany, the spirits of those unfortunates who fell on the plains of Pluvigner are doomed there to remain, restless and weary, until the judgement-day shall award to each his final destiny; and, it is said that, at the witching hour of night, at the time when the graves give up their dead, each hapless ghost is waked from his unblessed repose, and condemned to wander over the melancholy plain which was once his death-bed and his grave.

In the midst of much ignorance and superstition, there are classical breathings and poetical fancies, which attach to unhallowed soil, where neither heaven will receive nor earth retain the troubled spirit of those who die unshriven; but the simple epic of village life in Bucks is one dull, solemn round of birth, existence, and death with no ghosts either to affright the living or tell tales of harsh or evil treatment while in the flesh — whether their bodies fell from disease or starvation, or were deposited in unblessed mould, in coffin-planks so thin that human flesh and ligaments, and ligneous fibre, run a parallel race of decay and decomposition. Hence, we suspect that the Poor-Law Commissioner, Mr Baines [1], has given notice in parliament for a bill to provide more decent burial for the bodies of the poor than has hitherto been accorded them; and we trust that its provisions will be so stringent as not to allow the niggardly spirit of a squeezing guardian to mar and to blotch it — that a compulsory provision for coffins of appropriate size will be there found; and that the feelings of parents and relatives will be no longer slighted or insulted.

The Board of Guardians, at Thame, last week, was called upon to consider a communication made to the poor-law commissioners touching two instances where the coffins were such as to create disgust and a cry of shame in the minds and on the tongues of those who witnessed them.

In the village of Crendon, a few months ago, a child died belonging to a labouring man of the name of Cherry. The contractor for coffins at Thame on the solemn testimony of Esther Cherry, the wife, sent up a coffin for her babe, so shallow that the knees of the child were forced up an inch or two above the level of the coffin. And the lid of the coffin could not be applied without a most cruel pressure on the head and face of the dead. This information was sent to the contractor, who came up to the parents on the following morning, and took back the coffin with him, saying it was large enough, and using very rough language to Abraham Gold the messenger to him. He promised, however, to send up another on the following day, which was intended for the funeral; but, none coming, another messenger was sent, to whom was given the same identical coffin (as can be deposed to by three independent witnesses), and into this the body was squeezed. The os frontis and the nose were flattened to the level of the chin! and, when no screws could be found, long nails were driven in, in order, if possible, to keep the lid and the body of the coffin together; but, after all, the child could be seen in its coffin by the minister and those who attended the funeral. The case was mentioned by the minister to the relieving-officer, who promised that he would bring it before the Board of Guardians; but, from that day till lately, not a word about the matter had transpired, when another case occurred, certainly not quite so flagrant, but equally distressing and disgusting.

A letter, embodying these facts, it appears, was sent to the Poor-law Commissioners, who requested the cases to be investigated. Now, what was the process adopted by the Board? Did they send for any of the parents? Did they send for the carpenter (who was well known) who nailed down the coffin? Did they call for any witnesses to substantiate the facts? Nothing of the sort. They call the two delinquents — the contractor and the relieving-officer — before them; and the former asserts that the coffins were good and capacious, and the latter that he had never heard of any complaints!! and so, by the pleading of 'not guilty', the statements are said to be disproved. The testimony of six independent, disinterested witnesses is rejected. The Board seems satisfied that it has done its duty, that the insult to the dead has been amply avenged by a mock investigation, and that by their return the Poor-law

Commissioners will be satisfied, and that the Public shall hear no more of the matter.

But they may deceive themselves. Oppression may triumph for a time. But wrong and injustice done to the weak will call forth a retributive power, and some day or other it will mightily avenge itself; and such one-sided investigations — such sham pomposities, flanked with lies, and buttressed up with selfish sycophants — keeping down honesty and trust and fair-play — redound little indeed to the credit of men who have taken credit to themselves for justice and impartiality.

They may 'burke', if they like, by their closed doors and privacy, such funereal questions as these, but a question touching the living is before them, which they shall not burke — whether a poor starving applicant is, through a merciless order to the relieving-officer, on no occasion to be relieved, or whether the county and the parish of Thame are to be put to an expense of £40, when a simple fourpence might have prevented it.

We allude to the poor wretched female tramp, who after travelling for many miles, destitute for food for nineteen hours, weary and exhausted, was driven from the door of the relieving-office, and, in sheer despair and recklessness, thrust her hand through a watch-maker's window for the very purpose of procuring that substance which had been so cruelly denied her, thereby incurring an offence in law which has sent her to be tried for felony. The committing magistrate, feeling all the responsibility of his position, and touched with sympathy at the woman's tale, and hating an order which, on the face of it, the Poor-law Amendment Act never contemplated, has communicated (to his great credit) with the authorities at Somerset House, who have promised an investigation of the matter, which we trust will be thoroughly canvassed; and then will be solved the question which of late has been frequently canvassed — whether a RELIEVING-Officer be a reality or a nickname: it may bring the landowners also to ask themselves, whether this penny-wise and pound-foolish system is to be persevered in, their peasantry debased, and their lands mulct for their oppression.

M.H. 12/9738

1. Matthew Talbot Baines, 1799–1860; President of the Poor Law Board 1849 to 1852; barrister-at-law, Inner Temple (*M.E.B.*).

---

[122] To the Poor Law Board [1]

Crendon, 7 July 1855

Gentlemen,

As I am the clergyman alluded to in the article of the *Bucks Chronicle* of to-day, I beg to inform you that the carpenter alluded to has been summoned to appear before the Board next week; but the best proof is the Mother, *Esther* Cherry, & a Nancy Hicks of Burts Lane in this village. There are many other witnesses, & the thing created a great sensation. My attention was called to it at the grave, which made me complain to the Relieving Officer who promised to lay the matter before the Guardians. The carpenter, Wm Lovell, told me that the pressure was very great indeed, but he did not

95

examine closely after he had nailed it down & he hurried out of the room, the women complaining very much about it. I would not have troubled you with this communication, but the Board of Guardians has not treated other complaints with common respect.

I am, Gentlemen, your obedient servant,

Thos Hayton
Incumbent of Long Crendon

M.H. 12/9738

1. The Poor Law Board Act, 10–11 Victoria, c.109, received the Royal Assent on 27 July 1847. It established a Ministry for poor relief with a responsible minister in the House of Commons.

[123] To the Charity Commissioners

Crendon, 27 July 1855

Gentlemen,

In accordance with your intentions I saw Mr Hollier, the Solicitor for the objectors, Messrs Reynolds & Gibson, who said that nothing would satisfy him, except the continuance of the Trustees appointed solely by himself & Mr Reynolds in 1848, & they, the Trustees, choosing others as deaths might occur; this I replied, was, I conceive an insult to your decision & as such could not therefore listen to it. Since then I offered to recommend to you two or three others of their appointing. This appears to have been satisfactory, & I think will work its way (for all the nominated Trustees & others think it very liberal) unless the Solicitor persists.

My object, however, at present is, to request your opinion in reference to the persons who ought to be summoned to the Court, or, to whom notice should be given.

I have had two interviews with the Clerk of the Court & the local Solicitor, to both of whom these matters are quite novel. I was first told that all the living Trustees of 1848 would require to be summoned, viz. Mr Stone, living now in London & not living in the parish even when appointed by Mr Hollier.
Mr Robert Dodwell, who ceases in September to hold any farm here.
Mr Edward Shrimpton, aged 76 an occupier of only 18 acres.
George Gibson, collar maker.
Mr Joseph Dodwell, farmer.
Mr Henry Reynolds, farmer.
Mr J.K. Shrimpton, nominated under the new Scheme & assents fully.
Mr George Wainwright — occupying 15 acres but assents to the *new* Scheme & has no wish to be a Trustee.
To summon these 8 would cost it appears nearly £12 — half a charity.

At another interview yesterday, I read over the 'orders of regulating proceedings' & find that the plaintiff may summon whom he pleases; & as the objectors are only Messrs Reynolds & Gibson (for John Cozins Crook never was a Trustee & is a co-petitioner with Churchwarden Hanson, & a summons for him surely need not be required), I have thought it right, at a suggestion made at the office, to ask you whether you thought that two summons for the objecting parties Reynolds & Gibson would suffice, as in such case, in all probability the Judge, Mr Temple, would be satisfied.

Do you think *any notices* will be required to be sent to the persons to be appointed Trustees? They are all willing to become so. Then, as to the poor fellow William Syms whom Hollier & Reynolds made a Tool of to sign the Deed of 1848, would it, think you, be at all requisite to summons him, or leave the objectors to produce him.

I trust you will pardon me for teasing you so much, but we are anxious to do what is right at as little cost as possible; & as the legal gentlemen are quite raw upon the subject I have been compelled to apply to you, so that at the next sitting of the Court I may be able to reply to any preliminary questions which the Judge may think fit to ask me.

I am, Gentlemen, yours very respectfully,

Thos Hayton

[*Draft for reply* 31 July]
'it is for the consideration & decision of the Judge rather than the Board'.

Charity Com.

[124] *To the Charity Commissioners*

Crendon, 17 August 1855

Gentlemen,

Yesterday I attended at the County Court, had an interview with the Judge (Mr Temple [1]) who probably imagined that the power of adjudication was taken out of his hands by the recent Act of last week — This Act he has never seen; but promised against the next Court day to give an answer to my enquiries.

As doubtless its provisions are known to you, will you be so kind enough to inform me whether in the Charities alluded to you have judicial powers? Both the Churchwardens and myself will be glad to hear that it is so, as well as great numbers in the parish.

I beg to add that Mr Hollier, the Solicitor, who drew up the Deed of 1848 is now dead & I can hear nothing of any opposition — at least at present. The objector, Mr Reynolds, has said he wished he had nothing to do with it.

I am, Gentlemen, respectfully yours,

Thos Hayton

Charity Com.

1. Christopher Temple (1784–1871), barrister-at-law Lincolns Inn; County Court Judge (*M.E.B.*).

Crendon, 14 September 1855

Gentlemen,

I yesterday attended at the County Court to ascertain the preliminary proceedings. The Judge said he would require a notice to be affixed to the Church Door stating the day of hearing & the objects in view, & an assurance that the Trustees to be named should be willing to act.

It appears that two or three of the persons named in the Certificate & who formerly consented, are now disclined to act for reasons I am unable to give. I must therefore, be under the necessity of applying to others to affix their names to the Church door, unless the Scheme be altered to *three* instead of six; will this at all affect the 'Certificate of sessions'? After all my Endeavours & offers of the utmost liberality, I find an undercurrent of factious opposition existing — kept up by a leading dissenter & threats & intimidations given which shake the nerves of my Churchwardens & others who are perfectly satisfied with the proceedings.

Will you therefore, as an encouragement to cheer us, give me an Indemnity, under the 16th Clause of the Act of 1853? Should the Churchwardens demur to sign the required Notices, will you permit or authorize me to do it alone?

The shuffering conduct of certain individuals is truly contemptible.

I am, Gentlemen, respectfully yours,

Thos Hayton

P.S. Will you be kind enough to tell me whether you entertain any *doubts* about the validity of the Deed of 1848, made by the Heir at Law? I should not like to be 'floored' & give the Enemy an occasion to rejoice.

If you have, shall *we wait* till *judicial powers* be conferred as I am sure they will be & as the Judge . . . [torn] . . .

P.S. There is another contingency: there are no objections to the smaller charities; would it be proper, in case of the Deed being pronounced valid, that these Charities should have their Trustees *separate* from Sir John Dormer's?

I really would not so trouble you, but you can scarcely imagine how teazing this matter is. I, who am called upon to comfort require consolation myself the more. T.H.

Could you send any one down to assist.

Charity Com.

Crendon, 19 September 1855

Gentlemen,

I find that the Churchwardens *now* refuse their signatures to the necessary papers & notices in order to bring the case of the Charity before the

Court: so that under the present Certificate I can not do so myself; either I must have authority to do so myself, or you must give the business to the attorney-general, or advise, as in given judgement you may think best.

The Trustees appointed in 1848 by the heir-at-law which you pronounced to be an invalid appointment are still & will be unconvinced till they find a power over them. There are Trustees ready & willing to serve & would have readily signed the papers, but the Churchwardens told me that they thought their names sufficient. Do you see what a shiftless set I have to deal with.

I wrote to you on Friday last (the 15th) but, as I have not received the usual acknowledgement, perhaps my letter has not come to hand.

If you would wish to see me I will next week or the week following come up to London.

If I can be of any service in this matter & can be an instrument for the furthering of the objects in view, I will be happy to do so.

> Yours very respectfully,
>
> Thos Hayton

Charity Com.

[127] To the Charity Commissioners
Crendon, 21 September 1855

Gentlemen,

I duly received yours of yesterday; & whilst I thank you very sincerely for it, I cannot but regret the trouble to which I have put you, to say nothing of my own disappointment in having trusted to such unstable Churchwardens who, having lately each taken a farm of Mr Stone, one of the Trustees of 1848, are afraid I believe to sign either notice, or timorous for his attendance. I must therefore fall back upon myself; & I am really alone, tho' I can get others to join me if *absolutely* necessary to bring this matter before the County Court & do the best I can to effect its object.

Some begin to carp at the Scheme & say that the *shilling each week* ought to be continued; this is simply an attempt at the odd jobbing & to make the Church subservient to the pinching economy of the Board of Guardians to bring in their farm labourers to partake of it. I hope therefore any suggestion to that effect will not be sanctioned.

I am ready to sign any fresh notices, & will send you in a few days the names of the Trustees who will *promise* to act as you originally suggested, that two or three respectable persons besides the annual public officers would be deemed a competent number I really think it would be better than having a greater number — for very obvious reasons.

As I shall require the Deeds in reference to the smaller charities as well as the Minute Book since 1848 — all of which are in the possession of Mr Henry Reynolds of this parish & which he would not produce at my request, would you assist me in this matter & will you enable me to make out a requisition to the Clerk of the County Court agreeable with the objects contemplated by this Certificate, of course including subpoena to Reynolds to produce them.

> I am, Gentlemen, respectfully yours,
>
> Thos Hayton

Charity Com.

[128] To the Charity Commissioners

24 September 1855

Gentlemen,

As I feel very anxious that the poor should, if possible be partakers of the Charity at Christmas, I have lost no time in ascertaining the minds of the following persons, who pledge themselves to perform the duties of their Trust if nominated thereto, viz.
William Crook [1] landowner & farmer
Richard West [2] farmer
Joseph Hutt [3] farmer
Matthew Henry Shrimpton [4] house proprietor & needlemaker
Mr Watson (formerly specified) tells me that he thinks some are jealous of his having been nominated, as he is only a newcomer into the village, & that, as he is overseer, he would rather at present not be named.

Mr Reynolds, with some others of the Trust Deed of 1848, have become very sulky, intend to oppose the Scheme as entirely upsetting the Donor's will etc. I wish to stand alone as Petitioner, sink or swim with it.

There appears in the present scheme, in a reference to Hart's Charity [5], some little obscurity as to the application of the money in hand after a boy is apprenticed, as if some part of it was to be applied to other charitable purposes; at least I think it may be more clearly specified.

If Trott's Charity [6] is vested in the Churchwardens (as the Parliamentary returns of 1786 say) perhaps it might be as well to exclude it.

In this Scheme also there is a clause in Sir John Dormer's matter *where* the Trustees are to appoint a *person* 'to keep the monument'. This might clash with the power of the Minister & Churchwardens, as a person might be appointed whom they would exclude from the Vestry — 'the place where the Monument is' & therefore I respectfully suggest that the Minister & Churchwardens appoint the person (hitherto it has been the Clerk) & that the Trustees order payment of 12/— yearly as usual [7]?

I have thought it proper to make these remarks, as they might accelerate the business in hand.

> I am, Gentlemen, very respectfully yours,
>
> Thomas Hayton

Charity Com.

1. William Crook, farmer of Lower End.
2. Richard West, farmer, sub-tenant of the Dean and Canons.
3. Joseph Hutt, farmer and baker.
4. Matthew Henry Shrimpton, needlemaker of 76, High Street.
5. John Hart's Charity of 1665, consisting of a rent charge of £5, to be used for the apprenticing of boys.
6. Trott's Charity of 10s yearly from a rent charge on North Down Field.
7. 15s yearly was to be paid to the Clerk for the upkeep of the Monument and Aisle.

[129] Secretary of the Charity Commissioners to Hayton

12 October 1855

[Draft]
'I am directed to inform you in the first place, that the provisions of the Act of Parliament, require that two inhabitants of the parish should join in making any application to the Charity Commissioners — you are precluded from proceeding alone with any fresh application'.

Charity Com.

[130] To the Charity Commissioners

Crendon, 15 October 1855

Gentlemen,

        Your letter of yesterday I have duly received. Had not the Church-wardens prevented six others from signing, & then sacrificed their honest convictions to party spirit & unworthy fears, there would have been no stoppage in line to that proceeding; & now I could get twenty signatures to the application: However, as I have no object in view but a just administration of its Charity, & am as anxious as any person can be to allay any bitter feeling engendered, I have addressed to the Churchwardens & overseers, requesting them to call a public meeting & to discuss your communication & that I should be happy if all differences could be composed etc.

        I have ever conceived that the last administration of the Charity is at variance with the Founder's direction, inasmuch as he never could contemplate a *labourer's wages* being helped out of that charity or that it should be a premium for child-getting & that it was exclusively for farm labourers & such only that may have gained a legal settlement. — If you will define what a 'poor inhabitant' meant in 1620 & whether you conceive that a labourer at full weekly pay, whether he has a large family or a small one, is a fit recipient, you would much facilitate the matter: on this we are all at issue, & the commissions of 1830 fix it to the old, but such recommendation was soon broken through.

        Do you mean that at a public meeting of the Parish the recipients should be chosen, say in number 60 leaving the detail of the weekly number 8 to the approbation or selection of the Minister, Churchwardens & overseers, or that 8 are to receive the shilling *continuously or changeably* as circumstances may arise. If continuously for either a fortnight or a month, advantage will be taken of it at the Board of Guardians or in the pay of the surveyor.

It is this mean jobbery, & selfish principle which has brought the Charity into such disgrace.

*Then what is to be done about Hart's Charity? It has no Trustees whatever; & Canon's also with Westbrooke's: & that we are still in an anomalous position.

I propose to attend any meeting, & will be happy to be the means of communicating your wishes & report to you.

I am, Gentlemen, yours faithfully,

Thos Hayton

*These questions will all be mooted.

P.S. Since writing the above I have been consulting three or four of the most respectable of my parishioners as to your 'recommendation'. They think that as the present Trustees are not legally appointed & that there are no Trustees to the other Charities, we are virtually doing nothing; & such certainly is the case. They suggest that if a public Meeting of the whole parish was called & that twelve Trustees were chosen at that Meeting to be sanctioned by the Judge, & that the original Scheme was proposed with slight alterations, — every object would be obtained & that no opposition would be offered, — I myself accede to this. I think it right to inform you that for the last 9 months nothing but *private* Meetings have been held consisting of 5 or 6 Trustees — calling themselves 'the parish'; & that when last year I wished to submit every communication to them that I had from you, they refused to proceed in their business in my presence; & the Churchwardens requested me to withdraw, fearing a bodily & personal attack on me; so much for their liberal, enlightened men. T.H.

Will you recommend a public meeting to the effect recited? For these purposes it has been done at Oxford & elsewhere.

Charity Com.

[131] *To the Charity Commissioners*

Crendon, 3 November 1855

Gentlemen,

Mr Joseph Dodwell did at a public meeting of the inhabitants of this parish openly assert, in his usual blustering way that I had transmitted to you statements, not founded on facts — false & wilful misrepresentations — & that you now were fully convinced that I had done so; & as a consequence that you would not listen to any petition from me.

I beg you to allow me most solemnly to aver, that I have never made a statement to you which I am not ready to prove upon oath — I have never made a statement which did not come under my own intimate knowledge, I have never written anything but what was patent & notorious to all the village;

I publicly count on investigation into every part of my communications; & I have hardly conceived that you have ever uttered or expressed anything substantially the same as publicly proclaimed by Mr Joseph Dodwell. I have no object or view but trust-telling & justice to the dead & to the living (both of whom have been robbed for this last century by the foul . . . of authorities); & I have hitherto stood in estimation with my parish; but such a stalemate, I conceive, if made to you, is damaging to my character, & therefore I hope & conceive that you either give me an opportunity of publicly rebutting what I conceive to be a calumny in an open Court, or by a letter negating the statement.

I say again, what I have said before, that Sir John Dormer's Charity was not fairly administered — it was *exclusive* — it was never meant for day labourers at usual wages; & the reason why I would not act any longer was, because the monument to Sir John Dormer was virtually refused repair & because the farmers were ever foisting their labourers on the list; & this still is their wish — their open expression.

We held a meeting of the Inhabitants at large on the 1st Inst. when upwards of 300 persons were present; & the first proposition was Mr Dodwell's to make the meeting exclusive & was negated by 10 to one. Such a proposal was so exciting that I felt it my duty to dissolve the meeting & to arrange preliminaries for another to be held on Monday. The feeling of that meeting decidedly was to reject every Trustee of 1848; this does not accord much with Mr Dodwell's laudation of himself & his supporters — However as far as I am concerned I am ready to join with the Trustees of 1848, subject to their being approved of at a public meeting of Inhabitants or Householders, & a very fair way of getting at the public feeling, but I cannot identify myself with petitions, the County Court to confirm that which you yourselves have pronounced to be illegal — which in secrecy has been concocted & in secrecy confirmed, & which never has been approved of by the parishioners at large.

I am, Gentlemen, yours respectfully,

Thos Hayton

Charity Com.

[132] To the Poor Law Board

15 November 1855

Gentlemen,

The persons were were summoned to give evidence at the Thame Board of Guardians touching the narrow coffins, have requested me to write to you in order that their expenses may be paid, as they have been refused payment by the Guardians, laughed at and referred to Mr Pigott for payment. Their charges are as follows:

Solomon Shrimpton,	carpenter	3s.6d.
William Lovell,	carpenter	3s.0d.
James Cherry,	labourer	2s.0d.
His wife,		1s.0d.
Abraham Gold		1s.0d.

The reasonableness of the charge is obvious enough, especially as they had 2 or 3 journeys in vain for it.

I hope, therefore, Gentlemen, you will order the settlement of this claim as soon as it may be convenient.

Yours respectfully,

Thomas Hayton

M.H. 12/9738

[133] To the Charity Commissioners

Crendon, [received 16 November 1855]

Gentlemen,

Had Mr Joseph Dodwell showed me the letter addressed by you to him, I should have rested my vindication upon that letter & not have troubled you on the subject. I have to thank you for a copy which I read at a large meeting last night.

On the 5th of November by agreement a meeting was held composed of the Minister, Churchwardens, Overseers of the Poor & the Trustees appointed in 1848; the storm faded away, & we came to the following agreement.

That as Mr Stone & myself withdrew from being Trustees, there were four vacancies to make up the Twelve & we therefore added Mr James Dodwell; Mr William Crook & Mr Michael Rose [1] to the list subject of course to challenge; & as we had some doubt about what 'the approbation of the Vicar, Churchwardens & overseers' should mean, we agreed that the three officers should be ex-officio Trustees & be Entitled to be present at any Meetings whatever in reference to this Charity of Sir John Dormer & others Embodied in the Scheme, should such be the order of the Judge of the County Court. It was the opinion of the Meeting that both the *Aisle* & *Monument,* as expressed in the Deed of Sir John should be first thoroughly repaired from the funds now in hand [2]; & that the Trustees when appointed should hold a meeting, after further Notice given quarterly or oftener if found necessary, to select fitting recipients for the Charity, & that the Charity should be distributed at the Parish Church for 8 persons — one shilling each.

On Monday last these opinions were affixed to the Church door with a Notice for a further meeting of the Inhabitant householders [3] to consider whether the persons to be proposed as Trustees of Sir John Dormer's & others 'be generally acceptable to the parishioners' as required by you. The following are the Minutes of the Meeting — myself in the chair supported by the Churchwardens & overseers with upwards of 200 inhabitants.

As to Trott's Charity, it was the opinion & the wish of the Meeting that as the donor vested the Charity in the hands of the Churchwardens, the same

104

officers should continue to receive and distribute the Charity as they thought fit.

Then as to Hart's Charity about the apprenticing of Boys, the Church-wardens & overseers being considered legitimate Trustees, that they continue to apply that Charity as demised by the Donor.

N.B. Of course you will use your own discretions as to this.

Then as to Westbrooke's & Canon's Charities — they are at present without Trustees, the following persons were respectingly selected & recommended to the Charity Commission to be Trustees for those Charities, viz. Mr Jacob Watson, Mr Joseph Hutt, Mr Richard West, Mr Thomas Crook, Mr David Dodwell, & Mr Matthew Henry Shrimpton; &, should it be desirable that those Charities be Embodied with Sir John Dormer's that these six persons become ipso facto Trustees equally & in every respect with those who may be appointed for Sir John Dormer's Charity, & that they now form a committee with the Minister, Churchwardens & others to arrange an application to the Charity Commission.

It was also the universal opinion of the Meeting that these six persons should be added to the list of Trustees for Sir John Dormer's Charity, independently of any arrangement in favour either to Canon's or Westbrooke's Charity. (This resolution I beg leave to support most cordially. It will tend greatly to allay dissatisfaction & be a counterpoise to the clannish adherence of certain parties — If the number be only 12 — three Dodwells with dependants in that number will rule the whole; but if extended to 18 they will be a neutralising power; & the number of Trustees will not virtually be increased, as out of that number the overseers & Churchwardens must be chosen).

The Meeting agreed to the thorough repair of the Aisle & Monument out of the funds now in hand; & the Scheme of paying weekly to 8 poor persons named for Trustees was acceptable.

N.B. There were two or three objections too, but the objections were waived, thinking that with the addition of others there would be no necessity to wound the feelings of any one. Under these circumstances, therefore, I beg leave to urge upon you this addition to the number, as in this case all objections will be done away with & all parties satisfied. There will always be some grumbles; but I verily believe, nay I know it most assuredly, that such is the general feeling.

Perhaps you had better address your letters in future to the 'Vicar, Churchwardens & Overseer of the Poor' as I wish it now to be a joint concern.

I am, Gentlemen, respectfully yours,

Thos Hayton

Charity Com.

1. Michael Rose, farmer and tenant of All Souls. Superintendent of the Baptist Sunday School.
2. In November 1855, £45 was held by the trustees for the repair of the Monument. No payments were made to the poor from August 1854 to December 1857 (Dormer Account Book, pp. 42—47).
3. The rate-book of 1859 gives the names of nearly four hundred householders.

Thame, 12 December 1855

Gentlemen,

The Board of Guardians at the weekly meeting held this day took into consideration the orders of the Poor Law Board of the 1st November instant relative to the payment of witnesses attending an inquiry made by G.G.W. Pigott Esq in July last as to the sufficiency of the coffins supplied for burial of certain poor persons charged to the Parish of Long Crendon.

The Guardians direct me to express their regret of again returning to this subject, and to say that they cannot help remarking that after the steps which they had taken in this matter the proceedings were in their opinion somewhat uncalled for and not very courteously conducted by the Inspector, and they are convinced that the complaints did not originate from any regard to the poor, but on the contrary from a desire to annoy the Guardians and to create an ill-feeling among the Poor towards the Guardians and the Poor Law — the complainant not daring to sign his name to the communication to the Poor Law Board and (if the Guardians are correct in their surmise of which they have little doubt) being a person notoriously fond of mischief-making and chose highly coloured statements the Guardians think created erroneous impressions both on the Poor Law Board and on the Inspector which as it appears to the Guardians the latter was unwilling to have removed.

I have the honour to be your very obedient servant,

Richard Holloway
Secretary of the Thame Poor Law Board

M.H. 12/9738

[135] To the Poor Law Board

Crendon, 8 April 1856

Gentlemen,

I have again been requested to write to you on behalf of those poor men who gave evidence in a Court of Enquiry instituted by Grenville Pigott, Esq, touching some coffins which pressed down the features of the dead, & indecently exposed them in their coffins. The case was fully substantiated & application has been made 3 or 4 times in vain to the Thame Guardians, who treat the application with thorough contempt, as they do your 'order'. Last week again, one of the poor men applied, and they told him to tell Mr Pigott he might pay them himself — they would not do it, — although the sum is very trifling, it is rather hard that the poor men should be put to so much trouble.

I hope, therefore, you will exert your authority & do that justice which the Thame Board refuses to do.

> Respectfully yours,
>
> Thomas Hayton

N.B. The poor men are quite tired out — having lost 3 or 4 days labour already. Cannot the Relieving Officer who pays here, if payment is to be made or there be any value to your order, leave the money at their houses.

M.H. 12/9739

[136] To the Charity Commissioners

Crendon, 17 July 1856

Gentlemen,

In reply to yours of the 15 Inst I beg to say that it was only at the request of the Churchwardens that I wrote out the answers to the different questions or returns — I know nothing personally of the details, nor will I have anything to do with these, whilst in this disjointed & unjust state.

Your letter etc I will hand over to last year's Churchwarden on his return home; the Churchwarden for the present knows nothing about the matters.

In courtesy towards you, which I think I have not received at your hands, I beg to observe that payment is withheld from both the Canon's Charity & Westbrooke's simply on the ground of there being no Trustees: consequently there can be no 'collection' or 'distribution', as recommended by you; & I beg also to observe, that there is no likelihood of any one bringing your last scheme into Court; none of the 12 to be appointed Trustees will sign the Notice; those who hold the monies of Sir John Dormer's & Hart's Charities will not; & the others receipt the monies paid over to them or they are otherwise indemnified, & will not move; & those who would have brought the matter to bear, you have excluded by your Certificate. I look upon it as a shameful injustice to the poor & I will not be answerable for the consequences, unless you take steps forthwith to bring these things to a settlement. I have used all arguments & said that you would employ the Attorney General, but this, they say, you will not do. It is not the Scheme which is objected to tho' the parts of it are not agreeable, but it is to the Act of doing so — of going to the Court & advancing monies on a dubiety.

The acreage of the *Churchland,* so called (of which however, we have no original documents, or if so it is not forthcoming) I will willingly hand you; & I earnestly request you to order, if you have the power, the appropriate distribution of the rest. Hitherto we have looked upon it as land left for the restoration of the Church & applicable to the conducting of the Church service; lately the money has been given to the Clerk or Sexton who formerly, in addition to their fees, collected from house to house. A demur is made to a Church rate by some & for 3 years no rate has been made [1]; & I think that

107

the Church is virtually robbed of that money paid to the Clerk or Sexton; & therefore it is, that I request your advice, as suggested to me by the Archdeacon [2] : & in conclusion I beg to request your immediate interposition in behalf of the poor of my parish.

> I am, Gentlemen, yours respectfully,
>
> Thos Hayton

Charity Com.

1. A church rate was made on 15 February 1851, but was not enforced.
2. Edward Bickersteth (1814–1892), vicar of Aylesbury, and archdeacon of Buckingham 1853 to 1875.

[137] To the Charity Commissioners

Crendon, 11 August 1856

Gentlemen,

The result of a meeting to consider the purport of your letter of 2nd of August, we beg to inform you that [we decided that] the Scheme of the Charity should be carried into the County Court forthwith, & that a Notice to this effect would be affixed to the Church door on Sunday next, the 17th Inst.

> We are, Gentlemen, yours respectfully,
>
> Thomas Hayton, Vicar of Long Crendon
> J.K. Shrimpton
> M.H. Shrimpton, Churchwardens

Charity Com.

[138] To G.G. Pigott Esquire

Crendon, 15 August 1856

Sir,

I beg leave to state in reply to yours of the 13th inst that the witnesses in the Coffin Affair have not yet been paid according to the order of the Poor Law Board of the date you alluded to, that William Lovell, one of the Witnesses informed me that he had thrice made application at the Board; that he was treated with contempt & insult and that at his last application before the Guardians he was laughed at and told to go to *you* for payment with other rude jests and remarks; this application was made about *three months ago*.

108

These poor fellows have lost two days work and at least in application, and are so disheartened that they will not go again.

> I am, Sir, yours respectfully,
>
> Thomas Hayton
> Vicar of Long Crendon

P.S. If you wish me to prevail on the Clerk of the parish to apply again, I will do so, tho' it is quite unfair to take him from his work, when the Relieving Officer is so often in the village; and probably after all he will receive the same treatment as Lovell received. T.H.

M.H. 12/9739

[139] *From* Jackson's Oxford Journal

30 August 1856

To Sculptors and Builders

A Specification and Estimate of the Expenses of Restoring a Monument and its Railing, in the Parish of Long Crendon is required immediately by the Churchwardens of the Parish. Further particulars may be obtained by personal application to the Churchwardens of the said Parish.

[140] *To Grenville Pigott Esq*

Crendon, 26 August 1856

Sir,

William Lovell again (the fourth time) applied at the Board of Guardians at Thame on Wednesday last for the expenditure of the Coffin Affair, he got the usual sneering reply they would consider about it and when compelled they would do it. He also enquired of the Relieving Officer of what was the decision; and he said he knew nothing about it. They have displayed not only ignorance but a Brutish stupidity — careless of Justice either to the living or dead.

> I am very respectfully yours,
>
> Thos Hayton

M.H. 12/9739

Note: Grenville Pigott wrote to the Poor Law Board and enclosed Thomas Hayton's letter. The Board replied that the Guardians were compelled to make payment.

[141] Grenville Pigott to Holloway, Clerk of the Thame Guardians
                                               Whitehall, 8 September 1856

Sir,

Referring to your letter of the 3rd inst, I have to inform you that it is no part of my duty to notify the Witnesses that they may receive payments due to them from a Board of Guardians. Having been instructed by the Poor Law Board to ascertain from the Incumbent of Long Crendon (who first drew their attention to the irregularity inquired into) whether in accordance with your letter of the 9th July their order of the 1st November 1855 had been obeyed — I was informed by him that it had not been so although repeated applications had been made and one subsequently to my letter to you on the 19th ultimo.

I have now to state that although (out of consideration to the Guardians) I have long delayed to inform the Poor Law Board that this is still uncomplied with — I can no longer consistent with my own responsibility, & that I have therefore transmitted to the Poor Law Board the reply of the Revd. Mr Hayton to my inquiry together with your letter of the 3rd Instant.

                I am, Sir, your obedient Servant,

                Grenville Pigott

M.H. 12/9739

[142] Minute from Grenville Pigott to the Poor Law Board
                                               15 September 1856

The Guardians, or rather that portion of them who for some years have absolutely directed the affairs of the Union, have throughout this matter shown the utmost disregard of what is due to the Poor Law Board and to common humanity and justice — The Enquiry took place a year and a half since — the facts complained of were established beyond a doubt, & the Poor Law Board has more than once requested that their order of 1 Nov 1855, to be obeyed, and as it now seems, in vain. I think therefore that alteration to the communication suggested by Mr Lumly should be made with the addition of the word 'immediately' between the words 'Not' and 'Obeyed'. I beg to refer to my minute of the 15 Dec on 47405/55.

                G.P.

I think that the Revd. Mr Hayton should be thanked for his communication.

M.H. 12/9739

Crendon, 10 November 1856

Gentlemen,

I duly received your communication of Saturday last which I handed over to the Churchwardens. I only know that in August last a notice was affixed to the Church door signed by one of the Churchwardens & two other individuals; since that time no steps have been taken that I know of to further the business, except that the Churchwarden & myself advertised for Tenders in order to get at the probable expense of restoring the Monument of Sir John Dormer — we find that the monument must originally have cost upwards of £1500 & that to restore the colouring & the Tracing as it was formerly would cost £200, and to restore it creditably would require about £80; so that the Clause No 11 in the Scheme alluding to the Restoration should be altered inasmuch as the money in the hands of Mr Reynolds, will not suffice; for I will never consent for it to be done shabbily. Will you therefore so model the Clause as to make the Trustees to take not all the money in hand but any that may accrue to meet the expenses of the restoration? If not, I must request the Judge so as to alter it, but I should like to have your sanction — to this alteration see Clause 11 'out of the funds in the hands of the Trustees or monies hereafter to be paid to them' etc.

There are funds now in the hands of Mr Reynolds, Mr Hanson & Mr J.K. Shrimpton; but no one knows the amount; this is not my way but I conceive that the monies should be placed in the Savings Bank, as other parishes do, in order to increase the amount which for a great length of time has been kept waiting.

I beg also to state to you that altho' I am a Trustee with the Churchwarden & overseers over what is called 'the Poor Land', I cannot get the officers to let that land profitably & beneficially for the poor; I am therefore ready to include that Charity also with the others & I advise you strongly to do so.

I am, Gentlemen, yours truly,

Thos Hayton
Vicar of Long Crendon

Charity Com.

[144] [The Scheme of the Charity Commissioners]

SUMMONS.
In the County Court of Oxfordshire, holden at THAME
No. of Charity, 1.

In the Matter of the five several Charities in the Parish of Long Crendon, in the County of Buckingham, called or known respectively as—

111

First — Sir John Dormer's Charity
Second — Hart's Charity
Third — Westbrooke's Charity
Fourth — Canon's Charity
Fifth — Trott's Charity

To the Reverend Thomas Hayton, Clerk, Vicar of the Parish of Long Crendon, in the County of Buckingham; Matthew Shrimpton, of Long Crendon aforesaid, a Churchwarden of the said Parish of Long Crendon; Joseph Hutt, of Long Crendon aforesaid, Farmer, and Michael Rose, of Long Crendon aforesaid, Farmer, Overseers of the Poor of the said Parish; John Stone, of No. 28, Westbourne Terrace, Hyde Park, in the County of Middlesex, Esquire; Henry Reynolds, of Notley Abbey, in the Parish of Long Crendon aforesaid, Farmer; Robert Dodwell, of Long Crendon aforesaid, Farmer; Joseph Dodwell, of Long Crendon aforesaid, Farmer; William Hanson, of Long Crendon aforesaid, Farmer; Edward Shrimpton, of Long Crendon aforesaid, Needle-maker; George Wainwright, of Long Crendon aforesaid, Butcher; and the Dean and Canons of the King's Free Chapel of Saint George, in the Castle of Windsor, the Warden and College of the Souls of all faithful people deceased, in the University of Oxford; and the most Honourable Richard Plantagenet Marquis of Chandos, Lords of the Manor of Long Crendon, in the County of Buckingham; and William Parker, of Thame, in the County of Oxford, Gentleman, Steward of the said Manor.

You are hereby summoned to appear at a County Court to be holden at Thame, on the twenty-seventh day of February, 1857, at the hour of Ten in the Forenoon, upon the hearing of an application which has been made to the Court in the matter of the above Charities, by which it is suggested "That an Order shall be made by this Court discharging from the Trust the said John Stone, who is represented to be desirous or willing to retire therefrom, and appointing the Vicar for the time being of the said Parish of Long Crendon, and the Churchwardens and Overseers for the time being of the same Parish, and the said Henry Reynolds, Robert Dodwell, Joseph Dodwell, and William Hanson, John Kirby Shrimpton, of Long Crendon aforesaid, Corn-dealer; the said Edward Shrimpton and George Wainwright, George Gibson, of Long Crendon aforesaid, Collar-maker; William Crook, of Long Crendon aforesaid, Farmer; John Crook, of Long Crendon aforesaid, Farmer; James Dodwell, of Long Crendon aforesaid, Farmer; and the said Michael Rose, or some other proper Persons to be new Trustees of the same Charities, and vesting in the persons so to be appointed Trustees their heirs and assigns, without any other conveyance or assurance, all the real estate and hereditaments belonging to the said Charities, and the right of suing for, and recovering all arrears of the rent and rents charge, and all choses in action belonging to the said Charities or any of them, in trust for the same Charities respectively, and establishing the scheme referred to in the Certificate of the Board of Charity Commissioners for England and Wales, bearing date the eleventh day of November, 1856, for the regulation and management of the same Charities with or without modification or alteration, and for such further or other order or relief as shall be properly incidental to the said application, and as the Judge of the said Court shall think fit to make or grant thereon."

And you are informed that if you do not attend pursuant to the requisition of this Summons, the Court may proceed in the matter in your absence, and make such Order as may appear just therein. And you are

112

further informed that if you do not obey such Order you will be liable to be imprisoned by order of the Court.

R. Holloway, *Registrar of the Court*

Dated this fifth day of February, 1857

Charity Com.

[145] *To the Charity Commissioners*

Crendon, 4 March 1857

Gentlemen,

re Sir John Dormer's Charity

The petition touching this charity & others was heard last Friday at Thame, permit me to make a comment or two thereon.

In the first place I protest against the injustice of having as Trustees a predominating influence of dissenters who by electing themselves will in a short time completely swamp every Churchman; & as it is, it will be perfectly useless, for a Churchman to attend any Meeting; & as for myself, if I were to attend, it would be only to get insulted. The inference is obvious.

As for the money in hand, capable of meeting the required repairs of the monument, it will be seen by the estimate I enclose, as a perfectly absurd attempt & as it is best to be plain, I will resist to the utmost, & refuse access to the Church to all parties attempting to botch or daub over, under a smaller estimate, such a beautiful Monument as the Sir John Dormer's.

Another Estimate was made by a gentleman of the name of Hale, 65 Edgeware Road, within a pound or two of the one enclosed. If some alteration or arrangement can be suggested by you I will be happy to hear it; & as the repairs of the windows of the Aisle & other parts amounting to about £15 are not included in the estimate, we shall want in the gross £110; to meet the money in hand I am ready to subscribe £5; if the 12 Trustees will do the same, some hope may be entertained: otherwise I can see no chance for the repairs to follow the Order.

I also hope & trust that as 15/— a year was the sum left for a person to keep the monument; that is, weekly dusting & hosing it etc, to be that my Clerk will not be deprived of that sum.

If such payment is to be left to the Trustees at their option, he will never get it; to say nothing of the argument that such sum was not a part of the Charity for the poor.

There is a point in the 18th Clause to which the Judge seemed inclined — viz — to give the Charity *either* in money or in kind. I warn you against *all money* payments which are generally anticipated & mortgaged at the Shops — a regular trafficking went on under the old system.

[Footnote]

If the Board of Guardians know of some poor old creature getting an advance

113

in money, of that they will take & have taken advantage: I speak this of my own knowledge. Having seen the Charities so shamefully pirated, alienated, plundered, I naturally feel a warm interest for justice to be done both to the dead & living.

> I am, Gentlemen, yours respectfully,

> Thos Hayton

Charity Com.

[146] *To the Charity Commissioners*

> Crendon, 3 April 1857

Gentlemen,

It is now a month since I forwarded to you an Estimate of the expenses which would be incurred in restoring the monument of Sir John Dormer — with comments thereon, & also pointing out how weak the Law would be to order that which could not be effected. Touching that Estimate & letter, that I have received no announcement of its reception according to your usual courtesy.

Last week the Judge of the County Court made some remarks on these Charities & the repairing of the Monument, saying that he would order the amount in hand £62—64 to be applied to the Restoration. This, I fear will be a vain appeal unless two or three agree to it as a matter of revenge upon others; & of the Trustees I know some are both unwilling & unable to fall in with such a proposition.

As it appears that some ignorance in the mind of the Judge as to the amount of money in hand, & as His Honour promises to see you on the subject before he makes the order, allow me to specify the amount now due.

Sir John Dormer's in the hands of Mr Reynolds		£72
Westbrooke's Charity in the hands of Mr Hanson £12		
in the hands of Mr J.K. Shrimpton £12		£24
Mr Crook's hands (Canon's Ch.) £4		£4
Greening's received for 3 years		£2.5s.

The above is subject to correction in fractions: & as I conceive that it is a degradation to send Sir John Dormer a-begging on the plea of saving money for the poor, when the poor & the parish have had it, I trust that you will use your exertions to restore a beautiful structure without having recourse to what many may think a meanness.

> I have the honour to be, Gentlemen, yours respectfully,

> Thos Hayton
> Vicar of Long Crendon

Charity Com.

[147] to Mr Batcheldor

Crendon, 19 April 1857

Sir,

I beg to inform you of the dilapidated state of a part of the Court House where the Lords of the Manor held their yearly Court. The frames of the windows are knocked out; the bricks from the wall are being taken away; the inside is made a receptacle of filth & a harbour for nuisances, when a pound or two will effectively repair it.

Mr Parker, Solicitor of Thame tells me he has written to you on the subject but had no answer; may I respectfully entreat the College to assent to their trifling share of this repair?

I myself expended £1.11s. on the roof etc which the late Mr Hollier promised to pay me when the next proceeds came: I do not like, neither can I offer to lay out money on the building with so poor a living as this is. I threatened to turn out the mischievous parties who are a parcel of idle boys, but you know the trouble attending such things.

I am yours respectfully,

Thos Hayton
Incumbent of Long Crendon

Windsor

Letters of Thomas Hayton Galley 102 — AB

[148] To Mr Batcheldor

Crendon, 23 June 1857

My dear Sir,

I am very sorry to find that you are unable to come to the Court & the more so at the cause of it. I hope by this time you are better. I wished I had drawn your attention to the outside wall of the Court House, the tiles which require repair & are looking very shabby, the sparrows making ingress etc.

The cost will be no more than £2 & I have spoken to Mr Parker & shown him the requirements. I hope I shall have your sanction to the repairs, which the sooner done the better.

Yours very faithfully,

Thomas Hayton
Vicar of Long Crendon

I would get an estimate if required but the sum specified may be a few shillings under or over the above.

Windsor

115

[151] To Mr Batcheldor

Crendon, 7 August 1857

Dear Mr Batcheldor,

Some time ago I wrote to you respecting the Court Room here; & hope that your illness has left you & that you are yourself again. I therefore urge on your attention the little repairs — external — tiles, holes etc in the wall & through which the cold will shortly penetrate.

I have had one estimate & the cost will be under £3. Mr Parker only waits your sanction & this is the time of the year when the plaster fixes best.

Be so good then, as either to me or Mr Parker to intimate your assent & I shall on behalf of my poor children feel grateful to you.

Believe me, very respectfully yours,

Thos Hayton

Windsor

[152] To Mr Batcheldor

Crendon, [undated]

3rd time asking

Dear Sir,

Will you mention on behalf of the Dean & Chapter of Windsor the repairs which are actually necessary for the Court Room? The estimate is only £3, so only $\frac{1}{3}$ will be the amount of the College.

Pray let me hear from you as the wet is doing serious damage to the roof.

Yours truly,

Thos Hayton

Windsor

[153] To the Charity Commissioners

Crendon, 17 September 1857

Gentlemen,

Three months have now transpired since the Scheme was sanctioned of the Court at Thame, & not a word is heard respecting it. We are anxiously waiting to know what steps are to be taken, & whether a copy of the amended Scheme is to be sent us. If therefore you will communicate your wishes or orders, you will oblige

Yours respectfully,

Thos Hayton
Vicar of Long Crendon

Charity Com.

[149] To the Charity Commissioners

Crendon, 25 June 1857

Gentlemen,

re Sir John Dormer's Charity

I enclose you an extract from a local paper on the above named Charity, on which I wish to make a remark or two.

When the first petition was about to be presented, the very men who are now loudest for the Charity to pay the costs, were *then* the most adverse that such a payment should come out of the Funds. I hope you will refuse all such application. I claim for the monument of Sir John Dormer 3 years full rental without deduction for 'brandy and water' the expense of riding 2 miles to receive the rent when it may be taken any Tuesday at Thame Market [1]. Mr Dodwell's assertion that all the Trustees wishing for the weekly payments to go to their labourers — (for this in reality is the question) — is not correct; he had a meeting when only five attended and they were agreed; the others told me they cared nothing about it — & naturally the *Judge thought right, that would do*. Then as to the number of fitting recipients. There are upwards of 60 receiving about 1½d a day after rent and firing has been paid for, and nearly 70 persons eligible. So much for the assertions of Mr Dodwell.

I have heard of £3.15s more in the hand of Mr Reynolds of money for apprentices; but as none of us know much about the accounts — being kept nearly a mile away from the village — & this apprentice account being in the hands of three different individuals — it is necessary to draw your attention to this. Had the money been put, as is done in other parishes into the Savings Bank, there would have been enough to pay all expenses & more.

I hope if possible, that the monument will be restored this summer, the particulars of which you have in a paper sent by me to you.

I am Gentlemen, yours very respectfully,

Thomas Hayton
Vicar of Long Crendon

Charity Com.

1. Mr Reynolds was paid 2/– twice a year for collecting the rent charge payable on Chilling Farm, Brill (Dormer Account Book, pp. 11–13).

[150] To the Diocesan Church Building Society

4 August 1857

Application for aid towards enlarging & improving the Parsonage house at Long Crendon, Bucks, having been laid before the Committee, they greatly regretted that the application was not such as could be entertained consistently with the rules of the Society.

November 3rd confirmed

Bodl. Oxford Diocesan Papers d. 795

[154] To the Dean of Windsor

Crendon, 1 October 1857

Sir,

The Dean & Canons of Windsor with All Souls College & the Duke of Buckingham are respectively Lords of this Manor & there is a Court Room belonging to them conjointly where annually a Court is held in reference to customary properties.

Some years ago, this room was a miserable, dirty place, with nothing but wooden sliding windows & bare rafters above. I got permission from the Lords to use this as a Sunday school as we have no school of any kind whatsoever here. At great cost I removed the abominations, put glass windows in & plastered the ceiling etc. — the Lords undertaking to keep the roof & walls in order. This has occasionally been done; but at present the rain comes through the tiling, & the outside walls are detaching themselves from wooden squares into which brick & stone have been put. The repair of this wall a little while back is absolutely necessary & the estimated cost is only £3.5s.0d! but Mr Parker the Solicitor & agent for All Souls College tells me that he has no powers granted him by you to allow one third of the expense; consequently I wrote to Mr Batcheldor three times, but he has not deigned a reply. May I very earnestly request you to submit this to the Society at your earliest opportunity, so the repairs should be done forthwith; the orders from the other Lords have been given.

I am very sorry to trouble you; but I cannot afford to do it myself, as the Living is a miserable one, where dissenters abound. To help me along in Charities, my only assistance is from All Souls occasionally.

As your property is considerable here, perhaps at some Christmas you may remember us.

Yours very respectfully,

Thomas Hayton
Vicar of Long Crendon

Windsor

[155] From the Bucks Advertiser

12 December 1857

BRILL.
PETTY SESSIONS. — December 4.
(Before the Rev. George Chetwode; the Rev. J.S. Barron; and the Rev. Claud Martyn.)

UNFOUNDED CHARGE OF SHOOTING WITHOUT A LICENSE

A somewhat important and singular case came before the bench this day. The vicar of Crendon, the Rev. T. Hayton, was summoned by William Reynolds [1], not for trespassing upon another man's land, but for being out with a gun on his own, in search of game, with certificated and authorised persons, he having invited a party to shoot rabbits on his farm, who, after beating the covers, went into the turnip field adjoining.

Mr Griffits [2] supported the information, and Mr Hayton conducted his own defence, contending that he had a perfect right to act as he had done, and that no statute had been infringed. On this issue was joined.

Timothy Dodwell [3], who farms some land contiguous to the Vicar's, deposed, that on the 15th of October last, he saw through a hedge from the gate of his farm buildings, four persons beating some turnips, about four hundred yards distant, and heard three or four shots fired. He knew it was Mr Hayton and his servant, but did not know the other two, only he saw something like game on the back of the boy. He dodged the party into an adjoining field, where they beat some mustard, and soon after they came to some turnips, near which he and his men were at work. It was here he saw the boy with two hares on his back. He also saw a hare get up, at which Mr Hayton shot, together with others, and which, after running a distance dropped, and the boy went and picked it up. In his cross-examination this witness said, that besides being a farmer, he was a dealer in flour on the truck system, a speculator in thrashing machines, and did a little in the stone-pit line, but reaped no profits from any of these. He said he could see over a hedge eight-feet high, but could not see round a corner, nor through a deal board; knew a hawk from a hand-saw, though he once mistook an owl for an eagle. He swore that he was only ten yards from the hedge; that Mr Hayton was on the left-hand of the party, and that he shot the last, the hare running in an easterly direction.

A witness of the name of Saunders was then called, who said, he had been working all the morning in the same field, and that he heard no shots previous to the party coming near him. His master came up, and turning round, asked who were the persons down in the mustard field. He replied it was Mr Hayton, his servant, and a gentlemen whom he did not know. He saw them all beating the mustard field, with their guns ready to fire; and when they came up to the field adjoining that in which he was at work, he saw a hare, which Mr Hayton shot at and killed. On cross-examination he stated that he heard no shots before that time. Saw Mr Hayton on the right hand of the party. The hare ran upwards in a southerly direction.

A boy was then called, and swore that Mr Hayton was in the mustard field, and that he (witness) saw a hare get up in the turnips, which Mr Hayton shot at and killed. On cross-examination it was elicited that the witness was upwards of 100 yards distant from the hedge with his master and Saunders that only one gun was fired, and that Mr Hayton was on the right hand side of the party nearest the hedge towards which the hare ran.

The Rev. T. Hayton briefly remarked on the discrepancy of the evidence, denouncing the case as one of the most base and truthless that was ever brought into a court of justice. He could with great confidence have left it in the hands of the magistrates; but, to vindicate himself, and for the sake of the public, he would call two or three witnesses who would disprove nearly every statement made in support of the information.

The first witness called was Mr J. Stevens [4], of Thame, who said, being duly licensed, he had received an invitation from Mr Hayton to shoot rabbits on his farm on the 15th. He accordingly went; and having beaten the

119

middle cover proceeded over some adjoining lands towards another. There were no shots fired in the turnips opposite Mr Dodwell's farm-yard. He went down into a mustard field, into which Mr Hayton never entered, he saying that he would go round the cover to see whether Mr Dodwell would come and speak to him, as some difference existed between them. After that they joined Mr Hayton in a field of large white turnips, upwards of two feet high in which it was almost impossible to see a hare running. When in this field he saw Mr Dodwell and his men about seventy or eighty yards from the hedge, and nearly 200 yards from him, Mr Hayton being on the right-hand side and he on the left. From the place where Dodwell and his men were standing it was utterly impossible for them to see a hare get up in the turnips. They did not kill a hare that day, and if anyone had stated that he had seen their boy with two hares on his back he had stated what was an infamous untruth. If anyone had sworn that Mr Hayton had shot a hare that day it would have been equally false. The only hare shot at that day was by himself, on a road adjoining the turnips, but, though he hit her, she escaped. He did not see Mr Hayton shoot at a hare that day; but he saw Mr Hayton rise a covey of partridges which he did not shoot at.

Robert Hinton, Mr Hayton's servant, was then called. He said he was empowered, according to the Act of Parliament, to shoot hares, and that his master, in consequence of loss of sight, was unable to do so. He remembered the 15th of Oct. No shots were fired that morning opposite Dodwell's farm-yard; neither was Mr Hayton in the mustard field, having gone round the cover to draw Dodwell near the ground to ascertain the distance; but the height of the turnips was above two feet high, so that no person on the other side of the hedge could possibly have seen a hare get up in them. All that was shot that day was a couple of rabbits and a partridge by Mr Stevens, and one other rabbit by witness. His master, whom he was near all day, except for a few minutes, shot nothing. He never during the day saw his master shoot either at hare or partridge; and if anyone had sworn that three hares were killed, or that his master had shot one, it would be an abominable falsehood.

Mr Hayton, at this stage of the proceedings, said that he would call no more witnesses, as he felt sure that the magistrates saw clearly through this vile trumped up case, which he would leave in their hands, confident that the right he had to take a gun was unimpeachable, that he had disproved the statements made by Dodwell and his men, and that he had in no way infringed the law.

Mr Griffits argued that Mr Hayton had rendered himself liable to a fine by accompanying Mr Stevens, who shot at game; and that though there was a discrepancy in the evidence of his witness, it was easily accounted for by the lapse of time since the occurrence.

The Rev. George Chetwode, the chairman, remarked that the doctrine promulgated by Mr Griffits was monstrous and no farmer or owner of land, with a gun in his hand, would be safe if a sportsman walked with him over his fields if such was to be the case. The act of Mr Stevens could not implicate Mr Hayton, who was fully justified in carrying a gun; and, independent of this, the evidence in support of the information was so marked with inconsistency — so contradictory, that no decision against Mr Hayton could be pronounced; but, when Mr Stevens came forward and spoke in so straightforward a manner, he felt bound to give his evidence that weight which it was entitled to, to say nothing of the support it received from the evidence of Robert Hinton. He had, therefore, come to the conclusion that the case had not been proved, and that Mr Hayton left the court without the slightest imputation on his character.

The other members of the bench having concurred in the decision, the information was dismissed.

The announcement was received with great satisfaction by many farmers and others present, who heartily congratulated Mr Hayton on the result.

B.R.O. P.R. 134/1/4

1. William Reynolds, miller of Notley, brother to Henry.
2. Mr Griffits, member of the firm of Chilton and Burton.
3. Across a newspaper cutting in the Parish Register is written the following:—
   'This Timothy Dodwell who thus perjured himself & to prosecute whom I was offered percuniary assistance by different gentlemen, is the same person to whom I gave up the land which I have held of All Souls College.'
4. J. Stevens, grocer of Thame.

[156] [From an unidentified newspaper]

LONG CRENDON
THE CHARITIES

At the Thame County Court on Saturday week, the question as to the intentions of the donor, Sir John Dormer, came on for a final hearing before the judge, C. Temple, Esq., Q.C.

It will be remembered that, at the previous court, Messrs. Dodwell and Reynolds, and the other gentlemen who have of late years diverted the charities from the objects decided to have been intended by the donor, applied for an allowance out of the funds of the charity, to pay a solicitor and a barrister whom they had employed to endeavour to convince the judge that it was right and proper that the income of the charities should be appropriated in relieving ablebodied men having large families, instead of being limited to parties above 60 years of age.

As soon as the case came on, the vicar (the Rev. Thos. Hayton) called the attention of the judge to this point, who immediately stated that he had no power to order the repayment of any costs Mr Dodwell and his friends had incurred.

Mr Dodwell then rose and renewed the request previously made, that the trustees might be allowed to dispose of the charity to men with large families, irrespective of age, &c. He said that all the trustees, except the vicar, were agreed on this point; and that few deserving the charity could be found, without including labourers, as fitting recipients.

The vicar (Mr Hayton) was then heard. He said that the whole question depended upon what was meant in the deed of 1604 by a 'poor inhabitant'. He argued that it never could mean an able-bodied labourer, who was to be

121

brought out of the fields at three o'clock in the afternoon to the parish church, at evening prayer, to receive the dolement of a shilling – that the spirit of the will of John Dormer was altogether against such an idea – that, if adopted, it would have a tendency to pauperize every labourer, to lower him in his own esteem, to keep down the wages of labour, and to make him very serf; and that such a construction had been rejected by the commissioners, and every chancery barrister of note. (His Honour here intimated to Mr Hayton that he thought with him, and this spared any further remarks).

The judge then explained to Mr Dodwell his views on the subject. He said that he could not possibly allow the farmers to pay their labourers out of that charity, and the clause limiting the recipients to 60 years of age must stand.

Mr Hayton applied for an alteration in another clause, which, it appeared, deprived him and the churchwardens of a little patronage. The justice of this claim was recognized, and the clause altered accordingly.

Then came the place of payment, which the deed said should be at the church. It would seem that there was an attempt, on the part of Messrs Dodwell and Reynolds, to withdraw the payment from the church, or to set at nought the wishes of the vicar and churchwardens. His Honour stated that any such attempt was an infringement on the vicar's right, and said that he should make an order that the church should be the place of payment.

(We understand that, at a previous court, His Honour made an order that the money in hand should be paid into the Savings' Bank. To our surprise we now learn that this order has not been complied with, and that the money still remains in the hands of the parties upon whom the order was made. Whether this be so or not, of course, we have no means of ascertaining. We are content that, henceforth, these charities will be better managed. From all we can learn only four boys had been apprenticed during the last 50 years, at about £15 each, whereas the annual sum set apart for apprenticing boys is more than £200. We were told that the vicar has been endeavouring, for upwards of 20 years, to have these charities properly administered, and that he has consequently drawn upon himself, at different times, most villainous treatment, and the foulest misrepresentation were had recourse to. For eight years he was positively refused a sight of any documents bearing on the subject. About 1830, when the charity commission was issued, the deed of Sir John Dormer was brought out of Mr Stone's chest, and the undertaking by him and other farmers was to give a number of poor widows 1s. a week, and that regular accounts should be kept. This, however, was never done, and, soon after, the farm labourers were make partakers of the charity. A deed was made about ten years ago, the particulars of which few know; but this was pronounced to be an invalid deed, and that there were no regular trustees to any of the charities; thence the application to the court. We sincerely hope, now the trustees are appointed, that justice will be done both to the dead and to the living; and that the monument of Sir John Dormer will yet be properly restored, and receive an artistical embellishment, worthy of a man who, regardless of expense, caused it to be erected in his life-time, and added thereto an annual benefice of ... [torn]).

[attached to the approved Scheme]

Charity Com.

Crendon, 19 January 1858

Gentlemen,

I sent you a few months back a specification & Estimate of the cost of *repairing* the *monument* of Sir John Dormer. As the question is now under discussion, be so good as to return me such Estimate.

Two questions will be submitted to you officially; one in reference to the person who is to take the Chair at our meetings in my absence, which I think the Scheme insufficiently explains, in order to prevent any Cabal about the Election of a Chairman; & the other is whether an orphan boy, under Hart's Charity for apprenticing Boys, may be chosen by the Trustees to the exclusion of a 'son of creditable parents *resident* in the parish' [1]. The former is a move to ease the rate-payers; the latter I conceive is the True meaning & application of the Clause of the Scheme if the English language is to be taken in its plain sense — *resident* parents, implying living parents.

I do not wish you to notice this point in this letter, except you think fit courteously to do so; *but* the question may be so put to you, as to catch an inference to such purposes.

I am, Gentlemen, yours respectfully,

Thos Hayton
Vicar of Long Crendon

Charity Com.

1. Clause 16 states "in binding as an apprentice a poor deserving boy not less than 14 years, and not more than 18 years of age, and being the child of poor deserving parents, resident in the said parish of Long Crendon".

14 July 1858

Gentlemen,

At a Meeting of the Trustees of the Charity of this place your letter to the Minister & Churchwardens respecting the Charities of Westbrooke & Hart was duly read & an order given for returns to be made.

We are considerably puzzled as to the Restoration of Sir John Dormer's Monument, the estimates varying thus —

1. Mr Grimsley [1], sculptor etc of Oxford	£100	
2. Mr Gibbs [2], sculptor etc of Oxford	£84	
3. Mr Peyman [3] of Abingdon	£82.16s.	
4. Mr Hales [4] 65 Edgeware Road, London	£72	
5. Messrs Thompson & Mag [5], Aylesbury	£56	
6. Mr Holland [6] of Thame	£50	

(these latter — first a stone Mason & the other a Builder).

The first four I believe are quite competent to restore it, inasmuch as it is their special province & are experienced men; the latter on their own acknowledgement never attempted such a thing, & therefore I feel reluctant to assent to an Act for which the Churchwardens & myself under the Clause of the Scheme would have the blame, should the work be meanly or badly done, tho' many of the Trustees wish for the lowest sum to be expended.

The Monument was originally erected without any regard to expense in 1604 & is a beautiful structure with emblems, pillars & decorations by first rate Artists, the whole supposed to be of foreign workmanship with recumbent figures of Sir John & his Lady, both of whom have suffered in feet, head & nose.

The Keystone of the Arch over the figures has given way ½ an inch & there is a displacement or sinking on one side. Two of the best Sculptors say that the stones should be taken down to the Arch, & thus secure the keystone; others say it does not require it! I am inclined to think that no restoration can be called effective without the Arch repaired, the stones dried and sorted & then the colours purple, pink, vermillion etc. will last. & when we have had such a Benefactor & have hitherto treated him scurvily it would be ungrateful indeed not to do justice to him. Under this difference of opinion I have suggested the propriety of calling in Mr Street the Diocesan Architect [7] or Mr Scott [8] or any other skilled person & to decide upon the subject & advise touching the tenders which vary so disparately. Would you Gentlemen, venture a suggestion on this matter? It may not be really your province, still a friendly mediation may avail.

I have the honour to be, Gentlemen, yours respectfully,

Thos Hayton

Vicar of Long Crendon

Charity Com.

1. Thomas Grimsley, sculptor, 7a Park Villas, St Giles.
2. John Gibbs, stone & marble mason, 64 Cowley Road.
3. Henry Prince Peyman, statuary and stone mason, Oak Street, Abingdon.
4. Mr Hales, 65 Edgeware Road, London.
5. James Thompson, Station Street, Aylesbury.
6. Giles Holland, builder, brick and tile maker, Park Street, Thame.
7. George Edmund Street (1824—1881), diocesan architect; 1851 designed Cuddesdon Theological College; restorer of Bristol Cathedral and York Minster. (*M.E.B.*)
8. George Gilbert Scott (1811—1878). Knighted 1872; architect of the Gothic Revival. Designer of the Albert Memorial. (*M.E.B.*)

[159] *To the Chairty Commissioners*

Crendon, 25 August 1858

Gentlemen,

Sir John Dormer's Charity

Nothing has been done to the repairing of Sir John Dormer's Monument, nor is there this year any thing likely to be done. There are many differences of opinion in the *general meeting* called, & so few know anything at all about the matter, & your advice 'to call some competent person in & abide by his decision' not meeting with much favour, I am induced at the suggestion of my Churchwarden to request your interpretation of the 11th Clause in the Scheme as regards the Authority of the Minister, & Church-wardens whether they can choose a fitting person to restore the Monument & direct the amount & nature of the requirements,* in order that such inter-pretation may be inserted in the minutes, for the present as well as for the future reparation.

> I have the honour to be, Gentlemen, your obedient servant,
>
> Thomas Hayton
> Vicar of Long Crendon

*The person who offered to restore it for £50 after hearing the report of the Painter (who said it was extremely intricate & would require a great amount of labour) declined having anything to do with it even with an additional sum.

Charity Com.

[160] *To the Charity Commissioners*

Crendon, 24 December 1858

I have been anxious that all the Meetings of the Trustees of the above charities should be duly convened & notices sent to each Trustee: but I cannot prevail upon the Acting Trustees to do so. The Enclosed was the Notice on the Church door last Monday — without name of *place* or *date*. I declined attending such Meeting, & I write to ask you whether *any Notice* is requisite for either of the two half-yearly meetings; & if so, whether the enclosed is sufficient?

Am I at liberty to enter a protest on the Minutes should it be necessary, altho' I am not present at such meetings?

Nothing has been done yet to the repairing of the Monument, which to repair even moderately will require all that was in hand viz £72, & out of this sum the Court fees have been paid which were ordered, & the solicitors fees & Barristers fees for opposing the whole Scheme, which were not ordered, have been deducted; so that to undertake the restoration of the Monument under such circumstances would be absurd. What am I & the Churchwardens to do in such case?

A reply at your earliest convenience will oblige

> Yours respectfully,
>
> Thomas Hayton
> Vicar of Long Crendon

[*Enclosure*]
We the undersigned, being the Trustees of the Charities of this parish, hereby

125

give Notice of a Meeting of the Trustees to be holden at the Churchill Arms Inn on Tuesday the 21st at 6 o'clock in the Evening for the purpose of Auditing the Accounts and any other business relating to the above mentioned Charities.

James Dodwell
Edward Shrimpton
Michael Rose

Charity Com.

[161] *To the Charity Commissioners*

Crendon, 21 January 1859

Sir John Dormer's Charity

Gentlemen,

We have no exclusive Vestry Room in the Parish, but meet sometimes at one public house & sometimes at another, neither have we appointed by any resolution a place to hold our Meetings at; consequently the Meeting held on the 21st Dec must have been irregularly convened. Hence my complaint of the 24th Dec last.

It appears that the Trustees present at that Meeting voted monies etc & adjourned to do the like till Tuesday last, when without any Notice whatsoever (except a Boy sent round to certain Trustees, for I & others knew nothing about it) they met & voted other monies to be distributed. The three acting Trustees met & not being able to raise a Meeting of five persons, sent round the landlord to get two on the moment, which I hear with difficulty they effected. Now what I request of you is, to write to the acting Trustees telling them your construction of the 3rd Clause under the circumstances I have mentioned & also to inform me, in case of an *adjourned Meeting* for a *month* or so, what *kind* of *Notice*, whether in writing & how many *days previous* to the meeting such Notice should be sent, or whether any notice whatever is required [1].

They promised to get some printed forms, but that is an exertion too great for them.

I am, Gentlemen, respectfully yours,

Thos Hayton
Vicar of Long Crendon

P.S.
Since writing the preceding, I have seen the parish Churchwarden & we have thought it desirable to have your construction on the 18th Clause [2], as to two points. viz whether sick persons *transiently sick*, or having sickness in their house , tho' neither of the parents may be sick & neither 60 years of age

126

may be selected; & whether permanently unable is to be the rule. There is evidently a wish to get rid of what is stated to be the 'Duly qualified'. T.H.

Charity Com.

1. Clause 3 directed that the Trustees should have two Meetings a year. On the 25th of June and 21st of December. Any Trustees could summon a special Meeting on giving ten days previous notice. Five Trustees were to form a quorum at any Meeting.
2. Clause 18 laid down that money should be expended in helping any person over sixty years of age in the winter season. Recipients under sixty who through illness were unable to work were also eligible. A list was to be kept of the duly qualified (Charity Com. 1857 Scheme).

[162] Lower Winchendon Parish Register (Burials 1813–1859)

Many fine trees were cut down in the parish of Lower Winchendon this year after the sale of the property belonging to the Martyn family, which realized £25,000, five thousand below its value. Mr Bernard cut down in the avenue to his house & about the premises, many splendid and valuable trees [1], without one tear of sorrow for the deed, but as soon as I cut down the trees growing in the Churchyard which encumbered the ground, spoilt the herbage & endangered the Church, immediately did his anger boil forth & expressions of regret at their fall (strongly inconsistent with his own conduct) were multiplied, after the manner of sickly sentimentalism tho' not a single tree has any character about it for beauty or proportion. Strange that men should be so blind to their own deeds & so keen sighted in reference to deeds of others. I can justify my proceedings on grounds which any reasonable man would be satisfied with.

[*signed*] Thomas Hayton, Incumbent, in the 41st year of his Ministry [2], 1859.

1. The trees and herbage in the churchyard belonged to the lay Impropriator, & many large trees are preserved'. Lipscomb, *History of Buckinghamshire*, i, p. 531.
2. Thomas Hayton was appointed Curate in 1818.

[163] To the Bounty Board

Crendon, [Received 2 March] 1859

My dear Sir,

You were so kind a short time ago to send me an extract touching the lands belonging to the little Living of Lower Winchendon in the County of Bucks. The land belonging to the Living of Chearsley, the adjoining parish to Winchendon, abuts upon the allotment belonging to Winchendon [1], & the hedge between the two portions of land has never been set out. A dispute has arisen touching the boundaries — whether I am to make the Hedge or the Incumbent of Chearsley: I decline doing it, because it would make all the hedges round the allotment belonging to me, which is a perfect anomaly in the arrangement of lands.

Would you be so kind therefore as to tell me the exact measurement of the land belonging to Chearsley, specifying the amount of arable & grass respectively & whether there is more than one acre & ½ abutting upon my allotment of 20 acres & more: & what is the *description* of the lands in the deed of conveyance. I have been unable hitherto to get up to London, but if I am imposing upon you a duty or rather a task & you decline the trouble, I will try to be up next month & examine the map myself.

The inaccuracies which arise are astonishing; & I find that a Lordship of the Manor. viz, that of the Duke of Buckingham, claims trees growing upon the bank of a hedge which abuts upon a public road & is the boundary fence of the land belonging respectively to Winchendon & Chearsley.

Should you not comprehend clearly my request, I will come up and examine for myself.

> Yours respectfully,
>
> Thos Hayton

Ch. Com. F.1278

1. Marsh Farm, originally purchased by Richard Grenville in 1671.

[164] To the Charity Commissioners

Crendon, 6 June 1859

Gentlemen,

The enclosed paper is a copy of a Notice sent out to the Acting Trustees & others touching the restoration of Sir John Dormer's Monument, which, if neglected this month, will be difficult of accomplishment this year. I must therefore request your intercession on behalf of the dead, & to urge upon the Trustees the necessity of carrying out forthwith the Judge's order. Last year we had Meeting after Meeting — everyone having a nostrum of his own & none with any knowledge about the artistic Embellishments of such a structure. We had 6 or 7 tenders; from £50 to £150; & the best men said *that the highest* — could not restore it like the original. Some voted for yellow paint instead of gilt; I & others stuck to some local prejudice & that a common mason or head stone maker . . . [torn] . . . I saw it was useless to attend anything under such a variety of councillors; & therefore claimed with the Churchwardens the power under the 11th clause: & applied to a Mr Peyman, a builder at Abingdon to give an estimate which is £71.15s.0d. We have enquired as to his character, abilities etc, & find from Mr Noble [1], the sculptor of Bruton Street; from Mr Harcourt [2] of Nuneham Park for whom last year Peyman removed [and restored] a beautiful family Monument & from others, & have had the most satisfactory testimonials, & therefore I feel anxious that he should be employed — The sum of money in hand at the time of the order was £72; there will be now in hand about £20 more, unappropriated, so that on the score of funds there can be no objections. Besides there are other repairs required in the Aisle, windows, curtains etc which for these last two years have been thoroughly neglected. Under all the circumstances of the case, therefore I earnestly beg of you to communicate with the Trustees.

I am, Gentlemen, yours respectfully,

Thos Hayton

Charity Com.

1. Matthew Noble (1818–1876); sculptor; famous for his exhibits of busts at the Royal Academy (*D.N.B.*).
2. George Granville Harcourt of Nuneham Park (1785–1861); M.P. for Oxfordshire 1831–1861.

[165] To the Charity Commissioners
Crendon, 22 October 1859

Gentlemen,

Will you be kind enough to inform me at your earliest convenience whether you deem an agricultural labourer at full weekly pay entitled to Sir John Dormer's weekly Charity of one shilling simply on the ground *that his wife is unwell*, he being under 60 years of age? & whether the wife herself being unwell is an eligible recipient, she being under 60 years of age? & still bound to her husband.* Two or three cases of this sort have received the charity, & it is doubted whether the Trustees are justified in such appropriation.

I am, Gentlemen, your obedient servant,

Thomas Hayton
Vicar of Long Crendon

*under the 12th Clause [1].

[Draft answer 18 November]
The man if able to work is disqualified & the wife, if suffering from a permanent or chronic illness is eligible.

Charity Com.

1. Clause 12 laid down that recipients of the Dormer Charity should be over sixty, but persons incapacitated through illness should also be eligible as recipients.

[166] To the Charity Commissioners
Crendon, 19 April 1860
Private

Gentlemen,

The Trustees have held two meetings & since I read to them your letter of the 24 February last [1], but have not proceeded to the filling up of the two vacant Trusteeships, & I am informed (for I was not at the last meeting)

129

that not until after Midsummer will they do so — this was the decision of only 5 Trustees & it is so contrary to the spirit & letter of the 2nd Clause of the Scheme & your interpretation of it, that I have thought it proper to leave the matter in your hands, as I am sickened with such petty dilatoriness.

The Scheme provided that a box should be provided in which to place the books and documents [2], the box was provided about 3 years ago and till the death of Edward Shrimpton was used by him as a hat box! & not in proper use yet. At the monthly meeting we never see any books but the minute book, and people who would be inclined to look at them, dislike making application at the private house where they are kept.

If you think that these matters should be remedied, perhaps you will take some steps to that effect: I should only get abuse from dissenters were I to moot the matter.

I am, Gentlemen, respectfully yours,

Thos. Hayton
Vicar of Long Crendon & of Lower Winchendon

Charity Com.

1. This letter cannot be found.
2. Clause 7 said that the Minute and Account Books should be kept in a suitable chest in some convenient place of deposit.

[167] To the Charity Commissioners

Crendon, 20 June 1860

Gentlemen,

On the 25th Inst there was an Election here for two Trustees, the result of which has given great dissatisfaction & in due time I will state the objections. The person was proposed & seconded on the ground of his being the Eldest son of his father he was legally entitled to be a Trustee, grounding the notion on the preface to the Scheme which turns thus 'Vesting in the persons to be appointed Trustees their heirs & assigns etc'. The Trustees were divided in opinion about the matter, & when the person alluded to was proposed I put it chiefly on the ground of his being heir to his father; & on that ground he was elected: for on no other had he the least pretentions. He is a working needlemaker, owner & occupier of a cottage rated at £3.10s. & unable to write his own letters & otherwise in the opinion of every thinking man totally unfit for such an office.

Will you therefore be kind enough to inform me whether *such a claim* has any validity in it, in order that steps might be taken & real ones assigned to induce you to order a new appointment.

I am respectfully yours,

Thomas Hayton
Vicar of Long Crendon

Charity Com.

Crendon, 11 July 1860

Gentlemen,

Both the Churchwardens of this parish & myself together with the largest Landowners occupiers & the great majority of the poor of the parish are altogether dissatisfied with the recent appointments of Sylvannus Shrimpton & David Dodwell as Trustees of the Charity of Sir John Dormer & others & it has been requested, in consequence, to lay before you a plain statement of the case, in order to reserve the appointment on grounds which we hope will meet with your approval.

The following is a copy of the notice affixed to the Church door; 'The Trustees of the Long Crendon Charities give notice that at their half yearly Meeting at the Churchill Arms on the 25th of June *next* at 7 o'clock in the Evening they will proceed to elect two Trustees to fill up the *Vacancy* in their body caused by death & otherwise.

June 12/60. James Dodwell, Trustee'

1. The object of the Notice itself, as being informal, doubtful in its meaning as to time, nor in accordance with the 4th Clause of the Scheme which requires the signature of three Trustees; nor with your opinion of the proper construction of the 2nd Clause as given in your letter of the 24th of Feby last.

2. We object because an *undue* family influence will be given as well as a dissenting one, as the following statement will show: Trustees at present *all dissenters.*

1. Robert Dodwell (father to Andrew & David)
2. Joseph Dodwell (nephew to Robert Dodwell)
3. James Dodwell (nephew to Robert Dodwell)
4. David Dodwell (son of Robert) recently elected
5. Andrew Dodwell, overseer son of Robert
   David, Andrew & Robert, tenants of Joseph
6. Michael Rose
7. James Webster Shrimpton [1]
8. George Gibson
9. James Barry, overseer
10. Sylvannus Shrimpton [2] (recently elected)
11. William Crook more dissent than Church

Trustees at present Churchmen

1. The Vicar
2. Mr Reynolds of Notley Abbey
3. Mr J. Cousens Crook
4. Mr M. Henry Shrimpton
5. Mr Hanson (dead)

From this statement it will appear that nothing can prevent another dissenter being appointed in the room of Mr Hanson (who died about 3 weeks ago) the effect of which will be, as indeed it is already, to create a dissenting monopoly, if the appointments of Sylvannus Shrimpton & David Dodwell be sanctioned.

We also object more particularly to such an *array of family connections* in the administrations of a public charity (which has ever been doled out without reference to sect or party, tho' the spirit of each Deed loudly speaks 'Church' & nothing else) — as being fraught with a variety of evils on the very face of it, as having no precedent in public bodies, as guarded against with jealousy in our Collegiate Establishment, because of the well known tendency to create a monopoly & in consequence injustice.

I also object to Sylvannus Shrimpton on personal grounds.
1. Because he was proposed & seconded on *his right*, as the eldest son of the last Edward Shrimpton, to become a Trustee, every one admitting that neither his position nor habits of life entitle him to become a Trustee. He is simply a working needle maker, owner & occupier of a cottage rate of £3.10s., unable to write his own letters & never attended parish vestries in his life; & would be the willing tool of this sect.
2. As to David Dodwell, he is a rack renter & possessor of a cottage or two, & from family connection a decided partisan. I appeal therefore to you with all earnestness whether such appointments should be maintained to the exclusion of men of family, property & influence, & when I further add that, as neither Mr Reynolds nor Mr J.C. Crook (the largest occupiers of land in the parish) were present at the last meeting in consequence of their not knowing the day on which it was held, otherwise the result would have been different; & permit me on behalf of hundreds, that as the four defunct Trustees were all Churchmen, it does seem reasonable that men of the like sentiments should be chosen to counterbalance an already predominating influence.

     Yours very respectfully,

     Thos Hayton

Charity Com.

1. James Webster Shrimpton, b. 1822.
2. Sylvannus Shrimpton, 1810–1887; surgical needlemaker; member of the celebrated Crendon brass band.

[169] To the Charity Commissioners

            Crendon, 5 October 1860

Gentlemen,

Last night a Meeting of the Trustees of the Dormer charity was held when I brought forward your letter of the 26th July touching the appointment of David Dodwell & Sylvannus Shrimpton in order that a reply should be given to that letter.

After attending to the objections, I stated to the Meeting & recorded it on the minutes that if David Dodwell's appointment be confirmed, the case would stand thus; —

Robert Dodwell the Father
Andrew Dodwell the son ⎫
David Dodwell the son ⎬ overseers
James Dodwell nephew to Robert ⎭
Joseph Dodwell nephew also to Robert

From this there would be, *Father* & two sons & *two nephews; four cousins* & *two brothers-in-law* & the *first three* rack-renters under Joseph Dodwell, the truth was admitted.

Then as to Sylvannus Shrimpton. His 'position in life & habits'. He is a working needle maker, employing only one boy, occupying till recently a cottage at 2/— per week & rated at £2, never having fulfilled any parochial office till the present time, he now being a parish constable, tho' not venturing to make his own *returns;* at present he lives in his own cottage rated at £3.10s.

Not one particle of this could be denied. All is patent fact. And I beg to add, (as there seems to be a most dogged resistance among the Dodwells) that the said Sylvannus Shrimpton is completely under the thumb of Joseph Dodwell from a monied bond; that his associates are of the commonest order, himself playing in a band at Country Wakes & his daily habit — a round at each pot-house in the village, & yet he is chosen as Trustee to the exclusion of independent men!

A proposition however was made (of which you will have noted by a communication from James Dodwell) that, the Meeting of Trustees comprising eight in number, was satisfied with the appointments, & therefore requested your confirmation of them. The proposition was made by Joseph Dodwell & voted for by three other Dodwells, & their collar-maker George Gibson — two or three with myself not voting: the parish Churchwarden & Mr Reynolds the owner of Notley Abbey not being present, both asserting that until Messrs Dodwells put in a reply to the objections they would not attend & that with such a predominating influence it was idle to do so.

There was much loud talking about your authority & that certain parties would not be dictated to on account of the appointment etc.

At times it requires a manifestation of power to make some people feel or act.

Trusting that you will take such steps as may make us an independent body of Trustees,

        I remain, Gentlemen, yours truly,

        Thos Hayton
        Vicar of Long Crendon

Charity Com.

Crendon, 4 December 1860

Gentlemen,

I am at last happy to say that after upward of 30 years agitation in the face of the most dogged opposition of two or three individuals, the Monument of Sir John Dormer in the parish Church here has been restored according to the Order of the Court here & finished to the satisfaction of every one at the cost of £71.15s.0d. It is an Elaborate structure illuminated with Emblematics of the date of 1605. We trust to be able to carry out the restoration of the *railings* in the course of another year.

At a Meeting of the Trustees of the Charities on Friday last, your Letter touching the election of Mr David Dodwell & Sylvannus Shrimpton for Trustees was read, but no step was taken to-wards the carrying out of your recommendation, tho' there were vacant Trusteeships. The parish Churchwarden informs me that Mr Joseph Dodwell, the great leader of that name, avers that nothing shall induce him to listen to your recommendation; (nay I myself have heard him doubt your power) that he will call upon you shortly to state what he calls his 'case' & persuade you to confirm the appointment of his cousin & Tenant & Sylvannus Shrimpton: and, if he fails in doing so, he will retire from his Trusteeship & induce as many as he can to do the same, with a variety of rather minatory remarks. — Allow me, at the risk of being tedious, to tell you he institutes comparisons about his family & others that they hold one fourth of the Land & therefore that there should be 4 Trustees of that name! Certainly the Dodwells *rent* about 800 acres out of the 3500 in the parish; but that this should be a ground for monopoly in the distribution of the Charities is somewhat novel. — He also argues that because of some of the Trustees being *brothers-in-law*, that the same tie of relationship is on them as those of his name. This is utter nonsense; those who are brothers-in-law are independent of each other in every respect & have not acted in any combined manner. Then he compares Sylvannus Shrimpton with my Churchwarden Mr Matthew Henry Shrimpton as being equal in position etc, but tho' my Churchwarden is of the same trade, he employs three or four men, occupies land also, married into one of the most respectable families & is a man of acquirement, of uprightness & of unblemished moral character. — He also insists that the appointment was a fair one, whereas it was notoriously tricky & in violation of an understanding that a Mr Watson, one of the most respectable men in the parish & living in the House of J. Stone esq was to be chosen; & when accused of this by Mr J. Cousens Crook, he merely apologised by saying 'He would not pleasure the parson', a noble principle of action truly! Whereas I never requested anyone to become a Trustee. — As to Mr Dodwell resigning his Trusteeship, I have only to say that it would be received with delight; for he scarcely ever attends a Meeting but he creates a disturbance; & recently I was compelled from his blustering & insults to send for the Policeman to take him away — his object being, I am told, to disgust me & for himself to become Chairman! This is the acme of village ambition. You will find him very specious, & very stubborn. Mr Grenville Pigott of the Poor Law Board knows his obstinacy, having been compelled to put the law into force against him for his perverseness as a Guardian; & when he lived in a neighbouring village of Chilton (where Mr Vane's relation lives) he was ejected from his farm by the late Col. Jones in consequence of his overbearing conduct. I have been requested to put you in possession of these facts, because he will assert anything to carry his point, whilst I most solemnly testify that not one farmer, not being a Trustee, whom I have met with, nor one labouring man approves of the appointments of Sylvannus Shrimpton & David Dodwell.

Pray, Gentlemen, excuse this long explanate, which in justice to others & myself I have entered into.

Believe me, most respectfully yours,

Thos Hayton

Charity Com.

[171] [Notes in the Parish Register]

29 December 1860

This year has been marked with the loss of many friends of the Church here, by death & by change of residence. I found it a great trial; & my anxious wish was, if possible, to leave the pastoral cares in the hand of a substitute. This I could not conveniently effect for many reasons. The restoration of Sir John Dormer's Monument was at hand; & after all the opposition I had met with in my endeavour to see justice done to Sir John's Memory, I thought it my duty, as it was one of my greatest pleasures, to oversee the doing of it. I have lived to see partial justice rendered & hope, if God permit, to see in another year the rails & the windows put also in repair.

In the year 1821, after preaching a sermon on John the Baptist, an anonymous letter was sent me informing me that 'John the Dormer' was also a great Character & Benefactor to the poor, but that he had been in the wilderness for years & nothing had been heard of him. This alluded to the Charity not having been applied as the Deed of Sir John specified. Some years passed before I could get a sight of the Deed; at last it came forth about the time a Government Commission was issued (1827) and promises were given that for the future every thing should be done correctly. In two or three years, however, the charity became applied to the able-bodied agricultural labourers to the exclusion of the widows and aged & a kind of eking out miserably-paid labour. Hence application was made to the Commissioners of Charities for a scheme more in accordance with the will of the donor. To this the farmers were very adverse; & for three years opposition was made, but at length the Scheme as now in existence was carried through the County Court, & ordered the Restoration of the Monument. But who was to restore it? This was a mooted question & brought with it many difficulties & differences of opinion; & three more years passed before the matter was effected. The Trustees as a body asserted their right of selecting a person for the work & the amount of work to be done; I maintained the right of the Minister & Churchwardens to nominate the person, & that the restoration should be entirely under direction, which view was supported by the Commissioners as may be found by their letters & consequently light began to dawn & a Mr Peyman of Abingdon was chosen to do the work. His estimate was £71.15s. for the Monument without the Railing; & he has been most satisfactory [&]

135

carried out his undertaking. When the cause of justice suceeds, we cannot but rejoice & if my successor reads this with all its concomitant circumstances let him never despair when a good cause is before him.

[signed] Thomas Hayton, Vicar

January 1861

The last year 1860 was also remarkable for considerable excitement in Ireland, Scotland & Wales as to religious Revivalism. Many contradictory statements as to the result were made — *time* only will show whether the work was of God or man. In our village much apparent earnestness was shown; about thirty young girls & a few men, who to specify would be needless, sought for Baptism at the hands of strange preachers; were admitted into the Baptist connection without much ceremony, & for a time were very earnest. The Elders of the Baptist Connection did not rely much on this show of zeal, & others looking on, predicted nothing permanent from it, & as I had witnessed previous 'Rousings' & consequent 'lapsings' had not much faith in their religious, hysterical, demonstrations; & now on a calm review of the whole, I believe that religion has suffered in the House of its friends, by setting neighbour against neighbour, party against party, & by an assumption of spiritual pride & a craving for novelty which seems unable to satisfy itself. Nor during the last two years, since the Baptists starved out their Minister — a quiet & simple man — there has been upwards of a hundred preachers in the village — boys & men 18 years of age upwards (sent under the sanction of a Mr Spurgeon, a popular Baptist preacher in London) dealing out a quantity of Joe Miller's jests & pretending that God was blessing their Ministry by conversions wholesale, at the conclusion of their ranting addresses, coolly asked if any were labourers, under conversion from their words, if so to come to them in the Vestry, confess their sins & be comforted. This, however, has passed away, & the fair young females, who wept sentimentally their wonted smiles & human love has shown itself more active than divine. Even Mr Spurgeon himself who preached here under a large Tent has not produced any visible effect; indeed his address, I am told, was a quiet & sensible one, with strong rebuke at the want of order & unity in the Baptist connection which from distracted opinion cannot agree as to the choice of a Minister. One thing is very apparent — they are all deeply set against the Church of England & her ordinances, ignoring the Sacraments & using all their influence to misrepresent & to make proselytes. False-hearted ones have left us; & others, unstable, driven about with every wind of doctrine, come to Church occasionally & cannot discern between opposite principles; still, the Church has no reason to complain, tho' each shop in the village where human food & clothing is to be had, is under the influence of one family which monopolizes & makes each labourer purchase his goods of a relative under all the evils of the Truck System [1]. A day may come when the chains of an accursed system may be broken & moral & spiritual tyranny may cease to exercise that control which is degrading to the character of a Freeman and a Christian.

B.R.O. P.R. 134/1/8

1. Amos, Andrew and Ezra Dodwell were grocers, Edward had a general store and David, Samuel and James were bakers as well as farmers.

Crendon, 12 March 1861

Gentlemen,

Yesterday a meeting of the Trustees was called of which the following are the Minutes:

Notice

'We, the undersigned, being Trustees of the Sir John Dormer Charity do hereby give notice, that a special Meeting of the Trustees of the said Charity will be held at the Churchill Arms on the eleventh day of March next at 6 o'clock in the evening for the purpose of appointing three Trustees to fill up the vacancies in their number caused by the death of Edward Shrimpton & of William Hanson & by George Wainwright not having attended any meeting of the Trustees for a consecutive period of two years & upwards; to nominate acting Trustees for the current year, & to select fitting persons as recipients of the Charity, and you are hereby summoned to attend such meeting accordingly'

> signed Thomas Hayton, Vicar
> William Crook
> Matthew H. Shrimpton   dated this 25th Feb 1861

The above was served on each Trustee.
The following Trustees were present:
Thos Hayton, Mr Henry Reynolds, Mr Cousens Crook, & Mr Matthew Henry Shrimpton

'There not being a sufficient number of Trustees present, the Meeting was dissolved, sine die, with a request to be made to the Commissioners of Charity, either to send down as Inspector or to advise the best way of proceeding. T.H.'

I beg to add a remark or two to the above. All that we want is Fair play & independent Trustees, & that one family should not dominate over the whole The Messrs Dodwell (who are Legion) put a *fourth* of the name as *overseer* last year for the express purpose of adding another of their number. This was felt both out of the village & in the village as a grievous imposition.

Yesterday they agreed not to attend & to 'put the screw' upon two of their dependent tradespeople in order to thwart our purpose. The two Churchwardens & myself with Mr Reynolds of Notley Abbey the largest resident landowner in the parish were unanimous in the wish that you would settle the matter for us. William Crook also, who signed the Notice could not attend & another farmer was prevented. Your interpretation is really wanted; for all is at a standstill. A Box was ordered to keep the Books & Deeds in, but that was used as a *hat box* & is now without a key, & never seen nor used & the Deeds are still at Thame. There has scarcely been a legal notice given for years — a man being sent about on the day of the Meeting, very often only half an hour before the time; & the poor recipients of the Charity are held waiting shivering in the cold for upwards of an hour & then have to go to the House of the Acting Trustee, Mr James Dodwell, to receive their pittance. Consider these things & come to the rescue.

If you have power to select three Trustees & to do so would be gratifying to many, I append a few names who would work independently:

137

Mr Jacob Watson, farmer
Mr Charles Henry King, farmer [1]
Mr William Reynolds, miller
Mr Richard Hanson, farmer [2]
Mr Thomas Crook, farmer [3]
It grieves me to be so tiresome; but really it cannot be helped.

I am, Gentlemen, respectfully yours,

Thos Hayton

Charity Com.

1. Charles Henry King: tenant of Thame Mead Farm.
2. Richard Hanson; rented the Glebe Farm from Thomas Hayton.
3. Thomas Crook; farmed Butler's Hill.

[173] *To the Poor Law Board*

Crendon, 16 December 1861

Gentlemen,

Yours of the 16th I duly received; and I beg you to say that the *cool impudence* of the Relieving Officer, John Jonas Shrimpton, is most astounding. I myself called upon him about a year ago expressly on the very subject, of his referring applicants to the Guardian of the parish, showing him how unfair it was towards the poor, when his excuse was — his very words were — 'if he *did not refer* them to the Guardian, he would never hear the end of it and the explanation was, he would be bullied'. — I mentioned this to a gentleman at the time conversant with the Workhouse doings & he now can remember accurately what I said — I also spoke to a Guardian of the Union respecting such practice & he told me that it was an understood thing among them. It is not a month since a poor man named Thomas Ing of this parish aged 75, with a bed-ridden wife & a silly daughter & he himself suffering from rupture, applied to the said relieving officer for relief or admission to the workhouse & was refused (tho' he had been 3 weeks out of work) and *expressly referred* to Mr *Joseph Dodwell* the Guardian of the parish, & to this the poor man is ready to swear before any Commissioner or Tribunal. Indeed the whole parish knows it to be a patent verity.

Then as to George Gibson. The officer *knew* that Gibson had been without work for a month, & that the putting him off from the 21st to the 25th of the month was only a trick. Gibson's wife on the 22nd called for an order as she was led to expect, & was refused; hence her begging round the village for her starving children, the very words of Shrimpton, the officer being 'that from what he could see no man who rented any land would be employed either on the roads or by the farmers' — No *right* was claimed *for employment* at all. On the 26th the Surveyor put Gibson on the Road, saying, that he would occasionally employ him, just to keep him out of the Workhouse — *this* is the trick; & a man with a wife & 5 children under ten years of age received 8/— per week for their support!!! I think I have sufficiently replied to the impudent & lying assertion of the officer who mixes

138

up with his duties, Wesleyan tendencies as a local preacher, hence complaints of partiality are frequently made to me.

> Leaving this in your hands, Gentlemen, I remain yours truly,
>
> Thos Hayton

[*minute*]
20 December 1861
The state of feeling that has long prevailed between Mr Hayton and Mr Dodwell the head of the dissenting interest, is sufficiently clear by the tone of these letters.

M.H. 12/9740

[174] To 'The Poor Law Commissioners or to Colonel Pigott'
> Crendon, 22 November 1861

Gentlemen,

Many and loud are the complaints of the Laborers in this parish of the treatment they meet with at the Board of Guardians at Thame, & by the relieving officer who uniformly refers every applicant for relief to the Guardian of the Parish — Mr Joseph Dodwell — who also is the Chairman of the Board at Thame.

The following case has been submitted to me this morning & I have been urgently requested to write to you respecting it: — 'George Gibson, Laborer, age 34 — an able bodied man with wife & three children — ages 6, 4, & 2 — has not had 5 days work for upwards of a month; has not one sixpence of money nor one measure of corn of any sort, neither has the wife any means of subsistence. The husband attended at the Board of Guardians yesterday when he was refused an order for the House & referred to the Relieving Officer today who told him that there was nothing for him & that because he rented an acre of land neither he nor any others who did so would either be relieved or set to work by the Surveyor'. — I will offer no comment upon this; all Christian principle revolts at this petty grinding system — a mixture of meanness & revenge; & if you can do any thing in such matters either in the way of remonstrance or advice, you would be conferring a public benefit as this is but a sample of a system prevailing around us.

> I am, Gentlemen, respectfully yours,
>
> Thos Hayton
> Vicar of Long Crendon

N.B. Gibson is a steady, sober, civil & industrious man: as are many others — now unemployed, & to-day begging around the village.

[*Minute by Grenville Pigott*]
A copy of this letter should be sent to the Board of Health for their observations. The case, however extreme, is an individual case and the Chairman of the Board of Guardians & the Vicar of Long Crendon residing in the same

place have long been at variance — The Guardians may be told that the renting an acre of land is no sufficient grounds for withholding relief if the applicant is destitute. If this be doubtful — the Workhouse is the appointed test. G.P.

M.H. 12/9740

[175] *To the Editor of the* Buckinghamshire Advertiser

[Date unknown *c*. 1862—3]

Sir,

Will you allow me to make a few observations, through the medium of your valuable paper, upon the illtreatment of the poor of the parish of Long Crendon by its authorities. I will content myself by only giving you one case, as it would require too large a space to mention any more at this time. The case that I shall bring before you is that of a man, his wife and five small children — and here I would have you bear in mind this poor man was brought up a respectable farmer's son. In the year 1844 he entered into business, and with strict economy, combined with habits of industry, he could not succeed, and at length was brought to the condition he is now — a poor man. I shall pass over the history of this individual from that time up to the beginning of September in the present year, when his wife and eldest daughter were seized with the typhus fever. He then applied to the Chairman of the Board for a nurse, who, with a stern look and a few cross words — which the poor of this parish are familiar with, — sent him to the relieving officer [1] and the officer sent him one. Now, Mr Editor, this nurse could not stop with them at nights, but came at eight o'clock in the morning and left at eight in the evening. In the course of a few days the other four children fell ill with the same disease, so that you will perceive this poor man had to look after his wife and five children at night and then go to work all day. Application was made to the parish for some relief, but instead of relieving this distressed family, they did not so much as entertain the case, treating it with contempt, because he had two or three friends who very kindly stepped forward to render them assistance; and had it not been for this kindness, they must have been completely cast away. In a few weeks this poor man himself fell ill, and the nurse not being able to be with them at night, the whole family were compelled to be locked in by themselves. Now, Sir, suppose anything had caught fire in the night, they might have been burnt to death — some of them being delirious at the time. Mr Editor, this is indeed a hard case. Application was again made for relief, when the rigorous officer came to visit them, and going up stairs, said, 'Oh! oh! oh! oh! open your mouth and show me your tongue', pretending to know as much as a medical man, instead of giving them relief which was needed. On the 17th of November, this poor man arose at half past seven, and, having made a fire went up stairs to ask his wife to have a piece of toast and a drop of coffee, when, behold, he found her dead and yet then the case is rejected in disdain.

This state of things, Sir, is allowed to be carried on in the midst of an abundance of Christian professors; and it is a well-known fact that several

140

farmers of this village, for want of room in their rickyards, have been obliged to build their produce in the field after harvest. Oh, ye opulent farmers, and some of you profess to be Christ's disciples; how can you grind down and oppress the poor in this way? Talk about American slavery, you are equally as bad in principle, and some of you would be as bad in practice if you had it in your power.

Now, Sir, I will challenge the parish to say anything against the character of this poor man, or disprove any of the statements I have made. I am afraid of trespassing too long on your space, bidding you farewell for the present,

I am, yours, &c.,

CHARITY

[*Note in Thomas Hayton's handwriting*]
Jonas Shrimpton than whom no greater liar existed [1].

B.R.O. P.R. 134/1/4

1. John Jonas Shrimpton. Relieving Officer since 1841. He was responsible for giving outdoor relief. Resigned. (O.R.O. V/i/14).

[*176*] *To the Poor Law Board*

Crendon, 14 November 1862

Gentlemen,

I have been requested by the relations of 'Sarah Coles' to write to you touching her case which is to this effect:— Her Husband 'Benjamin Coles' is now in this parish which he avers is his settlement; he is dangerously ill — the last stage of dropsy, with *no means* whatsoever — indeed receiving with his three children 4 loaves and 1/6 weekly from the *Thame* Union. His wife 'Sarah' is now in the Bath Union Workhouse with three children, & she wishes to be removed to this place, or to receive assistance out of the Workhouse. — It appears that her husband has not been living with her during the last three years; & that some alleged impediment to her removal here exists in consequence of their temporary estrangement and of some recent enactment. Would you therefore have the kindness to make some enquiry on this really distressing subject, in order that either of the objects might be effected. The husband is very anxious to see his wife once more & be reconciled; & as the wife is respectably connected, her relatives are willing, if she were out of the Workhouse, to assist her in her endeavours to get a livelihood for her children. The Guardians of the Bath Union, have as I have been informed, refused any assistance in any way, pleading the force of some recent order or Act of Parliament.

If you could intercede in this matter, I am sure it would be beneficial for all parties.

I am yours respectfully,

Thomas Hayton
Vicar of Long Crendon

141

[*Extract from answer from the Poor Law Board*]
The Guardians, however, cannot legally take any steps to remove the woman
and her children to Long Crendon.

M.H. 12/9741

[*177*] To the Poor Law Board

Crendon, 18 November 1862

Gentlemen,

Yours of yesterday the 17th I have duly received. I am sorry to have
troubled you. Inasmuch as Sarah Coles through the medium of some local
charity at Bath, arrived here on Saturday, so that the parishes must fight it
out. The Father has been relieved here, and the Mother at Bath.

I am yours respectfully,

Thomas Hayton
Vicar of Long Crendon

M.H. 12/9741

[*178*] To the Poor Law Board

Crendon, 21 April 1863

Gentlemen,

Mr Joseph Dodwell is Chairman of the Board of Guardians at *Thame;*
Chairman of the Committee appointed to examine the returns of the
parochial rate; *overseer of the parish* of Long Crendon & has sent in a valuation
objected to by a great many of the Inhabitants — (indeed, *neither of the
churchwardens* approve of it) — who purpose to appeal, especially against the
valuation of his own farm & that of his brother overseer. A question has
arisen whether he should sit as Chairman or vote on appeals against his own
valuation. Many of us think it very unfair for him to do so, especially as he
has a brother on the Committee, thus in all probability, backing his own
opinion by three votes; will you therefore have the kindness to give us your
opinion on the subject & whether you think it accords with the practice of
English Courts?

I am, Gentlemen, yours very respectfully,

Thomas Hayton
Vicar of Long Crendon

[*Note:* The reply from the Poor Law Board mentioned that there was no
actual illegality in these proceedings.]

M.H. 12/9741

142

Crendon, 25 April 1864

Dear Mr Batcheldor,

The felling of the Elm Trees into the Churchyard has done much damage thereto; & the wall in different places is completely down. Will you have the kindness to represent this stage of things to the Chapter in order that the damage & repairs may be forthwith seen into?

The claimants for the Timber I would conceive are responsible for both the one & the other, especially as the wall became undermined by the roots of the trees, which wall of itself was substantial & perfectly satisfactory both to the Churchwardens & myself. An early reply will greatly oblige.

   Yours respectfully,

   Thos Hayton

Windsor

Crendon 6 June 1864

Dear Mr Batcheldor,

The enclosed is an estimate for the repairs of the ... [torn] ... damage done by the felling of the trees: I hope you will as soon as possible order their restoration.

The churchwardens have requested me to address them to you as requested.

   Yours very truly,

   Thos Hayton

Windsor

Crendon, 18 June 1864

Dear Sir,

My absence from home accounts for my not replying to your note.

Mr Crook, the Churchwarden & myself have been up the Churchyard & measured the dilapidated wall; & find it 60 ft in length by 2 yards high — this is what *Staples* [1] damaged in felling the Trees. — The other part of the wall including the gate way is in a rickety condition & the Churchwardens thought that by including it — the repair would be effectual.

I beg to inform you that the parishioners reject all ownership of that wall & the east wall which have uniformly been repaired by the Lessee [2]. In my 46 years residence here, I have known Mr Stone repair both walls as his Father always did.

This is frequently the case in these parts that the whole of the Church-yard wall does not belong to the parish as both Thame & adjoining places testify. I mention this because you seemed to express a strong opinion on this point.

I beg also to remind you of the damage done to the graves & to the daily damage of the herbage.

> Yours respectfully,
>
> Thos Hayton

Windsor

1. Staples, Timber Merchants, Middle Row, Thame.
2. The south wall is the garden wall of Windsor Farm (now the Manor House) and the east wall borders its paddock.

[182] To Mr Batcheldor

Crendon, 11 July [1864]

Dear Sir,

The Churchwardens & myself are about to give the Sunday School Scholars a Treat on Wednesday [1], and as our funds are not overflowing, will you kindly consider us with a trifle? I have never before asked you for anything (except to accommodate us with a speedy repair of the Churchyard wall — this is a last hook as you would say); & as I am told that an appeal of this sort you are not inattentive to, perhaps you will let us hear from you by return of Post.

> Yours very respectfully,
>
> Thos Hayton

P.S. I was too late at Winchester for the May fly, & the weather was too bright, I could not get one at all.

Windsor

1. The Church Sunday School had its party in the Vicarage garden.

[183] To Mr Batcheldor

Crendon, 19 August [1864]

Dear Mr Batcheldor,

May I remind you of your promise touching the churchyard wall? Mr

144

Watson is very anxious to hear from you. I am sure all your ecclesiastical sentiments would suffer at a second sight of such dilapidations.

> Yours very faithfully,

> Thos Hayton

P.S. No fishing weather yet. Respectful compliments to Mrs Batcheldor.

Windsor

[184] To Mr Batcheldor

Crendon, 5 November [1864]

Dear Mr Batcheldor,

Shrimpton has built up the wall to the satisfaction of the Church-wardens & myself & would be glad if you would send him a cheque for the amount of the contract £5.15s. He has done more than was specified, because a part of the standing wall should not be worked into. If you will make him a trifling allowance for that, he will point up & white mark the whole of the wall & then that side would correspond with the other.

May I request of you to remember Watson & his family? The dilapidated state of the farm yard wall would, if you saw it, enlist your sympathies with him.

If not done soon, it may be months before the repairs be done & you know that a hurdle is a poor defence against cattle. Do have the goodness to let us hear from you at your earliest convenience.

> Yours very respectfully,

> Thos Hayton

My respects to Mrs Batcheldor.

Windsor

[185] To the Revd Mr Moore [1]

Crendon, 16 November [1864]

Revd. Sir,

Shrimpton [2] the Mason of this place has requested me to ask you whether you accept his contract for £6 to repair the farm yard wall which the felling of the Trees so seriously damaged? The tenant, Mr Watson has been & is suffering from the continual neglect of repairs, & twice has Mr Batcheldor been written to without reply, to say nothing of a promise made to me when I called upon him in August.

I gave permission (with reluctance I will admit) for two of the large

145

trees to fall into the Churchyard, in order to avoid very serious damage to the Dwelling house & premises belonging to you, & was assured that recompense would be made for any displacement of graves & head stones. I find on examination that 26 graves require new turfing which at 6d per grave − 13/−, add to this the replacement of a head stone another 6d; & then after the Sexton I must make a claim for loss of herbage for a part of the Churchyard during 8 months & the cost of laying down new turf; this at least should be 10/−.

I make this simple demand on the score of justice − I might have pleaded for some acknowledgement either to the day School, Dorcas Society or Clothing Club, as I never received anything from the Lessee for any Institution.

> I am Revd Sir, respectfully yours,
>
> Thos Hayton
> Vicar of Crendon

Windsor

1. The Hon. Edward George Moore, Canon of Windsor 1834 to 1882.
2. John Shrimpton, mason. b. 1808.

[186] To Mr Batcheldor

Long Crendon, 19 November [1864]

Dear Mr Batcheldor,

Your not having replied either to Mr Watson's communication or mine, & Mr Moore having written to Shrimpton we inferred that you were unwell; hence my letter to Mr Moore.

If .the felling of the trees was a necessity, there was no necessity that they should be felled & damage the Churchyard. It was a favour granted to Mr Leper, which instead of a Trivial claim on the lowest estimate, ought to have been met forthwith in a liberal spirit.

As for the wall of the farm premises I should not have troubled you at all about it, had I not been requested to do so, & as for Shrimpton's charges, the acceptance rested with yourself.

The man has been employed all the summer by Lord Churchill & no demur has ever been made either as to work or charge.

Moreover, he works cheaper than any other mason in the neighbourhood.

I am sorry to have caused you so much trouble.

> Yours truly,
>
> Thos Hayton

Windsor

[187] *To the Revd Mr Moore*

Crendon, 12 December 1864

Revd Sir,

The Sexton has spoken to me again touching the payment of his labour, upon the graves, to the amount of 13/—! The reply I had from Mr Batcheldor was that he would *recommend* payment of this as well as the damage of 10/— done to the herbage [1] for 8 months. Would you have the kindness to interpose your authority for the settlement of this, or to tell me whether Mr Batcheldor is the accredited agent for you? It seems useless to write to him & everyone is astonished at the treatment received both by the Lepers & myself, — receiving damage at the profit of so highly respected a corporation as Windsor College.

I am respectfully yours,

Thos Hayton

Windsor

1. It was customary for vicars to let the churchyard for pasturage, hence the practice of the well-to-do to erect iron railings round the graves of their relatives. (J.H. Brown and W. Guest, *History of Thame*, p. 203.)

[188] *To the Revd Mr Moore*

Long Crendon, 20th [December 1864]

Dear Sir,

I enclose you a receipt according to your request & remain

Yours truly,

Thos Hayton

At the request of the sexton I have enclosed his Bill. T.H.

Windsor

[189] *Churchwardens' Book*

21 December 1864

Minutes of a public vestry held on the 16th December 1864 Notice affixed to the Church Door by John Warner, sexton of the parish.

In accordance with the Notice specified on the other side, a Vestry was held at the Church, but adjourned to the Courtroom when the object of the Vestry was explained to the Vicar; some suggestions were made to raise by subscriptions the amount of money required, but any Resolution to that effect the Vicar declined to put to the Meeting; but the following proposition was made by Mr Henry Reynolds & seconded by Mr J.C. Crook:

"the rate of one penny in the pound based on the poor rate of the parish be granted to the Churchwardens to carry out the repairs specified in the Notice & which an Estimate had been made, & as far as dissenters were concerned the money was to be collected on the voluntary principle."
signed Thos Hayton, Henry Reynolds, John Cozens Crook, Thos Crook, Jacob Watson

The above proposition was carried, 9 for the rate & 5 against it. The amount of the Estimate for the rate was stated at £21.0s.0d. The mode of collection for the dissenters was adopted with the Vicar & under a promise from some, that more money would be given than the ratal proposition:

T.H.

B.R.O. P.R. 134/5/1

[190] To the Charity Commissioners
Crendon, 11 December 1866

Gentlemen,

I enclose the Acceptance of Trust & the parties nominated.

Whether I clearly expressed one meaning or not in reference to Hart's Charity, your reply seems not to meet the case — which is 3 years Income of that Charity is now in our hands; & if we cannot find any one qualified, or anyone willing to take a boy for so small a sum, are we justified in carrying over to the Charitable Fund the *3 years accumulation.*

Yours respectfully,

Thos Hayton
Vicar of Long Crendon

A reply before the 21st Dec will oblige.

Charity Com.

[191] To the Bursar of Windsor
Crendon, 24 July 1867

Mr Bursar,

I wrote to the Dean [1] in reference to the repair of the Old Court Room here — rather urgently because it is in a dangerous state & because when I agreed to keep the internal part in repair, the Three Lords agreed to keep the covering etc. in good repair — I have the consent of the other Lords to do this needful repair, & I hope you will give your consent — the cost of your part will be only 33/—. You will indeed greatly oblige me by a reply by return of Post.

Yours respectfully,

Thos Hayton
Vicar of Crendon

Windsor.

1. Rev. and Hon. Gerald Wellesley (1809—1882); Dean of Windsor (1854 to 1882); 3rd son of the 1st Baron Cowley.

[192] To the Ecclesiastical Commissioners [1]

Crendon, 26 July 1867

Gentlemen,

In reply to a communication of mine to the Dean & Canons of Windsor, as one of the three Lords of the Manor, requesting their consent to the payment of a third share of certain repairs of the Room where the Court Leet is annually held, I was informed that their estates had passed into your hands [2], & that I must briefly state my case to you & respectfully request your earliest attention to it.

Some 30 years ago this old Court Room was in a sad, dilapidated, filthy state, with only wooden slide windows, unceilinged etc., I applied to the Lords for their consent (which I obtained) for me to make it suitable as a place for the Sunday Scholars (for we have no daily school in this large parish) on these conditions — I undertaking to put in new windows etc & keeping the interior in good repair, they promised to keep the roof & other parts in good order. It cost me nearly £50 to do this, & all except a portion of the roof is in excellent condition. The building is a quaint, ancient structure called the 'Staple Hall' in ancient writings: a few weeks ago the braces of the purlin on one side of the building gave way, & we are now fearful of some accident from a portion of the roof falling off, the repair of which will cost five pounds according to a given estimate, to which estimate & repairs the two Lords have given their approval; & as I conceive that you stand in relation as the other Lords of the Manor, may I request your sanction to such estimate & repairs? Your earliest attention will greatly oblige.

Yours very respectfully,

Thomas Hayton
Vicar of Long Crendon

P.S. The solicitor to the two Lords is a Mr Parker of Thame, who holds the Annual Court — a very respectable man and whom I confidently recommend to you. Mr Digby Green, — one of your secretaries knows the room & is partly acquainted with the Parish.

All Souls College — one of the Lords — feels interested about a daily School & the Warden has promised me help, perhaps you also could help forward such an object, for the farmers care very little about education, hitherto I have tried them in vain.

T.H.

[*Extract from the answer of the Commissioners*]
17 August
'The Commissioners are not prepared to comply with your request — the Commissioners generally subscribe only to day schools.'

Ch Com. F.37788

1. The Ecclesiastical Commissioners were created by an Act of Parliament in 1836 (6–7 William IV c. 77).
2. In 1840, the Dean and Chapter Act (3 & 4 Victoria c. 113) paved the way for reform by taking away patronage etc. from the Chapters. During the sixties, pressure was put on the Chapters to transfer their estates to the newly formed Estates Committee of the Commissioners.

[193] To the Ecclesiastical Commissioners
Crendon, 1 August [1867]

Gentlemen,

Mr G. of Lymington has somewhat urged me to send to you the enclosed extracts from the Parish Award, to which I have added a remark or two for which a Rectorial inference may be drawn [1]; but this I leave entirely to your better knowledge.

I have had a struggle against powerful opposition for nearly 50 years but am still hearty & strong & only require some extraneous assistance to institute a daily school, the want of which in this large village is a standing disgrace to us. Since one of the best estates has passed into your hands from the Dean & Canons of Windsor, I hope I may have the pleasure of hearing that you are willing to lend a helping hand to this desirable object.

Yours very respectfully,

T. Hayton

[*Answer (abstract)*]
17 August 1867
'The Commissioners are not prepared to comply with your request. The Commissioners only subscribe to day schools . . . Permit me to remind you that all letters addressed to this Office through the post are liable to postage, sixpence was paid here for the unpaid postage on your two communications.'

Ch Com. F.37788

1. In the Enclosure Award, Lord Churchill, the Lay Improprietor obtained 554 acres in lieu of tithes and Hayton 78 acres for 'half of the wool and certain grass ground called futhages.' (B.P.O. Long Crendon Enclosure Award).

[194] To the Secretary of the Ecclesiastical Commission
Crendon, 19 August 1867

Sir,

The repairs of the Building to which I alluded have been defrayed by the three respective Lords of the Manor (of which Windsor College was one) from the origin of the Court Rolls some hundreds of years ago. A Court Leet is held annually in this room and a dinner provided for the Copyholders of the respective Manorial Lords. As it was a fair agreement between the Lords, I hope on further consideration that the Commissioners will see the justice of the claim for such a small sum, and will not force a poor parson to do that which belongs to a wealthy body. I would not have urged the matter so soon, but the side-slip of the House is dangerous to the public.

> I am Sir, yours respectfully,

> Thos Hayton

P.S. I enclose stamps for the postage of my two letters.

Ch Com. F.37788

---

[195] From the Bucks Advertiser
27 July 1868

Correspondence
THE ARCHDEACON'S VISITATION.

To the Editor of the Bucks Advertiser & Aylesbury News

Mr Editor,

Last week you gave us a narrative of and comment on the Charge of your Archdeacon. Permit me as one of the working clergy to remark on the sequel of that gathering. After the Charge, which was less lengthy than usual, a charge was made upon the good things provided by mine host of the George Inn, advertised at 4s. per head and charged 4s.6d. The company was pretty numerous. The absence of many of the clergy and the presence of many churchwardens was remarkable, and herein nothing perhaps was lost. The Archdeacon took the chair, and in his usual mellifluous tones gave us a toast 'Church and Queen' or, as it was understood, 'Church and State', One rural dean, in his speech, thought the toast was coldly received; but after the 'Health of the Bishop and Archdeacon' met with such cordiality he could not attribute that coldness to any want of sympathy. This was a somewhat singular mode of inference, and not very logical; because these pillars of the Church were admired, it did not follow that the whole structure was in good order. Dogmatic toasts like dogmatic teaching are not in these days taken 'all for granted'. In the English as well as the Irish Church there are abuses which require correction; and a National Church Establishment should have clean hands and pure conduct, lest she loses her hold on the affections of the people. The Irish Branch of the Church is now the question of the day, and it is a difficult one [1]. More than half the tithes, which belonged to the

151

Church before the Reformation are now in the hands of laymen, who not only exact the payment of them most rigorously but do no service in return; for instance, the whole tithes of 115 parishes and a greater or less share of the tithes of 633 parishes, yielding £11,400 per annum, are in the hands of lay impropriators. The Marquis of Donegal has the tithes of 28 parishes; the Duke of Devonshire of 26; the Earl of Cork of 17; the Earl of Shannon of 11, &c. Are these tithe-usurpers to continue in quiet possession of this ill-gotten property, to which they have no rightful claim, unless time can alter the immutable nature of great moral principles? Had these abuses been fairly specified and the State pointed out as a Trustee or Guardian of Church property, not its Proprietor; had we been told in what the Union of Church and State consisted — and that the best of Dissenters, Dr Doddridge, Dr Owen, Mr Baxter and Mr Conder, held that giving Christianity the sanction of Law and the support of a public profession was the best policy — the acceptance of the toast would have lost its coldness and Mr Evetts been spared his floundering apology.

After complimenting the staff officers around him, it was suggested that the 'Working Clergy' should not be forgotten; but this was uncourteously ignored. There was, however, utterance given to what seemed like a libel on good old times, when* Heslop [2] and Hill were consuls. A rural dean in his speech stated that not long ago the clergy came to the visitation equipped for the hunting field, in top boots and riding whip! Having for half a century witnessed these meetings, I never saw one single instance of this. At any rate it was no great compliment to those clergy present who, if their garments were clerically *subfuss*,[†] many of them were bearded 'like the pard' — shaggy and *foxy* — with a certain costume in sympathy with Romish priests, barring the shaven crown and dangling cross. When the late Bishop of London was in a chrysalis state he appeared at a visitation at Aylesbury in a most *recherché* riding dress and whip; and on the Sussex Downs our eloquent Samuel [3] in former times disdained not equestrian dress and the cheer of the huntsman, so that which was meant for a complimentary comparison appears to fail in its application; and I verily believe that the churchwardens present prefer for their clergy the dress of country life to the prim formal cut of modern times, ecclesiastical millinery not being of their taste. This one-sided compliment was all that proceeded either from Archdeacon or Rural Deans in reference to the working clergy. Officers in a regiment are all very showy and well, but *they* never won a battle. 'It was my own serried ranks, my left shoulder forward men that won my battles', said Wellington; and it is the working clergy, who come in contact with poverty, ignorance, and vice, who have to endure the contradiction of sinners against themselves, who to the sick and dying have to administer consolation, who have to raise up the down-trodden and bind up their wounds and cheer the sufferers amid tyranny and wrong — these are the Church's mainstay — these are the real militant, oftentimes with[‡] narrow means to meet the daily calls upon them for help in time of need, and who themselves frequently have to struggle with oftentimes less than mechanics' wages, whilst the officers of the church riot in overflowing abundance. It is no idle office is theirs who have devoted their lives to religious instruction as a bond of union and moral obligation to the State, and many a bitter head and heart-ache have they to endure when doing battle against infidelity, hyprocrisy, and spiritual wickedness in high places. Surely a word of comfort and encouragement might have been spared for them among the soft and complimentary nothings; neither would it have fallen flat upon the

152

ears of the churchwardens, but would have elicited a cheer louder and more earnest than any abstract sentiment of Church and State, how necessary soever such an alliance may be. I might, Mr Editor, have told you of the sensible remarks of an inspector of schools, and of a layman who spoke modestly and well, but I have exceeded the bounds I proposed for myself.

I am, Mr Editor,

One of the Working Clergy

*Both these Archdeacons were disciplinarians; and the Bishops Tomline, Pelham [4], and Kaye were no ordinary men.
†Vide "Oxford Statutes."
‡Ita miseris succurrere discunt.

B.R.O. P.R.134/1/0

1. In 1871, the Church of Ireland was disestablished with compensation to existing office holders.
2. Luke Heslop (1738–1825); archdeacon of Buckingham 1778 to 1825.
3. Bishop Wilberforce had been canon of Winchester and rector of Alverstoke from 1840 to 1846.
4. George Tomline, bishop of Lincoln 1800 to 1820; and George Pelham, bishop 1820 to 1827.

[196] Bishop Wilberforce's Triennial Visitation

15 September 1869

1. *Name — Date of induction?*
   Thomas Hayton 1821.

2. *Has he, been resident for 275 days a year?*
   Yes.

3. *Whole duty?*
   Performs the whole duty.

4. *Other benefices?*
   Yes, Lower Winchendon.

5. *Is the Curate licensed?*
   ——

6. *What is his name?*
   ——

7. *Does he perform any other duty?*
   Yes: Lower Winchendon.

8. *State duty performed?*
   Two *full* services at Crendon ¼ before eleven & at 14 p.m.

9. *When do you catechise the children? By what method?*
   Every Sunday, questions out of catechism & reading.

10. *Lord's Supper?*
    Eight times yearly.

11. *Communicants at great festivals? Other seasons? List? Total?*
35; 25; yes; 40 to 45.

12. *Number of congregation. Increasing or decreasing?*
400. Increasing.

13. *Fair proportion of population?*
No; the great farms — impropriators & College Farm rented by dissenters.

14. *State object for which collections are made?*
The Infirmary: Clothing Club School: Teacher in singing & other Church purposes quarterly.

15. *School?*
Only a Sunday School — Dame School for children — from 170 to 180.

16. *Are you able to retain your young people in Sunday School?*
—

17. *Adult or Evening Schools?*
I have tried evening Schools, but the result was not satisfactory.

18. *Dissenting places of worship?*
Baptists: Wesleyan: Ranters 2 or 3 hundred: *others waifs* & strays from adjoining parishes who disregard all religion.

19. *What impedes your ministry or welfare of Church?*
The monopoly of land by dissenters & the carelessness of farmers who show much practical infidelity.

20. *Is Church in good repair? Do your Churchwardens discharge their duties?*
It is not in good repair; but we are moving to that end. I cannot say very much for that.

21. *Alterations in Church or Chancel?*
The Impropriator is now putting the Chancel in to excellent order.

22. *Any other matter?*
No.

> *signed* Thomas Hayton
> Incumbent

Bodl. M.S. Oxf. Diocesan Papers c. 334.

[197] *From the* Thame Gazette

4 January 1870

We are informed that the Vicar of Long Crendon has sent his adhesion to the Birmingham Education League [1], having been convinced from long experience from the state of parishes around, & from a callous indifference amongst all parties in his own parish for any scholastic institution, that nothing less than compulsory rates and attendance will avail for the education of the children of the poor. The programme which the League has issued seems to be making many converts, setting aside dogmas and denominational tactics.

1. This League was founded in 1869 to press for non-sectarian, compulsory and free education. Its Vice-President was Joseph Chamberlain.

[198] To the Charity Commissioners

Crendon, 4 April 1870

Gentlemen,

There is in this parish a charity issuing out of 12 acres of land, letting for £15 annually to be expended in fuel for the poor legally settled in the parish. This is the statement of the parish Award of 1824. The Trustees 'The Minister, Churchwardens & Overseers'. The money is laid out in coal which is distributed to the farm labourers yielding about 1 cwt to a household yearly.

As there is now no *parochial* settlement as in 1824 when the Award was made, a difficulty is felt as to its distribution, this parish being an open one where 'waifs & strays' from surrounding parishes flock into or are driven into — Are we justified in giving it to such? Or should we give it to the old & infirm alone? with certain restrictions as to age etc.

We are legally at a loss also as to the Dormer Charity which specifies 'Inhabitants' without reference to *settlement*. Some think that those who receive parish relief are not fair recipients, as Charities should not supplement rates.

As for myself I wish they were all taken for Education purposes the want of which is so much felt in so many parishes.

At your convenience, Gentlemen, I shall be happy to hear from you on these subjects.

I am gentlemen, yours truly,

Thos Hayton

Charity Com.

[199] To Mr Pringle [1] *, Secretary to the Ecclesiastical Commission*

Crendon, 25 May 1872

Sir,

Will you be pleased to lay my request before the Ecclesiastical Commissioners?

The parish of Long Crendon is very extensive, of which I have been Vicar since 1821; population now about 1400; formerly about 1740, but

155

owing to the miserable payment to labourers, many have been forced to emigrate. The farmers — the chief landowners are not resident — Churchmen & Baptists — have uniformly rejected all my overtures to establish either a National or a British School; consequently, I am about to apply for an order for a School Board [2]. In the first place a site must be chosen & there is no place equal to the piece of land which I have always maintained belonged to Windsor College, in lieu of the enfranchisement of a certain house & premises belonging to the Duke of Buckingham: as shown by the Parish Award & which the late Mr Batcheldor, Agent for the College, claimed as their right, & meant, if he had lived, to prevent the claim. The piece of land in question measures about 2 acres, 3 roods; & what I urgently & most respectfully request is to grant the parish one acre of it or a little more, & the remainder I will undertake to hold at as high a rent or higher than what is now given: indeed, it would be one of the greatest boons for the agricultural labourer to hold at 6d per pole — in allotments of 20 to 40 poles, & inasmuch as it is close to the village & centrally situated; whereas at present they have to go, after their daily labour, 2 miles to cultivate some barren allotments.

If you will be kind enough to urge this Treatment on the Notice of the Commissioners you will oblige

yours most respectfully,

Thomas Hayton
Vicar of Long Crendon

*an extract from the Parish Award which is to be taken by a Mr Clutton [3] will satisfy the Commissioners; tho' the Duke has paid no rent for years. I believe it is let at £4 an acre.

The commissioners say that they own the land & have written to the Duke's Agent & got no reply.

Ch Com. 37788

1. Later, Sir George Pringle; Secretary to the Ecclesiastical Commissioners.
2. The Elementary Education Act 33 & 34 Vict c. 75 laid down that local school boards should be elected by the rate-payers.
3. Mr Clutton of 9, Whitehall Place, surveyor to the Commissioners.

[200] *From the* Thame Gazette

23 July 1872

Pamphlets have been freely distributed at one penny each in Long Crendon, the authorship of the Vicar, implicating the Churchwardens with neglect of the repairs to Mother Church and of not realizing what ought to be had from farm lands etc. We hear from a confident source that a pamphlet, in answer to the above, is being entered at Stationers Hall entitled 'Fifty Years Ministerial Life in Long Crendon'. We hope it will clear up some mysteries in our village.

Corresponded.

[201] *A few words to the Parishioners of Long Crendon* by the Vicar.
Second Edition, 1872. W.W. Scadding, Printer, High Street, Thame.

17 January 1872

'Self-defence is a virtue Sole Bulwark of all right'.

Through severe indisposition I thought it my duty to express my regret at not being able to call a vestry to consider certain matters which equally appertain to Churchmen and Dissenters. As there are always captious people ready to comment upon what they do not understand, to get in fact, too large for their shoes and to give utterance to their foolish fancies, allow me to give a plain narrative of the causes which have led others, as well as myself to think that a vestry was desirable.

In Easter week the Churchwardens [1] called a meeting for their accounts to be examined; to appoint new Churchwardens and to consider other matters incident to the office of Churchwarden. No one attended the meeting, save the Churchwardens themselves, and Mr Thomas Crook, so that no business could be entered into. At the visitation in Aylesbury, I spoke to Mr Davenport in reference to this, and asked how it would affect certain questions; he advised me to call a public Vestry, especially as matters as that time were cropping up which were never anticipated; hence the expediency of regular appointments.

Many of you are aware that the heating apparatus in the church is a failure, Mr Harris being supposed never to have had fair play; the question therefore is, whether any further attempt at repair should be thought desirable, or relinquish the apparatus altogether; Mr Harris informs me that for £5 he will make it work satisfactorily, and for ten years keep it in order. Looking at it as a comfort to the worshipper and as beneficial to the entire building, this seems a question very desirable to be settled.

Then as to the better lighting of the Church, half of which has hitherto been in total darkness. So miserable was the gloom last winter that the congregation could not discern each other, a very serious matter for light-hearted people. The moderator lamps had either lost their power or were so clammed up with dust and filth that they languished and died before the end of the hour. Then as to the four-legged bilious looking candles in the pulpit which threw their dull sepulchral light so sparingly that brighter eyes than mine could not read thereby, I proposed to meet half way any expense for a modern light, and at my own cost to enliven the gloom of the chancel by suitable lamps. My proposition was entirely ignored and I was compelled to hold evening services in the Court Room, thereby incurring expenses nearly to the amount of five pounds. Surely this is a question well worthy of a Vestry's consideration (not to be left to the caprice of one or two individuals) in-as-much as it involves the opening and closing of the church in the winter evenings. I look upon these two questions in a Catholic light, based on the principle of a national Church, and open alike to Churchmen and Dissenters whose rights have never yet been compromised.

When we look at the inside of the church, we see walls damp scabbed and dismal, and which for upwards of 20 years have never undergone a cleansing; where spiders may be seen dancing about like dervishes, secure in

157

their ancient retreats: one might be led to suppose that the Churchwardens were nonentities, or had no money to spend on Mother Church, whereas they are both living men, active in the pursuits of their calling, but cold, torpid and indifferent as to the requirements of the House of God, or the support of those principles which they profess. One Churchwarden says there is £7 in hand; from another quarter I hear there is £17 in hand; and if the midsummer quarter be paid, as it should be there are ample funds for more than common requirements. As to the time and payment of these monies, I am wholly in the dark. Many find fault with the letting of the church land, viz 16 acres that is let under fair market value [2]; that the churchwardens have no powers of letting, save for one year, and that if there was public competition, a considerably higher price would be given. This is very true; and before the Inclosure of the Field there was a yearly letting and the last sum given for the open fieldland was £36 by Mr Briaris, and this amount might be realised at the present time. The Church with this amount carefully administered, would be able, except in certain cases, to meet her requirements, and God's house get her own again. Surely this is a consideration well worthy of a vestry of Churchmen and Dissenters who have an inherent interest with those who are called church people, and who, when appealed to, have never shown indifference but an alacrity which churchmen might do well to imitate. I need not specify examples as they are well known. I mention this in common fairness, for I wish for nothing from anyone save common civility, whilst I endeavour to act in the spirit of a Christian and the kindness of a Pastor.

We have a silent harmonium in the church — a silent memorial of an unfulfilled promise. When it was bought, there was a promise that it should be paid for by a subscription; this my churchwarden urged strongly; the parish warden was mute, but from that day to this I have not received a farthing. I was promised the benefit of a Reading and Concert by certain friends, but my churchwardens again thought it degrading to the congregation to ask of another parish aid and assistance in such a case; so I suppose I must sell it for half-price that for which I was promised to be thoroughly remunerated. On this I will leave the reader to make his own comment.

I have heard lately that the churchwardens themselves differ as to what ought to be done to the church; one wishes some outside work to be done, the other the purification of the inside. I wrote in as polite a manner as I possibly could to ascertain what they meant to do, so that I might make arrangements as to the services. My application was disregarded — no reply has been given to this hour. Different treatment might have been expected especially when no offence has been wilfully given, and the question one in reality relating solely to myself; a man with common sense and unbiased mind will see in all this a strong argument for the appointment of new churchwardens or a plain declaration of mind from the old ones.

Finally, as to the 'Poor's' Allotment which is theirs and nobody else's [3], and no Trustees nor body of Trustees have any right to let the land at half its value, I have long been dissatisfied both with the administration, and distribution of the charity, as the Award speaks of the improved rental, which has never been called for. The mode of letting has no fixity in it, and an attempt to recover the rent, if refused, would puzzle a county court Judge. What has that Charity to do, says some captious critic, with an Easter vestry?

158

much! every way. The Overseers of the poor have never taken any interest in it, so that the management of it virtually has been in the hands of the Minister and Churchwardens, and at the annual meeting a verified statement of receipts and expenditures is to be statute-required and to be sent to the Charity Commissioners. In consequence of my having been refused a list of the recipients of the charity and looking at nearly half of the charity being lost to the poor who have no benefit in the occupation, and of doubtful benefit accruing to the laborer who after nine and a half hours thumping for his master has to walk four miles and toil two or three hours more and returning to his home hungry and thirsty and wayworn, with Poll not in the best of humours, I withdrew from all responsibilities as Trustee having intimated the same to the Charity Commissioners. My churchwarden also the other day when applied to for his sanction to a transfer of a portion of the land, declined to have anything to do with it, so that the parish churchwarden is now virtually the sole Trustee. Under such circumstances a better understanding might be arrived at and more satisfaction given by the deliberations of a public vestry and this justifying the advice given by Mr Davenport. Trusting that this plain narrative of facts will show at least the expediency if not the necessity for some action to be taken on these subjects, I leave them for your reflections. Casting aside little prejudices which blind, and expanding your orbit of vision, you will see that I have not said without a cause that which I have said. Suffering from the weakening effect of a severe indisposition and little inclined either to call a vestry at the present, or to enter into personal discussion may I venture to hope that the Churchwardens will rouse themselves from their lethargy and will not allow bad feelings to sway them, but energise forthwith in those matters of paramount importance which refer to the comfort of the worshippers at the Church and to the honour of Almighty God.

I am respectfully yours,

Thomas Hayton

If anyone should think that the letting of the land to a day laborer is a boon, how much more would a smaller portion of land near the village be beneficial, even if the laborer gave double the rental the farmers give, instead of charging him £8 an acre. Some people like to be Liberal at other people's expense, and the administration of this charity is an example of it. Whenever a laborer is taught to look to a charity for help, this is helping him to pauperism, in fact degrading him, making him lose all feelings of independence and of social position which he has as much right to as the best in the land. But the time is coming when 'Hodge' will lift up his head, feel no longer old Cedric's collar and be what God meant him to be, a man earning his daily bread by receiving fair wages for a fair day's work.

Shortly a short Tract on Education and poor administration by the Monks of Notley contrasting it with protestant education and poor relief as now administered.

Bodl. M.S. Top. Oxon. d. 41 page 154.

1. Jacob Watson, Vicar's Warden; J. Cosins Crook, People's Warden.
2. Sixteen acres of land down Westfield Road, given for the upkeep of the Church.
3. Twelve acres of land down Westfield Road, given to the poor in lieu of grazing rights etc. Number 53 on the Enclosure Award.

Crendon, 25 September 1872

Gentlemen,

The case I have to submit to you is simply this — a Trustee became Bankrupt about 2½ years ago; tho' disqualified he occasionally attended our meeting [1]. As Chairman I thought it invidious to interfere unless some one should moot the question. This was done frequently in private to me, but never at the Meetings. On the death of another Trustee, notice was publicly given by two Trustees that the vacancies should be filled up. A question arose whether the disqualification of the Bankrupt still continued; or as he had attended the Meetings without rebuke, whether his Bankruptcy had ceased its effect upon him as a Trustee, or whether a new Election should take place as that seemed involved in his disqualification.

The Meeting thought that a new Election was not necessary & that the Bankrupt might act on the ground that no objection had been made to him during the time that had passed.

Do you think, Gentlemen, that the decision of the Trustees is a proper one?

As Chairman I would be obliged by giving me your opinion.

I have the honour to be, Gentlemen, your obedient servant,

Thos Hayton
Vicar

Postscript 28 September
Since writing the enclosed I have been told by one of my parishioners that the Bankrupt alluded to, viz. John Dudley has been in communication with you & that your reply to him was that as 12 months had elapsed since his Bankruptcy he might still attend the Meetings. I give this as I heard it; but if you know the antecedents of this man & his present position (which if required I will give you) you would hesitate to admit such a fellow to a Trustee's Meetings.

Any remark you may make on this, let it be distinct from the question.

Charity Com.

1. Any Trustee who becomes bankrupt, ceases to be a Trustee under Clause 2 of the Scheme.

Crendon, 14 December 1872

Sir,

I have just had an interview with Mr Thomas Crook, one of the acting Trustees of the above Charity, & he tells me in reply to your letter to him, he named only three of the Dodwells being first cousins; I beg to state that there

160

are now four Trustees of that name including one as an overseer; & that the relationships are not only first cousins but brothers in law & one a son of a Trustee. He admits having made this error; and I have thought it right just to tell you so, — of course from your letter to Crook such information is superfluous — only I thought I ought to make it.

Yours very truly,

Thomas Hayton

Charity Com.

[204] *To the Charity Commissioners*

Crendon, 7 March 1873

Sir,

The 21st of December falling on a Saturday; partly prevented me from attending the Annual Meeting; independently of this, I was told that John Dudley would again force himself to abuse me; as it was he did make his appearance, & was publicly convicted of having uttered an untruth as to your being satisfied with his continuing to act as a Trustee.

The Acting Trustee (Mr T. Crook) has requested me to reply to your letter of the 8th March last touching a resolution (if it may be so called) entered in the Minute Book of the 21st Dec, at which the following were present —
c. John Cosens Crook
c. John Cooper [1]
c. John Crook [2]
c. Stephen Cook [3]
b. James Dodwell Brother in law & cousin to John Dodwell
b. David Dodwell Cousin to John Dodwell
b. Timothy Dodwell Cousin to John Dodwell
b. Herbert Dodwell Son of David
b. Michael Rose

Mr James Dodwell proposed that they should abide by their resolution at the previous Meeting touching John Dodwell, this was seconded by Mr Rose, but it was never put to the Churchmen of the Meeting nor any show of hands called for — it was a simple entrance in the Minute Book. Mr T. Crook had never been in the Chair before & he afterwards saw his mistake. The Meeting had been speedily called to elect & nominate 3 Trustees & this proposition of James Dodwell was to get rid of the question & to retain the nomination of John Dodwell — to have so many of the same family is esteemed highly objectionable by nearly all the Inhabitants & as there are others eligible I hope & trust that you will not sanction any more of that name.

I am, Sir, respectfully yours,

Thos Hayton
Vicar

P.S. The Acting Trustee will also write to you, & I do so as his acting co-partner.

This nomination had only three hands held up for it; the rest were silent, thro' fear of offence to a certain individual.

P.S. The Poor allotment Charity is in a very unsatisfactory position still.

Charity Com.

1. John Cooper from Thame Mead Farm.
2. John Crook from Peppers Hill Farm.
3. Stephen Cook, dairyman and smallholder. He was vicar's warden for many years.

[205] To the Secretary of the Education Department
Lower Winchendon, 1 June 1873

Sir,

I am the Incumbent of Lower Winchendon as well as Long Crendon, both of which places have uniformly repudiated Education; & after 50 years ministration I may be permitted to know a little of the requirements.

I hear that a petition has been sent you from certain non-resident land-lords who have never given a sixpence even to the Sunday School, but who now seem inclined with singular Zeal to induce you to change your correct policy of joining Winchendon & Chearsley together — by one-sided represen-tations. If you think it proper to send me the grounds of their petition, I will reply to them seriatim as I feel confident that you will recognize the force of my objections & I have to urge against building a school contiguous to the Churchyard without a sufficient guarantee for its establishment & support [1].

I have the honour to be, Sir, yours respectfully,

Thomas Hayton

E.D. 21/1348

1. This applies to Forster's Education Act of 1870 (33–34 Vict c. 75) which compelled parishes to provide education for children.

[206] To the Secretary of the Ecclesiastical Commissioners
Crendon, 19 December 1873

Sir,

In the Spring of this year, at the suggestion of Mr Clutton, after he had examined the Parish Award, I wrote to you petitioning for a portion of land, formerly belonging to the Dean & Canons of Windsor, on which to build a school, for the poor & ragged population of this Village. I called at Whitehall in Summer, & was told that, as the Duke of Buckingham had paid no rent for upwards of 20 years 'his Grace pleaded the Statute' [1]! To ask his Grace for

162

any land would be useless — He would be as deaf as 'Ailsa Crag'. A legal authority told me the other day that no claim would be valid *against the Church:* if, however, the Commissioners sanction the Claim I have no more to say.

Mr Clutton also asked me the value of my Living — whether it was £300 per annum: I replied 'It was on the gross' without entering into any particulars. Let me state the case as briefly as possible. Having a curacy in an adjoining parish in 1821, this Living of Crendon value £70 a year, was offered to me & I accepted it; worked up the Inclosure of the Parish; thereby raising the value of the Living to about £150 per annum by draining, building, subdividing, & there being only a cottage for the Glebe land, I built at my own expense a parsonage house with its adjuncts. A friend lent me some money to carry out my plans, & I have now to pay out of my £300 a year — £100 per annum to meet the requirements of a Life Assurance held by my *friend.*

The lay Impropriator has 700 acres of land in the parish rented by dissenters; (Baptists). All Souls College, 300, rented by dissenters; some 400 acres belonging to absentee landlords who never contribute one shilling either to Sunday School, Dorcas, or Clothing Club. The best 400 acres belonging to Notley Abbey is held by one who recognizes no form of religion & contributes to no Institution; so all I get for the Sunday School is about 50/— annually, & not a farthing to the other Clubs, save £2 from Lady Churchill for the Dorcas & £3 which the Warden of All Souls sends me for the Clothing Club. The Estate, under lease & other property belonging to the Ecclesiastical Commissioners yields, I believe upwards of £300 a year, gives me not the least assurance on the Charities or otherwise.

I am 80 years of age, hold a small Living near this place, have performed 3 full services every Sunday since 1821 & am now anxious to have an assistant curate but cannot afford it. Is it therefore in the power of the Ecclesiastical commissioners to assist me in this object or am I precluded by its rules from any aid?

If so, would the Commissioners as landlords of the Ecclesiastical property give me a yearly donation or subscription to the Charitable Institutions alluded to? There is no resident gentlemen in this parish & the farmers are rack-renters & more than half of them Dissenters, so that from these sources I get nothing. If Mr Secretary can help me in any of these objects, I will be very thankful, *but* most of all for that which refers to myself as thereby the others might be better met.

I have the honour to be, yours very respectfully,

Thos Hayton
Vicar of the parish of Long Crendon

[*Note from the Commissioners on the letter*]
The Commissioners have recently sold their land in this parish — they have now only the manor copyhold [2].

Ch Com. F.37788

1. This refers to the Statute of Limitations of 1623. 21 Jac. 1 c 16.
2. The 'manor copyhold' refers to the house next to the church: considerable amounts of land and farm buildings were included.

[no date — after 1873]

Memorandum

as to the Pew in the Church called 'Notley Pew' [1] — Some think there is a faculty for this unseemly erection denounced by every Visitor as an ugly excrescence fit only for the burning!

In the year 1827 the Church was thoroughly repaired by the parishioners & this pew especially was made new by the parish rate & not by the owner of Notley Abbey; so that any claim for proprietorship is utterly baseless. Indeed, by the late Bishop Wilberforce the pew was ordered to be pulled down, & recently the idea has been mooted, but from personal feelings the order has not been carried out. Time however will do away with this deformity.

T.H.

B.R.O. P.R. 134/1/9

Date: Bishop Wilberforce died in 1873.
1. This pew belonging to the Reynolds family was perched up in the south aisle.

[208] To the Secretary of the Educational Department

Crendon, 14 June 1875

Sir,

The Vicar of Chearsley [1] has shewn me your request as to the 'Promoters of the School' at Nether Winchendon, of which place I have been Curate & Incumbent more than half a Century, & therefore may be permitted to enter into some details as to that parish.

A few years ago we had a day school there conducted by two mistresses, this soon collapsed from want of support & other reasons I need not specify. The School which is now partly built — with no seeming probability of being finished — was promoted by the Duke of Buckingham; Richard Rose Esq. of Aylesbury [2] & the Revd. A. Isham of Weston Turville [3], each one having an estate at Winchendon. They held private meetings among themselves, sometimes at one place & sometimes at another, for the express purpose of thwarting the junction of Winchendon & Chearsley. Once I was requested to attend, but I declined doing so, inasmuch as I neither liked the object in view, nor the projected site for the School, nor could I see how afterwards the School was to be supported, knowing too well the reluctance of rate payers to meet expenses. The site chosen for the School was an old piece of waste ground, boggy & wet & abutting on the Church yard — the very worst site that could be chosen, as the Archdeacon & others all testify; and the Builder himself tells me it is over an old pond, disfiguring alike both the Church & the village scenery, in short an act of pure vandalism.

The Duke of Buckingham's Tenant is now suffering under mental derangement & about to be removed to an Asylum, having attempted self-

164

destruction; Mr Isham's tenant tells me he will have nothing to do with the School, whilst his wife avers that it will be useless & thinks nothing more desirable than a good district School where an efficient Master may be over it, as no female teacher could possibly manage the unruly boys of the village; Mr Rose's Tenant seems indifferent as probably he may not be long there.

As to the other owners & occupiers of land in the parish, one gentleman holding about 200 acres lives 5 days in the week in London & 2 at Thame; another owner of land lives entirely at Thame; a third at Chilton & another at Chearsley. All these are in favour of the junction of the two parishes together with the two Incumbents.

I suppose the School at Winchendon finished, of which the Builder seems dubious for reasons personal*, there will be none to conduct the School — I cannot find any one at all likely; but if the two villages elect a School Board, these may carry out The Act — the Voluntary principle I am sure will not work, inasmuch as Education in these small villages is not much prized either by parents or rate payers.

At this my parish of Long Crendon three years are expiring and nothing done! The Site hastily approved of by Mr Prichard [4], is not by many thought a proper one; it adjoins a Public House, is in front of a Blacksmith's shop & a busy thoro'fare, & above all, is in Chancery & when out of it none can tell, so that the Fabian policy is still indulged in to the grief & murmurings of many of the Inhabitants. I thought I should live to see something done in the way of Education, but I begin to despair, unless my Lords exert themselves more effectively;

I have the honour to be, Sirs, yours very respectfully,

Thos Hayton
Vicar of Long Crendon & Nether Winchendon

*It is currently reported that the Builder has urged legal means for ½ his pay for work done.

E.D. 21/1348

1. Revd. Andrew Hamilton, M.A. Cantab; deacon 1870; vicar of Chearsley 1872 to 1876; vicar of Chilton 1876 to 1883.
2. Richard Rose, of 'The Chestnuts' Aylesbury.
3. Revd. A. Isham (1809–1892), Fellow of All Souls; rector of Weston Turville. Author of theological works. (M.E.B.)
4. Mr Prichard, Assistant Inspector of Schools.

[209] *To the Secretary of the Educational Department*

Crendon, 9 August [1875]

Sir,

I have had a communication made to me by one of the absentee Landlords of Lower Winchendon to permit my Church to be opened for a Divine Service in aid of the School built (but not finished) by certain owners of land; my reply is the following — 'When the Education Department has issued its *final* order in reference to the two villages of Chearsley & Lower Winchendon, *then* it will be time enough to take note of your request. I cannot entertain the idea that My Lords will stultify themselves in violating the plain meaning of the 9th Section of the Elementary Education Act, especially after having given so much time to object or to show cause why a severance should be made & after their expressed opinion on the matter to the Vicar of Chearsley'.

To separate the parishes would be an Act of Cruelty; & I am now more convinced than ever from weekly communication with the rate-payers, that to adopt the *Voluntary principle* would be a failure. This anxiety to launch the Embryo School is looked upon as a kind of sham; its meaning is to get rid of Chearsley — currently reported to be urged on by Ducal Influence on Lord Sandon [1]. The floor of the School is not yet finished; no mistress secured; & no funds in hand; & for a female to manage the rude boys of a country village is quite impracticable, & therefore I cannot lend myself to an object, the failure of which I unhesitatingly predict, from a variety of local considerations.

The village of Chearsley is worse off than Winchendon. Two farmers are the landowners of two thirds of the village & the other third is held by Dissenters, so that the Vicar is hopeless as to a School on the Voluntary principle. The only alternative under these difficulties is a School on the borders of the two parishes — as at first projected — to contain about 130 Scholars — conducted by a *Master & Mistress*. This view is concurred in by all most interested & who are anxious for an effective education.

I most respectfully submit these remarks to the consideration of My Lords, and will be glad, as also will the Vicar of Chearsley, that some definitive order should be issued.

I have the honour to be, Mr Secretary, yours very truly,

Thos Hayton
Vicar of Lower Winchendon & Crendon

E.D. 21/1348

1. Dudley Francis Stuart, Lord Sandon (1831—1900); eldest son of the 2nd Earl of Harrowby; Vice-President of the Committee of the Council for Education.

[210] From the Bucks Advertiser

21 August 1875

LOWER WINCHENDON.
OPENING OF THE VILLAGE SCHOOL

On the greensward between the churchyard and the highway has lately risen a pleasant looking red brick building, that tells you at once it is the village school. It is in form a long room with the gable to the road, a class-room projecting from one side of it. It has been a rather considerable time, we believe, in development, but at last it is finished, and on Thursday no less a personage than the Lord Lieutenant of the County, the Governor select of Madras, the Most Noble and Duke of Buckingham and Chandos, attended at that little village school, assisted in the brief devotions that had been arranged, and then formally opened the building for teaching uses with an address.

But we are hastening rather too rapidly. We learn, from whispered confidences, that the Vicar of the parish, the Rev. Thomas Hayton, has not felt called upon to interest himself greatly in the project of a village school. The time has gone by when a Vicar of Lower Winchendon might be accounted rich on £60 a year; and we must have regarded it as one of the mysteries of an established church that a parish so poorly endowed should even rejoice in the services of a curate, had we not alighted on the name of the Rev. Thomas Hayton as Vicar also of Long Crendon, with £200 a year, and some thirteen or fourteen hundred souls, located on considerably more than three thousand acres, under his spiritual care. The school of Lower Winchendon owes, then, little or nothing to the Vicar; but it is the result of a determination on the part of the landowners of the parish to provide a means of instruction for the children of the parish, the Rev. A. Isham, of Weston Turville, giving the undertaking his kindly and zealous aid, and even liberal pecuniary assistance, the furniture of the school being most of it, we believe, provided by him. The architect of the school is Mr H.H. Smith, of Leicester; the builder, Mr Holland, of Thame. It is intended to accommodate fifty children in the large room, and twenty-eight in the smaller, the latter being for use as a class-room or sewing-room. The site was given by Mr Bernard, of Winchendon Priory; and the cost of the building has been £500.

[211] To Bucks Advertiser & Aylesbury News
Lower Winchendon, 24 August 1875

Sir,

The writer of the article on the jubilant gathering at Lower Winchendon, on Thursday last, having made statements which are at variance with fact, and having brought my name forward in a way which might lead to erroneous conclusions, be pleased to allow me space for a reply, which shall be as succinct as I possibly can make it.

In the first place let me inform you that history recognizes no Priory at Winchendon, that being an assumed name of recent date, instead of Winchendon House, the worthy occupier of which requires no ecclesiastical association with the plunderer of Notley Abbey to raise his reputation or respect with his neighbours. The title of Priory is a myth, founded on the idea that there was an underground communication with Notley, and thence on to the Prebendal at Thame. All this is fudge, the offspring of some fanciful brain. The monument in the churchyard requires no sentimentality, it being the roseate repose of certain members of a very respectable family which have held an estate in the parish for a great length of time. Had the traveller cast his eye on the old quaint building adjoining the churchyard, formerly the abode of Sir Francis Knollys, he might on enquiry have found matter of Romance, which by a little ornamental verbiage would have tickled the fancy of his lady readers, who might have been stirred up to discover the means of a lady's flight with her Romeo.

The green sward (how Arcadian!) alluded to is four feet or more below the level of the churchyard, receiving the drainings from it, making the place in winter a very bog, over which few would venture. No grave can be dug in the church-yard without water rising in it to a foot or more in height. On this damp ground a school has been built, showing its unseemly parts to the church, thus marring the old picturesque view of it, and making, as a result, the churchyard a playground. This I publicly denounced as thorough Vandalism.

Now, more immediately to the point. I have uniformly advocated that education, to be effective, should be unsectarian, free, and compulsory — of course, with modifications; and I knew very well that, under such auspices, which have been elaborately paraded, these sentiments would not be entertained, and therefore I withdrew altogether from the undertaking. A few years ago, Miss Bernard supported a school in the village, but when she married [1] the school collapsed. No landlord, no farmer came forward to take her good work in hand, and then things went on till the passing of the Elementary Education Act. Soon after the Act came into operation I called upon Mr Bernard, asking him what steps should be taken; his reply was 'Leave the Education Department to act as it liked'. On this hint I acted. Her Majesty's School Inspector visited the three parishes of Cuddington, Winchendon, and Chearsley, putting those three into a district. Winchendon looked sweet on Cuddington; meetings were called; plans for enlarging Cuddington School were called for, (which plans, by-the-bye, are not yet paid for); but a change came of the dream, objectors arose, repudiated the contemplated alliance, pleaded the 9th section of the Act, an Inspector came (as I was informed), and the result was a divorce, thus throwing picturesque Winchendon into the Fuzzy arms of Chearsley. These two parishes are still a limited district, and both the Vicar of Chearsley and myself have urged upon the Education Department the propriety of issuing their final order for the parishes. Last month a letter was received from my Lords saying that they regretted no action had been taken by them in reference to the parishes, and that was partly owing to the Duke of Buckingham who had not replied to their queries nor taken the steps required by the Act. This letter, handed to me by Mr Hamilton, I read to the two churchwardens of Winchendon, in order that they might see we were acting openly and fairly in the matter — using no sinister or back-stairs influence or personal power to sway public policy, both of us being convinced that a rate-school would be less expensive and more effective, situate at the junction of the two parishes (which are contiguous) with suitable buildings for a master and mistress, and that these little fid-fad schools, with a certified mistress barely out of her teens, would have no power over the rough and rude lads of a country village, rendered impudent and insubordinate from certain addresses of vagrant spouters. These views are entertained by many whose tongues are tied.

The village of Chearsley (noted for Cerdic the Saxon) contains about

900 acres, with a population greater than Winchendon, two-thirds of the land belonging to the Church of England farmers, the residue to Dissenters, who cannot be expected to contribute anything to a school on the voluntary principle. It would be hard indeed for these two farmers to be called upon to build and support a school entirely alone, feeling assured that neither of the villages separately could make a Committee of Management to carry on the school with success. They might puddle along through the 2nd or 3rd Standard, but would never reach any efficiency contemplated by the Act, and thereby be debarred of a grant [2]. During the last week a letter has been received from the Education Department by Mr Hamilton, the Duke of Buckingham, and myself, appointing Sept. 14th as the day when their Inspector will visit the parishes. What his recommendation may be, remains to be seen — what it would have been under Mr Forster is pretty well known. I must not omit to notice the speech of his Grace the Duke of Buckingham, the *jupiter tonans* of the party. It was plain and practical, but specious and one-sided. Like a skilful tactician his Grace shirked the point at issue. In fact it was a specimen of Utopianism which he will never live to witness, until the school be converted into a Temperance Hotel so much required in a village where thirsty souls abound, and making the room at the Dancing Bear a place to lecture on *Incendiarism and its kindred vices.

> I have the honour to be, Mr Editor, your obedient servant,
>
> Thos. Hayton
> Vicar of Lower Winchendon

*Some villain in January last set fire to the cottage adjoining the Inn; by rare chance the good lady of the Inn escaped being burned out.

1. Sophie Elizabeth Bernard married Joseph Napier Higgins in June 1861. Their son, Francis, born 1864, eventually inherited the estate, taking the name of Higgins-Bernard.
2. Grants were given if children reached Standard IV.

[212] To the Editor of the Bucks Herald

21 September 1875

As the Incumbents of Weston Turville and Chearsley have now exhausted the subject of the Winchendon School, as far as regards themselves, allow me, Mr Editor, a space in your columns to pacify the perturbed spirit of Mr Isham, especially as he seems labouring under the idea that I was more in the secret of Mr Pickard's visit to Winchendon than himself, and that he was not fairly treated in the matter, — neither one nor the other is truth. In Mr Isham's last letter there oozes out a peevishness which I did not expect from his usual placidity, and a tu quoque suspicion as to myself; and from these feelings the composition is of a slip-slop character, unworthy of an old controversialist. I give Mr Isham credit for much zeal and perseverance and self-sacrifice in rearing this boggy building for the benefit of my parishioners and their offspring, whilst I denounce the site as the worst, the cheapest, and the dirtiest, that could have been chosen. In fact, the landlord promoters, to get rid of the school being built on their own land, where sites of sanitary character were patent and picturesque, thought anything good enough for the brats of the village, for whom during these 50 years and upwards no regard had ever been paid, always excepting the kindness of Mr Bernard, who did not 'offer', as asserted, this site, but was pressed to do so by an influence he could not well resist, and this after his expressed opinion to the contrary.

When I received a letter from the Inspector of Schools that he would visit Winchendon on the 14th of September and that he had written to the Duke of Buckingham and Mr Hamilton to the same effect, I felt rather astonished that he did not specify the object of his visit, which I neither courted nor desired, and therefore doubted with myself whether I would attend or not; still, for courtesy's sake, I did attend, having written to him on the 10th to this effect, which will prove to Mr Isham that his suspicion is unfounded. The cool and self-complacent speech of the Duke of Buckingham at the opening of the school, and from his Grace's assertion, previous to the commencement of the school, that he had seen Lord Sandon, who had promised that the landowners of Winchendon should have a school separate from all the other parishes, and this is in the very teeth of the Council's Order for one to be built at the junction of Winchendon and Chearsley, adding to this Mr Pickard's passing over in silence in his annual report the name of either parish — all accounting for the reckless defiance of the Order and abnormal proceeding. I conceived that such conduct showed a weakness and vacillation in the Government department, and made the public to believe that jobbery was as rank among Tories as Whigs. This made me look upon the whole as a foregone conclusion, and that my attendance at the school would be a farce; and such it proved to be. On the 14th Sept., however, we met — a Duke, two country parsons, and Mr Pickard — the Council's embodiment — a four-cornered conclave — no reporter that day — we knew not why we had met, except to admire the flooring of the school, and the back settlements of a Mr Moule. His Grace, however, began by asking Mr Hamilton what site he proposed? The reply was, 'I have nothing to do with any site — that was a side issue away from the main point. Had the promoters of the school acted legally or not?' Mr Hamilton proved to the satisfaction of the Inspector that they had not; the Duke, feeling himself floundering, rather pettishly replied that they would oppose the first general order. 'I will join issue with your Grace on that head', was Mr Hamilton's reply. Here the debate ceased; and thus ended the farce in the school, with his Grace's *brutum fulmen* — a kind of Quixotic flourish at a windmill. After the departure of Mr Pickard, his Grace condescended to hold a long conversation with the Vicar of Chearsley and myself about schools, parents and children, and a variety of other topics not pertinent to the meeting; and, after wishing him a bon voyage to the mixed population of Madras, we parted more kindly affected than when we met.

One word to Mr Isham, and I am done.

I appreciate his kindly feelings towards me; and whatever may be the determination of the matter, I trust that we will mutually accord each other's good intentions towards the children and the parishes.

I have the honour to be, Mr Editor, yours very respectfully,

The Vicar of Lower Winchendon

Curate
I have no assistant Curate, save occasional help from Mr Hamilton, the Vicar of Chearsley.

Services
Every Sunday morning & evening in full — at a quarter before eleven & a quarter before three in winter, in summer six in the evening.

Intercession for Missions?
Yes, Sunday after St Andrew's Day.

Absent from Church? Number of Population?
A great many. I think one third of the parish recognise no divine service. One third dissenter and the rest Church people.

Collection
Yes, one for foreign missions: none for diocesan purposes. We have eight for *local purposes!*

Schools. Religious instruction
I am sorry to say that the farmers would never help me to build a school; and now do everything to delay building the school ordered by the Education department.

Fabric of the Church. In good repair? Can the poorer people kneel?
Yes, in *fair* repair but much is required externally. The parish churchwarden is a Wesleyan Methodist & useless. When got rid of, I expect a better & the poorer classes will then be more accommodated than they are.

[signed] Thomas Hayton, 25 March 1875

Bodl M.S. Oxford Dioc. papers c. 340

[214] From the Parish Register

22 July 1876
Year 1874—5—6,

In November 74 a School Board was chosen — any thing but in a fair way. Meeting after Meeting nothing was done, except it might be to prolong or put off as long as possible the Evil Day. At last after two years gestation & threats from the Council of Education, plans were submitted & tenders made, & the amount for building a School for 180 children was £2500; — money to be borrowed & repaid in 50 years: and the foundation of the School was begun Jan 3 1876 to be finished about Midsummer next.

5—25 February 1877

The Building was finished about Michaelmas 1876; & then Left to its fate for a time. — In the interim, Nov 9th there was a contested Election for the School Board, there being 7 candidates — John & Wm Crook; John & Timothy

171

Dodwell; R. Coltman; M. Rose & the Revd Thos Hayton, the first four were elected with the Vicar; the Crooks heading the Poll, the Vicar next and the Dodwells followed, leaving Coltman & Rose out of the running. Meetings were held to procure seats, desks etc. & to choose a Master; the latter, a Mr Dunkin [1], was preferred before other applicants. At the early part of this month he arrived with his family; but no opening of the School has yet taken place, owing to some difficulty in getting desks etc. & to a somewhat dilatory movement on the part of the Board of which I make no comment.

The School was opened formally on the 27th March with only half the number of forms & desks, but in 2 weeks the number was 172. — I was requested to address the children which I did briefly & all went off satisfactorily.

B.R.O. P.R.134/1/11

1. Mr Dunkin from London was paid £70 a year, plus house, garden and 'school pence' (each child paid 2d a week and the second and subsequent child, one penny.) Long Crendon School Log Book.

[215] *To the* Thame Gazette

10 June 1882

Mr Editor,

The remarks in your last issue touching the decorations to the Parish Church here were true as far as they went; but in fairness to others who aided in the decorations, allow me to say that the gallery, side walls and font were respectively ornamented by the Misses Cooke, Miss Edith Smith, and Miss Pritchard, a teacher at the Sunday School, who worked earnestly for the roseate bindings of the font.

As to the candlesticks in the reading desk, I must own they were in a dingy state, and altogether unworthy of their place, as being loose in the sockets they fly from one angle to another, unless held, and had it not been for an active young man the minister lately would have been in a flame when the surplice was ignited by one of these movements. Lamps in accordance with the pulpit have been talked about by the Churchwardens, but nothing more has been done.

Then, as to the chancel, repairs of which are vested in an estate belonging to Mr J. Dodwell [1], who a few years ago spent a considerable sum of money on certain parts of it, leaving others to get worse. The sorry state of the dado painting is a picture of 'mouldy melancholy' shedding tears of grief at the neglect of degenerate sons, whilst the chancel door with its broken panel has not for these 20 years felt the pressure of a paint brush.

I am, Mr Editor, yours truly,

Thos. Hayton

1. In 1874, Lord Churchill was in financial difficulties and sold the Manor Farm estate to John Dodwell for £19,000.

*[216] To the Ecclesiastical Commissioners from the Rev. T.G. Williams,
Rector of Waddesdon and Rural Dean [1]*

We beg respectfully to draw the attention of the Ecclesiastical Commissioners to the accompanying memoranda, and wish to state that the aged Incumbent in his 90th year has to hire a conveyance weekly to take him to and from Nether Winchendon, thus reducing his income considerably.

Ch Com. 48831

1. Rev. John Thomas Williams. Scholar of University College, Oxford; Deacon 1856; rector of Waddesdon 1869; Rural Dean 1881.

[217] To the Ecclesiastical Commissioners

Crendon, 19 November 1883

Dear Sir,

On the 17th of last month an Enquiry under the Bishop's sanction was made here touching the value of this Living: & also what I received from the little village of Lower Winchendon. On the 24th question I added some remarks which might show, my Lords, what hard work I had to go through; & as I am on the point of paying £50 per annum for the service at Lower Winchendon Church such amount was not alluded to in the remarks. If you will be pleased to lay this before the Lords you will oblige

yours respectfully,

Thos Hayton

[Draft for reply]
The Commissioners agree to pay an extra £6 a year, the patronage being private, upon condition of the same sum being raised from non-ecclesiastical sources.

Ch Com. 48831

[218] To the Ecclesiastical Commissioners

Crendon, 13 December 1883

Dear Sir,

There is not a shadow of a chance of the proposition specified in your letter received this morning ever being met. The only consolation I have is that soon I must leave the Living for which I have expended all I have.

Yours,

Thos Hayton

Ch Com. 48831

To the Secretary of the Ecclesiastical Commission

Crendon, 17 December 1883

Dear Sir,

Would you be so kind enough to inform me who was the mover in the 'Committee of Enquiry into the Crendon Living' as I never authorized one, or requested any aid? Indeed I have only once asked you for aid for the Sunday School & Clothing Club. The smart negation was quite a deterrent for other applications. The mighty Benefaction of £6 yearly has caused much amusement among clerical friends and others, reminding them of the late Bishop Wilberforce's remark on the dryness of the 'old Len'. In reality the proposition is a farce. The other day a 'reserve' pensioner in the Marines 'had his long finger cut off and the admiralty added £6 a year to his pension': and the wealthy Commissioners now offer me 2/3¼ per week conditionally. Is it not a burlesque on charity, unsought?

The gentlemen appointed to enquire say the treatment towards me is shameful.

Yours respectfully,

Thomas Hayton

[*Draft for reply*]

As however the Vicarage of Long Crendon is a private patronage, the Commissioners, in conformity with their rule of practice in such cases, offered to contribute one half (i.e. £6) of the annual sum needed to raise the income to £300 per annum.

Ch Com. 48831

[220] *From Lower Winchendon Parish Register*

Wet and boggy. In the year 1886, the Vicar's prediction has been justified, & new floor & a better system of drainage was acknowledged to be necessary, & to be undertaken forthwith.

[221] *To the Editor of* The Thame Gazette

Crendon, 15 September 1887

I am sure, Mr Editor, you would not wittingly give insertion in your paper to anything like a cool deliberate falsehood bearing either on the living or the dead. In your paper last week, on the character and doings of the late Mr J.C. Crook, however correct some of the statements may be, there was one ascribed to him which was in patent contradiction to truth, namely, his

174

having been the originator of the annual dinner given to the aged and the poor of this parish. This was not so; he had nothing whatever to do with the origin of that dinner which has become an institution. Nay, he refused like some others to give a helping hand, and the reasons given for refusal were: The poor were well enough provided for by the Guardians, that there was no complaint, that the example set by the parish of Brill was not worth following, and that one individual is reported to have said, rather than any fuss should be made about contributions, he would pay for a dinner himself — this, however, was a vain brag and a nonentity — with a sneer at those who were attempting to carry out the projects in the parish, no-one willing to undertake the arrangement of it until the late Mr. Coltman [1], who at that time was almost a stranger in the parish and was induced by the Vicar to make the attempt. Contributions were at once given, and Mr Coltman with an energy most praiseworthy, with Mr Kirby Shrimpton, applied to some friends, not parishioners, who liberally promised them support. Concerts, at considerable expense, were got up by Mr Coltman and many Thame friends came forward who praised, with kindly speeches, the undertaking taken up under adverse circumstances. This was carried on until the death of Mr Coltman, and then it was that another set of men, ashamed of their former reluctance, came forward in support of the institution. At a recent dinner at the Bells Inn, no-one even alluded to the first originator and those who assisted him. Such is poor human nature, which, when its ends are obtained, forgets the means which raised them to it. I have been requested by friends of Mr Coltman, to give a flat contradiction to the paragraph in question, and especially that part of it which ascribes to others the credit due to the late Mr Coltman.

I am, Mr Editor, yours obediently,

The Vicar of Long Crendon

1. Richard Coltman, a London business man and a great benefactor to Crendon. He lived at Perrotts, afterwards buying the Prebendal House in Thame.

[222] *From the* Thame Gazette

8 November 1887

We regret to report the death of the Rev. Thomas Hayton, B.A., Vicar of this parish, at the advanced age of 94. His demise was not unexpected, as during the past two or three weeks, as has been announced in these columns, he has lain seriously ill, his condition being such as to occasion grave anxiety to his friends. The end, however, came on Wednesday morning, when the deceased gentlemen passed peacefully away in his sleep. Born on November 17th 1793, the son of Mr John Hayton, of Wigton, Cumberland, he matriculated at Queen's College, Oxford, March 12th 1815; receiving at Mr Keble's hand a second class in literis humanioribus in Easter Term, 1818. He graduated B.A. in the same year. He was a personal friend and contemporary of the late Lord Westbury, of the Rev. Dr. Wilson, Dean of Queen's College, and of the Rev. Frederick Lee, M.A., of Thame, through whom he received his first appointment. Deceased was ordained Deacon in 1818, and Priest in 1820, by Bishop Pretyman of Lincoln, at Buckingham, who was consecrated in 1787, and who had been senior wrangler in 1772 — 115 years ago! A link in the past. Bishop Pretyman, advising his candidates for holy orders about hunting, enjoined them not to pride themselves on riding the best horse nor being the foremost in the field. Mr Hayton became Perpetual Curate of Long Crendon in 1821, and by the presentation of the late Sir Thos. Bernard in 1832 he was also perpetual Curate of Nether Winchendon, in which parish he has ministered continuously nearly 70 years, being his first curacy when he was ordained in 1818. He well remembered the Jubilee Day of George III — a period before he was in orders — having taken part in a grand amateur wrestling match on that day, in which it is believed he came off the winner of the match. In the following year (1810) on the occasion of some riots at Carlisle, he acted as a special constable. Mr Hayton also distinctly remembered a man who had fought at Culloden in 1746, when the adherents of the Young Pretender, Charles Edward Stuart, were defeated under the Duke of Cumberland, and the rebellion crushed. Deceased knew intimately Sir Francis Burdett, and in 1820 met the widow of that eminent statesman, Charles James Fox, at Winchendon. Mr Hayton was one of the few now living who saw Mrs Siddons, the great actress, on the stage, she retiring from the profession in 1812. He had met, at St. Bees, Admiral S. Lutnidge, who died in 1814, and who commanded H.M.S. Carcass, which went on the Arctic Expedition in 1773. Lord Nelson, who was then a boy of 15 years, served on board. In 1843 the churchyard at Long Crendon was enlarged on the north side, Mr Hayton having planted the seven trees standing there on the additional ground. Deceased was a gentlemen of high intellectual attainments. As a polemical writer he was clever, keen, and incisive, and in any prolonged controversy his opponents always found him a 'Foeman worthy of their steel'. In politics he was, in early days, a great Radical and Reformer, having a very just disgust at the constitution of the House of Commons before the Reform Bill of 1832, but at the last election he had so far modified his views as to give his tacit support to the Conservative candidate — more particularly as to the Irish Question. Deceased married in July 1827, Adelaide, daughter of Mr Stevens, of Rickmansworth, and celebrated his golden wedding more than 10 years ago. He lost his wife in 1884. Mr Hayton was the oldest clergyman but three in England, the oldest being the Rev. B. Edwards, Rector of Ashill, Norfolk, since 1813, who is in his 99th year.

[223] Notice of the Sale at the Vicarage, Long Crendon, from Jackson's Oxford Journal

26 November 1887

THE VICARAGE, LONG CRENDON, BUCKS

Two miles from Thame Station, G.W.R.

The whole of the Genteel HOUSEHOLD FURNITURE, including the contents of the Dining and Drawing Rooms and ornamental items; the well-appointed Bed Room appendages; the China, Glass, and Linen; a small

Library of BOOKS; the SILVER and PLATED ARTICLES; JEWELLERY, WINES, KITCHEN REQUISITES, and numerous other items; also the Outdoor Effects,

TO BE SOLD BY AUCTION

By MUMFORD and BOND

On the premises, on Wednesday, Nov. 30, 1887, at Ten o'clock punctually, in consequence of the number and importance of the lots.

On view the day previous to the auction, and catalogues may be had of the auctioneers, Brill and Thame.

177

LETTERS AND NEWSPAPER CUTTINGS STUCK IN THE
PARISH REGISTERS

B.R.O. P.R.134/1/4   Case of Alleged Poaching, 12 December 1857. [Newspaper unknown].

Its Poor and their Treatment. *Bucks Advertiser*, c. 1865.

ibid   8   Chandos and the Farmers, signed Z. *Aylesbury News*, 20 January 1838.

To the Marquis of Chandos, signed Z. *Aylesbury News*, 27 January 1838.

Dinner to Disraeli. *Bucks Advertiser*, 19 July 1847.

Two letters from Hayton, 1860 and 1861.

ibid   9   Curious Vestry Doings at Long Crendon, c. July 1838. [Newspaper unknown].

To the Marquis of Chandos, signed OMEGA, c. 1838. [Paper unknown].

Memorandum — Notley Pew.

Restoration of Sir John Dormer's Tomb. *Jackson's Oxford Journal*, 21 December 1860.

ibid   10   The Archdeacon's Visitation. *Bucks Advertiser*, 27 June 1868.

Assessment of Long Crendon. *Thame Independent* [date unknown].

Smallpox and how to treat it.
     Letter 1. To *Bucks Advertiser*, 27 January 1865.
     Letter 2. To *Bucks Advertiser*, 13 February 1865.
     Letter 3. To *Bucks Herald*, [date unknown].

ibid   11   Dinner to the Aged Poor, c. 1870. [Paper unknown].

A Gypsey Marriage, c. 1870. [Paper unknown].

Hayton's account of Crendon School Board.

APPENDIX

Charity Com. 252518 A/1

INDEX OF PERSONS AND PLACES

IN THE LETTERS

The references are to the serial numbers of the letters, not to the pages.

Place-names not followed by the name of a county are in Buckinghamshire.

182

Hobart, Hon. H.L., Dean of Windsor, 42, 50, 54
Hodgson, Christopher, 2, 6, 7, 31
Holland, Giles, 158, 210
Hollier, John, 74, 77, 81, 101, 108, 116-17, 119, 123-4, 147
Holliman, Richard, 51-2, 74
Hollis, John, 79
Holloway, Richard, 67, 134, 144
Hopcroft, William, 40-1, 44, 78n, 92
Horsenden, 89n
    rector of, see Partridge
Horspath, Oxon, 110
Howlett, Thomas, 110
Humphrey, Mr, 74
Hutt, Joseph, 114, 128, 133, 144

Ickford, 26
Ing, Elizabeth, 96
    Thomas, 173
Isham, Revd A, vicar of Weston Turville, 208, 210, 212

Jamaica, 29, 30
Jackman, Mr, 42
Jackson's Oxford Journal, 94, 139, 223
Jeune, Dr Francis, 85
Johnstone, ..., 96
Jones, Col., 170

Kaye, Rt Revd John, bishop of Lincoln, 11-23, 39, 45, 59, 60, 71-2, 84-8, 195
Keble, John, 222
King, C.H., 172
Kingsey, 26
Kipling, Revd John, vicar of Oakley and Chearsley, 12, 69n
Kirby Beard, Messrs, 100
Knight, T., 64
Knollys, Sir Francis, 211

Langston, S., 86
Lee, Dr, of Hartwell, 27-8
    Revd F., 64, 69, 222
    Richard, surgeon, 33, 85
    Timothy Tripp, vicar of Thame, 33n
Leper, Mr, 186-7
Lester, Joseph, 92
Lewis, Thomas F., 34
Lewknor, Oxon, 64
Lincoln, bishops of, see Pretyman, Tomline, Pelham, Kaye
Littlejohn, Revd W.D., 94
London, bishop of, 195
Long Compton, Warks, 82
Longford, Ireland, 118

Lowell, William, 120, 122, 132, 138, 140
Lumly, Mr, 142
Lupton, Harry, 64n, 69
    Henry, 67-9, 71, 73
    Mrs Henry, 69
    Sackville, 64, 67
Lutnidge, Admiral S., 222

Markham, Mr, 69
Meare, Mr, 109
Moore, Revd & Hon. D.G.V., 185-8
Moreton, Oxon, 26
Moule, Mr, 212
Mumford & Bond, Messrs, 223
Munday, George, 95-9

National Society, 42-3, 45-6, 48, 55, 57
Nelson, Lord, 222
Neville, Revd & Hon. George, 100
Nichols, George, 34
Noble, M., 164

Oakley, 69
    vicar of, see Kipling
Owen, Dr, 195
Oxford, 65
Oxford, bishops of, see Wilberforce, Fielding
Oxfordshire, County Court of, 144, 156
    Judges of, see Temple, Wing
    Registrar of, see Holloway

Paine, Mr, 89
Palmerston, Rt Hon. Lord, 95-9
Parker, William, 65, 75, 144, 147-8, 151, 154, 192
Partridge, Revd E.W., rector of Horsenden, 89n
Peaceful, William, 58
Pelham, Rt Revd George, 2, 195
Pembroke College, Oxford, 82
Peyman, Henry P., 158, 164, 171
Pickard, Mr, 212
Pigott, G.G.W., 120, 132, 134-5
Poor Law, Commission of the, 24-6, 29, 30, 34-8, 47, 52-3, 62-6, 78, 80-1, 120-2, 135, 173, 176-8
    Assistant Commissioners of, see Gulson, Hill, Parker, Power
    Commissioners of, see Lewis, Nichols
    President of, see Baines
Power, A. (later Sir Alfred), 78, 80
Praed, Mr, 27
Pretyman, Rt Revd George, 222

Williams, Revd T.G., rector and rural
	dean of Waddesdon, 216
Willis, John, vicar of Haddenham, 84
Winchendon, Lower, Nether, 11, 13,
	60, 65, 82, 162, 205, 208-12,
	216-17, 220, 222
Winchester, bishop of, 85, 87
Windsor, Dean and Canons of
	St. George's at, 42, 56-7, 80,
	101, 144, 206
	Agent for, *see* Batcheldor
	Bursar to, 191
	Chapter Clerk of, *see* Croix
	Deans of, *see* Hobart, Neville,
		Wellesley
Wing, J.W., 116, 119
Wotton Underwood, 58
	Wotton House at, 67

Young, ..., 27